GOSPEL, TRUTH, & INTERPRETATION
Evangelical Identity in Aotearoa New Zealand

The story of evangelicalism in New Zealand is almost as old as the history of European contact. The earliest missionaries to New Zealand included evangelicals who spread the features common to global evangelicalism from Cape Reinga in the North to Stewart Island in the South. This two-hundred year history of evangelicalism "down under" has created a lively Christian subculture which, while sharing much in common with evangelicals around the globe, nevertheless has its own distinctive character and gravitas, not to mention its own set of characters, defining moments, and contextual issues. The essays in this volume exhibit much of the breadth and depth of this evangelical witness, divided as it is into two sections: historical and theological. As David Bebbington says of the historical essays in this volume, "what is most striking about the members of the evangelical bodies depicted in this volume is their variety. These people were not uniformly *anything*, let alone joyless or humourless. The evangelicals of New Zealand were by no means monochrome, and least of all black." Derek Tidball says of the theological essays in this volume, that they exhibit four hallmarks: they are evangelical, contextual, creative, and courageous, before concluding: "These papers show skilled evangelical theological acrobats in action, not for the entertainment of us all but for the instruction of us all."

Tim Meadowcroft is Senior Lecturer in Biblical Studies and Head of the School of Theology, Mission, and Ministry at Laidlaw College in Auckland, New Zealand.

Myk Habets is Head of Carey Graduate School, Carey Baptist College in Auckland, New Zealand.

ARCHER STUDIES IN PACIFIC CHRISTIANITY

This series explores the experience of Christians in this vibrant region. The best research of new and established scholars will build a more profound understanding of Christian communities, their sense of themselves, and their attempts to engage their unique contexts.

GOSPEL, TRUTH, & INTERPRETATION
Evangelical Identity in Aotearoa New Zealand

Edited by Tim Meadowcroft and Myk Habets

Archer
Press

2011

ISBN 978-0-473-23363-1

Archer Press is an imprint of the New Zealand Baptist Research and Historical Society. PO Box 12149, Auckland, New Zealand

© 2011

The editors offer this volume in thanks for the contribution to evangelical identity in Aotearoa New Zealand made by their two institutions: Laidlaw College (previously the Bible Training Institute and the Bible College of New Zealand) and Carey Baptist College (previously The New Zealand Baptist Theological College).

Contents

Contributors	11
Preface	14

I. Historical

Introduction to part one *David Bebbington*	17
Chapter One: furloughs and catechisms: formative strands in New Zealand evangelicalism *John Hitchen*	20
Chapter Two: the foundation of the Bible Training Institute *Peter Lineham*	49
Chapter Three: "Baptist and Evangelical": changing perceptions of being evangelical among New Zealand Baptists, 1926-1946 *Martin Sutherland*	68
Chapter Four: spirit and reason: Canon Orange and Professor Blaiklock as contrasting exemplars of evangelical identity in mid-twentieth century New Zealand *Stuart Lange*	85
Chapter Five: evangelicals equipping Melanesian men and women: an interpretation of the training ministries of the Christian Leaders' Training College of Papua New Guinea, 1965-2010 *John Hitchen*	110
Chapter Six: the role of the Evangelical Unions and Inter-Varsity Fellowship in defining evangelical identity in mid-twentieth century New Zealand *Stuart Lange*	137

Chapter Seven: does a rose by any other name still smell the same? 153
Kevin Ward

II. Theological

Introduction to part two 171
Derek Tidball

Chapter Eight: locating the church in evangelical theology 174
Murray Rae

Chapter Nine: evangelical ecclesiology? Witness, faithfulness, and "success" in the gospel 191
Andrew Burgess

Chapter Ten: beyond Henry's nominalism and evangelical foundationalism: Thomas Torrance's theological realism 205
Myk Habets

Chapter Eleven: Stanley Grenz' theological method: revisioning evangelical theology or business as usual? 241
Brian Harris

Chapter Twelve: hermeneutics and evangelical identity: a literary critical appreciation 266
Tim Meadowcroft

Chapter Thirteen: music as revelation: a comment from over the fence 289
Judith Brown

Chapter Fourteen: is an evangelical New Zealand contextual theology possible? 305
Martin Sutherland

Contributors

David William Bebbington is Professor of History at the University of Stirling. His publications include: *Evangelicalism in Modern Britain: A History from the 1730s to the 1980s* (Unwin Hyman, 1989; 2nd edn, Routledge, 1993); *Victorian Nonconformity* (Headstart, 1992; 2nd edn, Wipf and Stock, 2011); *The Dominance of Evangelicalism: The Age of Spurgeon and Moody* (IVP, 2005); and *Baptists through the Centuries: A History of a Global People* (Baylor University Press, 2010). He has just completed a study of global Victorian revivals.

Judith Brown is an occasional lecturer in theology at Laidlaw College, Auckland, and in church history at St John the Evangelist College, Auckland. She has published on both Ernst Bloch and theology and the arts, including the work of Colin McCahon. Her current projects include a book on theological method.

Andrew Burgess is Vicar of All Saints Anglican Church, Nelson, and Senior Lecturer in Theology at Bishopdale Theological College. In 2012 he will become Dean of Bishopdale Theological College. His concern is for theology in the service of God's Church, and his research includes work on Karl Barth and Jesus' Ascension, the Church in witness, and the unity of the Triune God's judgement and grace. He is the author of *The Ascension in Karl Barth* (2004).

Myk Habets is Head of Carey Graduate School, Carey Baptist College, Auckland. His publications include *Theosis in the Theology of Thomas Torrance* (Ashgate, 2009) and *The Anointed Son* (Pickwick, 2010), and numerous journal articles, and he has edited a number of works such as *Trinitarian Theology After Barth*, with Phillip Tolliday (Pickwick, 2011).

Brian Harris is the Principal of Vose Seminary in Perth, Western Australia. His PhD was on the theological method of Stanley Grenz and has been published by Mellen Press (2011). Together with Derek Tidball and Jason Sexton he is currently editing a volume in honour of Stanley Grenz which is due to be published by Wipf and Stock. His other research interest is in the area of quiet leadership, and he is presently working on a text on this topic which is due to be published by Paternoster in 2013.

John Hitchen is a Senior Lecturer in mission studies in the Laidlaw-Carey Graduate School of Theology, Auckland, New Zealand. He is a previous National Principal of Bible College of New Zealand and of the Christian Leaders' Training College in Papua New Guinea. His Aberdeen, Scotland doctoral study focused on nineteenth century missionary formation and mission in the South West Pacific. Recently he has also helped establish a Master of Theology programme in Papua New Guinea.

Stuart Lange is a Senior Lecturer at Laidlaw College in Auckland, where he teaches courses in church history. His primary research interest is the history of Christianity in New Zealand, especially its evangelical streams.

Peter Lineham is the Regional Director of the College of Humanities and Social Sciences at Massey University's Albany Campus, and Associate Professor of History. He has written extensively on the religious history of New Zealand.

Tim Meadowcroft is Senior Lecturer in Biblical Studies and Head of the School of Theology, Mission and Ministry, Laidlaw College, Auckland. His research interests include hermeneutics and the biblical texts of the Second Temple period. His most recent books are *Haggai* (Sheffield Phoenix, 2006) and *The Message of the Word of God* (IVP, 2011).

Murray Rae is Professor of Theology at the University of Otago and Head of the Department of Theology and Religion where he teaches courses in systematic theology and ethics. His research interests include the work of Søren Kierkegaard, theological interpretation of Scripture, theology and architecture, and Māori engagements with Christianity.

Martin Sutherland is Vice-Principal at Laidlaw College in Auckland. He has published widely in Baptist and evangelical history and in theological method.

His most recent publication is *Conflict & Connection: Baptist Identity in New Zealand* (Archer, 2011).

Derek Tidball is a former Principal of London School of Theology and currently Visiting Scholar, Spurgeon's College, London, and Vice-President of Evangelical Alliance UK. His many publications include *Skilful Shepherds* (Apollos, 1986); *The Message of the Cross* (IVP, 2001); *Ministry by the Book* (Apollos, 2008); *The Message of Holiness* (IVP, 2010); and *In Christ, in Colossae: Sociological Perspectives on Colossians* (Paternoster, 2011).

Kevin Ward is Senior Lecturer in Church and Society at the Knox Centre for Ministry and Leadership and Adjunct Lecturer in Theology at the University of Otago, Dunedin. His research interests include the place of church and religion in contemporary society and congregational studies.

Preface

This volume is a result of two colloquia put on in Auckland by Laidlaw-Carey Graduate School on the subject of evangelical identity in Aotearoa New Zealand: one, in 2006, on historical matters and the second one, in 2007, on theological aspects of evangelical identity. Most of the essays herein represent work presented at those colloquia. The historical forum was privileged to hear also from David Bebbington who provides an introduction to part one of this volume. The theological forum was similarly privileged to hear from Derek Tidball whose introduction to part two is also herein. We are grateful to these two men for the sharing with us of their vast experience and knowledge on the matter of evangelical identity, and also to all participants in the colloquia and contributors to this volume. Thanks must also go to Martin Sutherland, at the time Dean of the Laidlaw-Carey Graduate School, who was responsible for conceiving and setting up both events. Rebecca Little's proof reading was an important part of the final stages of production. And we are grateful to Archer Press for the inclusion of this volume in their stable of material on Pacific Christianity. We offer these essays in the service of the unfinished mission of evangelical theology in Aotearoa New Zealand.

Tim Meadowcroft (for the editors)

**Part One
Historical**

Introduction to part one

David Bebbington

Evangelicals in Aotearoa New Zealand have often received a bad press. One of the most distinguished of the nation's historians, James Belich, has voiced the views of many by expressing, albeit with a phrase that distances the author from the evaluation, a strong sense of antipathy towards evangelicals. "From some modern perspectives," wrote Belich in 1996, "the evangelicals are hard to like. They dressed like crows; seemed joyless, humourless and sometimes hypocritical; [and] they embalmed the evidence poor historians need to read in tedious preaching..."[1] Clearly when Belich refers to the crowlike appearance of evangelicals, he has in mind pictures of Samuel Marsden, the leader of the Church Missionary Society's pioneering venture to New Zealand, wearing the black clerical garb of the early nineteenth century. That dress, however, was confined to clergy and was superseded long before the nineteenth century was over. Yet the image is applied to all evangelicals. It may be surmised that the attributes of being joyless, humourless, and hypocritical were as rare amongst them as a resemblance to crows. Certainly the tedium of their preaching is a matter of opinion. Many published sermons of the nineteenth century contain challenges and encouragements for those who have ears to hear. Yet Belich is making a weighty point. What he describes is indeed a powerful image among many New Zealanders (and others elsewhere) living in the twenty-first century. Evangelicals of the past are commonly seen as gloomy or worse.

How can that situation be remedied? By exploring more of the evidence to which Belich refers, and not only in sermons. The magazines and manuscript records that evangelical denominations, organizations, and congregations generated in abundance during the

---

[1] James Belich, *Making Peoples: A History of the New Zealanders: From Polynesian Settlement to the End of the Nineteeenth Century* (Auckland: Allen Lane / Penguin, 1996), 135.

nineteenth and twentieth centuries can be quarried for material showing what evangelicals were really like. Hypocrisies will undoubtedly emerge, but so will other attributes. It will be found that evangelicalism was near the core of family life at all social levels. It will appear that evangelicals discovered a reassuring sense of community in their Christian congregations. And it will be established that evangelicals, again and again, were responsible for enterprises that helped the poor and needy. It will emerge, in short, that, by even secular criteria, evangelicalism was on balance a good thing. The historical record will prove to be among the most powerful apologetic weapons of the twenty-first century.

In the historical section of this volume there are efforts in that direction. There is discussion by Peter Lineham of the forces that did so much to embed evangelical religion in New Zealand society. Martin Sutherland explores how in the earlier twentieth century the evangelicalism that owed a great deal to revivalism was transformed in popular perception from a simple eagerness to evangelize to a set of doctrinal markers. That contributed to a tendency among conservative evangelicals towards fundamentalism, a process that was sustained in the later twentieth century and that is explored by Kevin Ward. The InterVarsity Fellowship, Stuart Lange shows, often formed the crucial glue of the conservative coalition, generating bonds that had an impact far beyond the colleges where the organisation primarily operated. In another paper Lange also demonstrates the variety of styles within IVF circles by contrasting Canon Orange of Christchurch with Professor Blaiklock of Auckland. The missionary impetus in the evangelical movement, so powerfully embodied in Marsden, also found expression in James Chalmers, whose visit to New Zealand in 1877 is analysed by John Hitchen. The training given in a missionary college in Papua New Guinea in the late twentieth century is authoritatively described by John Hitchen, himself one of the providers. These cameos go a considerable way towards dispelling myths about evangelical motives and methods. If members of the evangelical congregations were occasionally short-sighted, they could also be visionary.

Two features of the evangelicals considered here deserve particular comment. One is that they were part of a broad international movement. The revivalism of nineteenth-century New Zealand, for example, was a dimension of a global phenomenon. Later on new organisations from Britain were often matched by fresh ideas from America. Because they were evangelicals, many New Zealanders read about developments in other lands with much more frequency than their neighbours. Furthermore their activism drove them to apply the lessons from abroad that they had seen described in their newspapers. Again, their missionary consciousness made them eager to put some of the schemes into practice beyond their own islands. So New Zealand evangelicals participated in a worldwide network of evangelicals. They often contributed decisively to developments elsewhere. The Brethren of New Zealand, for example, played a disproportionate part in that movement's changing ethos in the 1960s. Whether receiving or giving influences, the evangelicals of New Zealand formed part of a transglobal phenomenon of great moment during the epoch of the nation's existence.

Partly because they received and gave so much, the evangelicals, in the second place, were immensely diverse. The contrast between Orange and Blaiklock, contemporary leaders in the same organisation, illustrates that dissimilar stances were normal within the evangelical world. In the previous century there were vivid differences between members of the various denominations with their distinct origins in England or Scotland and their establishment or Nonconformist roles. The denominational traditions, still vigorous in the twentieth century, ensured a heterogeneity in the evangelical movement to which they all belonged. Perhaps what is most striking about the members of the evangelical bodies depicted in this volume is their variety. These people were not uniformly *anything*, let alone joyless or humourless. The evangelicals of New Zealand were by no means monochrome, and least of all black.

Chapter One
Furloughs and catechisms: formative strands in New Zealand evangelicalism

John M. Hitchen

To unpeel the layers of influence shaping evangelicalism in early colonial New Zealand is no easy task. This essay explores two such layers which seldom receive attention, but which come together during the visit to New Zealand from 13 June to 24 August 1877 of James and Jane Chalmers. As London Missionary Society missionaries the Chalmers had been stationed at Rarotonga in the Cook (or as they were then known, Hervey) Islands for the previous decade, and were en route to their new appointment to the recently opened LMS work in Papua New Guinea. This New Zealand visit gave the Chalmers experience as "missionaries-on-furlough" sharing awareness of Christian mission in the Pacific region and thereby helping to shape one formative layer of colonial Christianity in the late nineteenth century.[1] The rapport and relationships the Chalmers established with the colonial settlers and their children also leads us to explore the way the Westminster Shorter Catechism provided the common core of religious understandings supporting those relationships, and illustrated the Catechism's role as another layer of mind-shaping influence.

---

[1] Reports of the visit, as well as in New Zealand newspapers cited below, are found in James Chalmers, "Through New Zealand to New Guinea," *Chronicle of the London Missionary Society* (1878): 153–56; in James Chalmers, "Rarotonga to Stacey Island" (Congregational Council for World Mission/London Missionary Society Archives, School of Oriental and African Studies, London, Papua Journals, James Chalmers, 1877), also on Inter Documentation Company (IDC) Microfiche version of the CWM Archive (Fiche # H2123/359: Frames 12–20). These two latter sources are henceforth referred to as Chalmers, "Rarotonga to Stacey Island," followed by the frame number for the IDC Microfiche version.

James and Jane Chalmers on furlough in New Zealand 1877

Like most missionaries of his time, James Chalmers' image as a career missionary developed through his "deputation" work on behalf of LMS in the missionary sending countries. He began such work in Australia on his initial voyage with his wife Jane to Rarotonga,² but it became the central feature of his later furloughs. Not that Chalmers longed for furloughs! Like his older colleagues he regarded regular furloughs as a measure of incomplete dedication to the work. Departing for missionary service in 1866 he "fully intended never to return."³ When the Chalmers left Rarotonga for Papua New Guinea in 1877 Joseph Mullens, LMS Foreign Secretary in London, expected them to furlough in Britain after a brief orientation in their new place of service.⁴ Chalmers complained about having to return to Britain "so soon" and suggested a call at New Zealand on the way to Papua New Guinea would suffice.⁵ They spent ten weeks in the young colony. In Auckland, James Chalmers had one friend,⁶ and publicity about Chalmers' part in the liquor and cross-cultural marriage questions

---

² See John Hitchen, "Training Tamate: Formation of the Nineteenth Century Missionary Worldview: The Case of James Chalmers of New Guinea" (PhD Thesis, University of Aberdeen, 1984), 547–48, and A.T. Saville, "1866 Journal" (LMS/SSJ, IDC H2125/1683).

³ James Chalmers, "Notes for Lizzie" (LMS/Papua Personal, Box 1, Folder 1; IDCH2123/378:1–381:21). These autobiographical notes written for his second wife in the final years of his life (1895-1901) are reproduced in Hitchen, "Training Tamate," Appendix A; the citation above is on page 23; cf., Chalmers-Whitehouse 9 Janaury 1883, cited in Richard Lovett, *James Chalmers: His Autobiography and Letters* (London: Religious Tract Society, 1902), 222.

⁴ Mullens-Chalmers 24 December 1875 (LMS/SSLOut, Box 11).

⁵ Chalmers-Mullens 24 May 1876, (LMS/SSLIn, Box35/1/C, IDC H2125/997).

⁶ A Captain Daldy had for ten years sent Chalmers newspapers and forwarded his letters on to England. Daldy was a deacon in the Congregational Church, Auckland. Chalmers, "Rarotonga to Stacey Island," 12.

on Rarotonga prepared the way somewhat.⁷ Jane Chalmers' family had migrated to Dunedin and she had visited them twice previously.⁸ But this was James Chalmers' first New Zealand visit and he was virtually unknown. Their plans "to spend a few quiet weeks with [their] friends" soon changed.⁹

From the first Sunday the Chalmers found themselves engaged in four kinds of mission promotional meetings. Each Sunday James addressed morning and evening services in Congregational and Presbyterian pulpits in Auckland, Dunedin, Oamaru, Timaru, and Christchurch.¹⁰ Chalmers' comment after the first such church service at the Auckland Congregational church pastored by Mr Robertson, set a developing pattern: "I gave them a missionary address."¹¹ For good measure in the Oamaru Presbyterian District he preached to "a good, large and attentive audience" in the Otepopo congregation in the morning, at a Kakanui gathering in the afternoon, and at the Maheno congregation in the evening.¹² One Sunday in both Dunedin and Christchurch a combined

---

⁷ Chalmers-Mullens, 7 September 1875 (LMS/SSL, Box34/6/B, IDC H2125/991), 10; cf., Rarotonga Report 1874, (LMS/SSR 1874), 22.

⁸ See Hitchen, "Training Tamate,"460–62, on the Hercus Family. Jane Chalmers spent 3 weeks in Dunedin in 1866 while the *John Williams* travelled from Adelaide to Sydney, and recuperated there from November 1875 to April 1876. In Oamaru in August 1877 James and Jane stayed at the farm of Jane's cousin, Mr Elder, and while in Oamaru they also spent one night with "our old family friends Mr and Mrs Flett," presumably friends of Jane's family from Greenock or Glasgow days. Chalmers, "Rarotonga to Stacey Island," 17; cf., also Hitchen, "Training Tamate," 460–62.

⁹ Chalmers, "Rarotonga to Stacey Island," 14; also in *Chronicle of the LMS* (1878): 153.

¹⁰ Their itinerary was: Auckland, 13–17 June 1877; Dunedin, 25 June–10 August; Oamaru and Otepopo–Kakanui–Maheno parish, 10-13 August; Timaru, 14 August; Christchurch, 15–24 August. Chalmers, "Through New Zealand to New Guinea," *Chronicle of the LMS* (1878): 153–56, and Chalmers, "Rarotonga to Stacey Island," 12–20.

¹¹ Chalmers, "Rarotonga to Stacey Island," 12.

¹² Chalmers, "Rarotonga to Stacey Island," 17.

churches' after-church evangelistic rally drew good numbers to a down-town theatre.[13] Sunday afternoon in both these cities also gave opportunity for major combined inter-church Sunday School rallies of up to 2,500 children, to which we shall return shortly.[14]

This Sunday pattern was supplemented by weekday public missionary meetings on behalf of the London Missionary Society. The final such gathering in Dunedin doubled as a farewell valedictory for the Chalmers. A "complimentary tea meeting," it cost two shillings a head, and was chaired by a resident magistrate, Judge Bathgate. The local newspaper coverage illustrates the varying impressions a missionary meeting can convey. The *Otago Daily Times* noted one leading minister's cold kept him from attending, and that the proceedings lasted "till nearly ten o'clock," but said nothing about Chalmers' message.[15] The *Otago Guardian*, however, showed Chalmers' human side in reporting that he publicly wished his recently deceased mother could have shared with his parents-in-law on the platform. It also reported his comments about missions bringing out hidden heroism in men like Williams and Patteson; the progress of the New Guinea Mission to date and his confident hopes, "... to labour long there. I have a hope within me that in a year we shall be stationed close by Mount Owen Stanley. (Cheers)... and New Guinea shall be a glorious stone in the Redeemer's crown, and Dunedin shall help it. (Cheers)."[16] *The Otago Witness* gave the fullest account, detailing not only the titles of

---

[13] *Otago Daily Times* (23 July 1877): 2, commented: "Considering the unfavourable weather there was a good attendance of the Queen's Theatre service last evening, when the Rev. James Chalmers from Rarotonga, delivered an address," cf., Chalmers, "Rarotonga to Stacey Island."

[14] Combined Sunday School rallies were held at Knox Church, Dunedin and Trinity Congregational Church, Christchurch.

[15] *Otago Daily Times* (8 August 1877): 2.

[16] *Otago Guardian* (9 August 1877). See also other impressions of the same meeting, *Chronicle of the LMS* (1878): 153; C. Stuart Ross, *Tamate: The Apostle of the Papuan Gulf* (Melbourne: M.L. Hutchinson, 1902), 10–12.

the hymns, choir items, and Chalmers' speech, but also those of the chairman and the four others who shared the platform.[17]

The Oamaru reporter tells that at the rain-dampened Monday 13 August meeting, Chalmers,

> gave a vivid and interesting account of the introduction of Christianity among the natives by John Williams and the native teachers with him. He painted the hardships and dangers cheerfully undergone by these men for the spread of the Gospel. He related numerous anecdotes tending to prove with what noble self-sacrifice the work had been carried out.[18]

Chalmers also challenged the impression left by the Earl of Pembroke, G.R.C. Herbert, and "The Doctor," G.H. Kingsley, in their recently published *South Sea Bubbles*, that it was advisable to leave the "noble savage" alone in his "virgin state."[19] Chalmers suggested that had it not been for the principles of the gospel which the Earl and Doctor denigrated in their writing, they could not have visited in safety the places of which they wrote.

Chalmers concluded each such meeting with "a most eloquent appeal" for financial support for the LMS. Having emphasized the partnership between European and Pacific Islander missionaries in the evangelization of the Pacific, he particularly sought to link New Zealand audiences in what today we call "partnership in mission." He encouraged his hearers to support a specific Pacific Island missionary working for the LMS in Papua New Guinea, noting that their "annual salary amounted to only £15."[20]

By the time of the 22 August "large public meeting" in Christchurch the regular pattern for such deputation meetings was firmly established. Chalmers suggested to the Christians of the

---

[17] "Missionary Meeting," *The Otago Witness* (11 August 1877): 10.

[18] *North Otago Times* (14 August 1877): 2.

[19] G.R.C Herbert [The Earl] and G.H. Kingsley [The Doctor], *South Sea Bubbles* (Melbourne: George Robertson, 1872). See Hitchen, "Training Tamate," 17, 73.

[20] *North Otago Times* (14 August 1877): 2.

twenty-seven year old settlement that Australia and New Zealand's wealth should enable them to relieve Britain of all responsibility for Pacific missionary outreach. He then:

> gave an interesting account of his twelve years' experience in Polynesia; his voyage out, and introduction to the mission field in the New Hebrides; the event of his being wrecked on Savage Island and subsequent visit to Tahiti and other islands in the Society group; and entered minutely into the description of mission work in Rarotonga.[21]

His final emphasis was again on the need for support for Pacific Island evangelists to Papua New Guinea.

By most modern standards these deputation meetings had significant flow-on effects. The Otago auxiliary of the LMS was born at one such deputation meeting.[22] We can trace at least six churches, sunday schools, or individual donors who committed to support a Rarotongan evangelist in New Guinea for at least a year – with one donor guaranteeing the needed £15 for each of three years.[23] Chalmers spent time with the Presbyterian and Congregational ministers in each centre. He addressed a meeting of the Presbytery in Christchurch and came away convinced Canterbury Presbyterians were ready to support a Presbyterian missionary if such were seconded to LMS for work in Papua New Guinea.[24] The impact on particular churches varied, but the following comments, penned thirty six years later in the church's *Jubilee Souvenir*, pay tribute to the Chalmers' influence in the Andersons Bay, Dunedin, Presbyterian parish:

> The representatives of the London Missionary Society for some time kept missionary enthusiasm alive. The Rev. James Chalmers ('Tamate') twice spent two or three days at Anderson's

---

[21] *Christchurch Press* (23 August 1877).

[22] *Chronicle of LMS* (1878): 153; Chalmers, "Notes for Lizzie," in Hitchen, "Training Tamate," Appendix A, 25.

[23] *Christchurch Press* (23 August 1877); Chalmers, *Chronicle of the LMS* (1878): 153–55.

[24] Chalmers, "Rarotonga to Stacey Island," 20.

Bay as the guest of the Hon. Matthew Holmes, and about this time the Sunday School kept a native missionary, Piri, up to the time of his death.[25]

The Chalmers' visit was also a major stimulus, if not cause, of Rev C. Stuart Ross, the minister at Andersons Bay, commencing *The New Zealand Missionary Record*, which served as a children's missionary information magazine from 1882 until 1885 when it was absorbed into the denomination's official magazine, *The New Zealand Presbyterian*. Unsurprisingly, James Chalmers contributed no less than twenty items, half of them extended stories of Papua New Guinean people and experiences, to the *Missionary Record*.[26] This visit also stimulated fundraising for mission vessels, and the donation of a six-ton yacht to enable Chalmers to establish better supply lines for the Pacific Island teachers, and thereby answer the

---

[25] *Jubilee Souvenir of Anderson's Bay Presbyterian Church: From the Settlement of the First Minister July 9th 1863 to July 9th 1913* (Dunedin: J. Wilkie, 1914), 34. C. Stuart Ross documents the on-going exchange of correspondence, sending of boxes of clothes for Piri, the Rarotongan evangelist Anderson's Bay Church supported, and arranging the needed mission vessel, as examples of their partnership with Chalmers (Ross, *Tamate: Apostle*).

[26] Several of these stories would re-appear in Chalmers' own and other later writings, e.g., "Granny: A Friend of the New Guinea Mission," *NZ Missionary Record* [henceforth *NZMR*] 2(6) (April 1884): 82–84 and *NZMR* 2(7) (May 1884): 87–88, reappeared in Chalmers, *Pioneering in New Guinea* (London: Religious Tract Society, 1887), and again in Chalmers, *Pioneering Life and Work in New Guinea, 1877-1894* (London: RTS, 1895). Ross republished other stories from the *NZMR* in his own biography of Chalmers, published after Chalmers' death in 1901, e.g., "Kone, the New Guinea Rainmaker," *NZMR* 2(2) (December 1883): 17–19 and *NZMR* 2(3) (January 1884): 36–38, reappeared in Ross, *Tamate: Apostle*, 67–79. I express sincere gratitude to Jane Bloore of the Presbyterian Church of Aotearoa New Zealand Archives, Dunedin, for her generous and detailed help sourcing references for this section.

growing chorus of critics of the LMS's standard of care for their Pacific missionaries in Papua New Guinea.[27]

On this kind of "furlough," then, for a limited period the normally isolated Christian worker of humble origin shared platforms with resident magistrates and (severe colds notwithstanding) church dignitaries. He became the focus of the best organising and cooperative effort in ecclesiastical circles. In town and rural congregations, in Sunday Schools, theatres, and at public dinners he enthralled the audience with selected illustrations of his missionary work. He was expected to stimulate spiritual fervour amongst the committed, effectively challenge the non-committed to come to faith, and regularly to call for prayerful and financial involvement in his work. Throughout he had no settled abode, but was feted from centre to centre with hospitality in excess of his usual experience and living standards. While thus engaged the missionary's psychological, moral, and spiritual integrity were severely tested.

Such was the pathway by which Chalmers conveyed an appreciation of mission work to the colonial churches in New Zealand, adding one stream of understanding and opinion to colonial attitudes towards the wider Pacific and New Zealand's place within it. Chalmers' summed up his own impressions:

> What a grand country this New Zealand is! The Britain of the South will some day be worthy of its parentage as in its childhood it gives good promise. God grant that it may grow up a truly Christian country and do much for the evangelisation of the world.[28]

---

[27] On the need for a boat: *NZMR* 1(1) (November 1882): 8; *NZMR* 1(12) (October 1883): 150; and *NZMR* 2(8) (June 1884): 101. On the gift of a vessel: *NZMR* 2 (7) (May 1884): Supplement; and "A Munificent Gift," *NZMR* 2 (10) (August 1884): 135. These same notices were reproduced in Ross, *Tamate: Apostle*, 80–97. On the criticisms of LMS, see Hitchen, "Training Tamate," 83–86 and 592–95.

[28] Chalmers, "Rarotonga to Stacey Island," 21.

One aspect of this visit suggests an intriguing link to a basic influence underlying this missionary input to colonial life. To make the link we pose the question: how does a childless missionary who has lived in another culture for a decade, apparently instantaneously relate to crowds of up to 2,000 colonial children more than once, and communicate with them so as to leave a lasting impression? As we have noted, in both the central Knox Presbyterian Church in Dunedin, on Sunday 5 August 1877 and again a fortnight later at the Trinity Congregational Church in Christchurch, Chalmers addressed large combined rallies of Sunday School children. The leading Dunedin newspaper's succinct report noted three features: the numbers of children and their adult teachers present; the denominational ecumenicity of the event; and the fact that Dunedin children gave close to twopence each for the offering.[29] Two nights later Judge Bathgate reported one measure of the impact of Chalmers' message on the children: "A boy who had been present on Sabbath came to one of the teachers on Monday, and said, holding up a penny, 'I hadn't a penny yesterday, but I bring a penny to-day'."[30] Reviewing the year, the Kirk Session noted under "Sabbath Schools": "the Rev. James Chalmers also delivered an address, when the children from various Sunday Schools in Dunedin were present to the number of about 2500, and a large sum was collected for the New Guinea Mission."[31] What, then, was the link by which Chalmers bridged from his missionary life to establish his evident rapport with young and old alike on this New Zealand visit? One factor, I suggest, was the one fundamental worldview-shaping reality Chalmers and the children held in common: the Westminster Shorter Catechism. We turn now to

---

[29] *Otago Daily Times* (August 6 1877): 2: "It is estimated that about 2500 Sunday School children - and adults of various denominations were packed into Knox Church yesterday afternoon when the Rev. James Chalmers late of Raratonga (sic) delivered an excellent address regarding his missionary work. The collection on behalf of the New Guinea Mission amounted to £19.10.5."
[30] "Missionary Meeting," *The Otago Witness* (11 August 1877): 10.
[31] *Annual Report of the Session & Deacons' Court of Knox Church, Dunedin. For Year Ending 31st December, 1877* (Dunedin: Coulls & Culling, 1878).

explore this common link and its worldview–level influence in the relationship between the missionary and colonial Christians and their children.

The Shorter Catechism's contribution to worldview formation in the nineteenth century: an underlying link between Chalmers' and colonial Christian worldviews

James Chalmers and the Presbyterian and Congregationalist Christians he impacted on his 1877 New Zealand visit shared common theological assumptions and worldview tenets received and shaped by the Westminster Shorter Catechism. It is doubtful whether any of the church's worldview-shaping tools today exerts an influence comparable to that wielded by the Shorter Catechism upon the Scottish communities in which James Chalmers grew up, and from which the Free Church of Scotland colonists had come to Dunedin in 1848. Television and modern information technology carry great mind-shaping influence. But the basic assumptions they commonly inculcate derive from and support worldviews very different from the emphases of the Catechism.[32]

Mission educators and deputationists of the nineteenth century could, and did, assume a common catechetical worldview as the basis for further missiological informing and formation. Today we have few, if any, comparable broadly accepted theological starting points for shaping future generations of missionaries, or for sharing missionary vision. Even in church traditions where catechetical instruction continues and is positively encouraged today, the Catechism is just one among many voices shaping the worldview of young people.[33] In the nineteenth century Scotland where our

---

[32] Note the comment on the same contrast in Wilbert R. Shenk, *Changing Frontiers of Mission* (Maryknoll: Orbis, 1999), 123.

[33] See, e.g., the appeal to present-day North American Reformed churches to re-prioritise catechetical instruction in, Starr Meade, "Evangelism Begins at Home," *Modern Reformation* 14 (March/April 2005): 17–21. Cf., G.S. Hendry, *The Westminster Confession for Today: A Contemporary Interpretation* (London: SCM, 1960).

missionary candidate-to-be and original Dunedin colonists grew up, the Catechism competed with little comparable to the broad range of today's alternative contenders for the young person's mind. We need to identify and explore those catechism-based assumptions, which, we suspect, contributed largely to the affinity Chalmers found with his New Zealand church audiences during his 1877 visit. In so doing, we may also be exploring basic worldview components influencing both the Pacific missionary enterprise, as I have developed more fully elsewhere,[34] and the colonial church-life of the second half of the nineteenth century.[35]

Surveying the place of the Catechism in Chalmers' own upbringing illustrates its role in the lives of British-born young people of his generation. Born in Ardrishaig in Argyllshire, Scotland, 1841, Chalmers was brought up in villages within a few miles of the district's centre, Inveraray.[36] Work on the Inveraray pier had enticed his stone-mason father, John Chalmers, from Aberdeenshire in the mid-1830s. Chalmers would write in later life, "Of course at home and at school we had the Shorter Catechism ad nauseum..." His reminiscences suggest both parents took his moral and spiritual training seriously.[37] Until James was eight years old his father usually worked away from home, ever seeking more lucrative work than proved available. But in the son's memories his father's economic situation was incidental and his religious influence paramount. The father, whom James described theologically as "...a thorough old moderate churchman, a steady auld kirk,"[38] took the

---

[34] Hitchen, "Training Tamate," 209–29. This essay draws heavily from this section of my thesis.

[35] The Catechism was not the only formative influence on a Scots youngster's worldview. In "Training Tamate," 177–269, we also explore in Chalmers' case, the influence of socio-economic and family background, schooling, the wider intellectual climate, and other specific church influences.

[36] For a concise biography of Chalmers, see J. M. Hitchen, "Chalmers, James," in *Dictionary of Scottish Church History and Theology* (ed. Nigel M. de S. Cameron; Edinburgh: T. & T. Clark, 1993), 158.

[37] See his "Notes for Lizzie," in Hitchen, "Training Tamate," Appendix A.

[38] Hitchen, "Training Tamate," 189–92, and Appendix A, 6.

initiative in teaching the son to memorise Scripture, in Bible reading in the home, in questioning him on the catechism, and in encouraging him to attend Sunday School. John Chalmers did not send his son to church or chapel on Sabbath; he took him to both: "Blow high, blow low, rain or snow, sunshine or storm all were alike, to church he would go and I must accompany him… and when on a Sunday evening we were not at chapel we had a chapter of the bible and then were catechized."[39]

Though deep in the Scottish highlands, and never beyond the influence of the established Presbyterian Kirk, the Chalmers regularly attended the United Presbyterian Secession Chapel, which James regarded as his home church.

Chalmers' school in Glenaray was conducted by the Society in Scotland for Propagating Christian Knowledge. Something of a missionary confrontation existed in SSPCK schools between the Christian catechism on one hand and a traditional worldview and alternative moral standards on the other.[40] Chalmers was to find a similar situation in his Pacific missionary experience. In 1899 Mackay explained the place of the Catechism in an SSPCK school:

> The Society man, it must be remembered, was more than an instructor in the Three R's. The [SSPCK] scheme of 1710 bound him to be particularly careful to instruct his scholars in the principles of the Christian reformed religion, and for that end to catechise them at least twice a week, and to pray publicly with them twice a day.[41]

When Chalmers "wonders what effect that Catechism has had on [his] life," and refers to having it "ad nauseam" at home and in school, he was by no means rejecting the doctrines expressed in it.[42]

---

[39] Chalmers, "Notes for Lizzie," in Hitchen, "Training Tamate," Appendix A, 6, 8.
[40] See our detailed discussion in Hitchen, "Training Tamate," 196–98.
[41] William McKay, *Education in The Highlands in The Olden Times* (Inverness: Printed for Private Circulation, 1899), 18.
[42] Chalmers, "Notes for Lizzie," in Hitchen, "Training Tamate," Appendix A, 8.

He never deviated from the doctrinal emphases of the Catechism, although he did supplement them with further biblical emphases. Nor was Chalmers rejecting the pedagogical method of catechesis by rote learning, as his continuing use of catechisms in his missionary service confirms. Rather, Chalmers questioned the proper place in which the Catechism should be taught. For him, the day school did not provide the appropriate context for religious teaching. Only the personal and experiential context of home and Sunday School provided the sympathetic appreciation necessary for the proper grasp of the Catechism's content and meaning. When taught in a day school context alone he feared that "in many it has soured them against religious things." But, in his own case he conceded that even this overdose at school "may have been a help to me."[43]

Due caution is appropriate in assessing just how well lads like Chalmers or his colonial counterparts understood and embraced the theology of the Catechism. The weaknesses of rote learning, the immaturity of a child's intellectual development in comparison with the gravity of the Catechism's content, and a child's meagre experience of the categories to which it referred, would have all limited the comprehension of its precepts. But, through memorisation, revision, and repeated explication these concepts were fed into the child's conscious, and no doubt subconscious, thinking. They formed a major foundation for developing desires, goals, conscience, and value system. This provides a partial, but crucial, explanation of key experiences in Chalmers' later life. His apparent rejection, or at least neglect of spiritual interests in his mid-teens, with his missionary call immediately before, and conversion immediately after that rejection, are three such experiences.[44] I have documented the way the Catechism's themes

---

[43] Chalmers, "Notes for Lizzie," in Hitchen, "Training Tamate," Appendix A, 8.

[44] See Hitchen, "Training Tamate," 277–93 and 316–27.

motivate and recur throughout Chalmers' missionary service in Rarotonga and later in Papua New Guinea.[45]

As A.C. Cheyne pointed out in 1963, the role of this Catechism in the life of nineteenth century Scottish children stands not only as "a symbol of the penetration of Scotland's soul by the work of the Reformers. But of course it also stands as a monument to a vanished world of thought and belief."[46] The questions now are to what extent that "world of thought and belief" was still alive for the pious early New Zealand colonists and their children who listened to Chalmers the visiting missionary in 1877, and just what were the leading themes of the Shorter Catechism's influence?

The content and "logic" of the Shorter Catechism

The "Assembly of Divines at Westminster with the assistance of Commissioners from the Church of Scotland," presented to the English Parliament on 14 April 1648 "a Directory for catechizing such as are of weaker Capacity."[47] This "Shorter Catechism"

---

[45] See Hitchen, "Training Tamate," Chapter Four, "Prospective Candidate's Worldview," 340–453; and Chapter Six, "Missiology Confirmed and Applied," 557–739.

[46] A.C. Cheyne, "The Westminster Standards: A Century of Re-Appraisal," *Records of The Scottish Church History Society* 14 (1963): 199, where he illustrates his point by citing American evangelist D.L. Moody's surprise at a children's meeting in Edinburgh when in response to his rhetorical question, "What is Prayer?," hundreds of voices chorused back the answer to Question 98 of the Catechism. See Hendry, *The Westminster Confession for Today*.

[47] From its full title: *The Shorter Catechism, Agreed upon by The Assembly of Divines at Westminster, with the Assistance of Commissioners from the Church of Scotland, as a Part of the Covenanted Uniformity in Religion Betwixt the Churches of Christ in the Kingdoms of Scotland, England and Ireland, and approved Anno 1648, by The General Assembly of The Church of Scotland to be a Directory for catechising such as are of weaker Capacity, with References to the Proofs from Scripture*, (Various Editions). For details of its formulation and acceptance by the General Assembly of the Church of Scotland, see Benjamin B. Warfield, *The Westminster Assembly and its Work* (New York: Oxford University Press

comprises 107 questions and their answers with a number of proof texts from the Bible for each answer. The questions fall broadly into three sections.

Questions 1–38 address basic Christian doctrine, opening sublimely with God's glory and enjoying God as humanity's highest goal. The questions proceed to knowing God, what he is like, and his relationships with this world. From God, the focus moves to human beings and especially humanity's fall from communion with God and resulting need. This leads in turn to a summary of Christ's person and work as redeemer from that need, how to secure this redemption, and the Christian's relationship with God both now and in the future.

After summarising the Christian faith and Gospel, the next and major part of the Catechism – Questions 39–84 on moral law, divine requirements, and human need – studies the Ten Commandments in detail. The logic of this progression is two-fold: a grasp of the law explains the inner attitudes and behaviour God requires of humans, and convinces of the need of redemption. The section on moral law concludes by stressing human inability to attain these requirements unaided.

The final section – Questions 85–107 on divine provisions for receiving and sustaining Christian life – tells how to receive the needed help and share the benefits of this redemption through the Word of God, the sacraments, and prayer.

Thus the Catechism's teaching was set within two major parameters: the theocentric and the evangelistic. On the one hand stood God's active rule over women and men, the requirements he placed upon them, and their consequent dependence upon him. On the other hand were God's active decrees on humanity's behalf and his offer of redemption in Christ. The catechumen was to experience two fundamental realities: to know God, and to become rightly related to him. In its overall sweep the Catechism challenged

---

1931), 63–69; and for its Scottish use, see Cheyne, "The Westminster Standards," 199–214.

human self-competence. It allowed no room for a secularism that ignored or rejected God's sovereign rights over his people. It also challenged human self-righteousness. Though its emphasis on law may have been seen as binding legal restrictions, the intention was to inculcate humility and consequent dependence upon God in Christ for all that is of most value in life.

James Chalmers' whole missionary career was consciously lived out within these theocentric and evangelistic parameters. The overall logic of the Catechism formed a key platform of his worldview.

Leading worldview-forming themes of the Shorter Catechism

Five major themes or emphases permeate the Shorter Catechism. First, God is the Living Lord of Human affairs. As Warfield put it:

> No Catechism begins on a higher plane than the Westminster "Shorter Catechism". Its opening question... sets the learner at once in his right relation to God. Withdrawing his eyes from himself, even from his own salvation, as the chief object of concern, it fixes them on God and His glory, – and bids him seek his highest blessedness in Him.[48]

The Catechism confirmed this centrality and lordship of God repeatedly. He alone was the living and true God [5],[49] whose will controlled all history as he actively created, preserved, and governed all his creatures [7–11]. He entered into a covenant of grace to rescue the elect and provided his eternal son as a redeemer [20–21]. He effectually called believers by the work of his Spirit [31]. By his free grace he gave justification, adoption, and sanctification to the Christian [33–35]. Love for God summed up all the commandments [42]. His own nature and his work for them were sufficient basis for making demands of his creatures [44]. The first commandment required humans to acknowledge and worship him

---

[48] Warfield, *Westminster Assembly*, 379.

[49] Henceforth numbers in square brackets refer to the numbered questions of the Shorter Catechism.

and make no ultimate commitment to anyone or anything else [46–48]. He held men and women accountable for their transgression and to apply the means of grace he offered [84–87]. He invited them to draw near to him through prayer as trusting children [100]. Concern to glorify him and obey his will should come first, and he alone was the source of encouragement and theme of praise, in prayer [101–103, 107].

The Catechism presupposed that God was actively involved in the most intimate activities of his people. Recurring concepts such as God's "will," "covenant," "counsel," or "good pleasure," and his "glory," further emphasised this presupposition [7, 20, 24, 39, 98, 103]. Five questions stressed his contractual agreement with his people [12, 16, 20, 92, 94]. More often it taught of his dependability as law-giver and judge. To glorify God was our chief human goal in the first, and our highest privilege in the last, question, and a recurring theme throughout [2, 6, 7, 46, 47, 66, 101].

From the start this God-centred focus both established our human duty and called for response: indeed, to "enjoy Him forever." Only here, perhaps, was there mitigation for the otherwise inexplicable omission of any focus upon the love of God. The emphasis on the sterner aspects of God's nature meant we could easily miss the passing reference to assurance of God's love as one benefit flowing from justification, adoption, and sanctification [36]. To give God due honour and to find satisfying fulfilment in him were the Catechism's primary precepts for humankind. Little wonder Chalmers in reflective mode commented, "the God of the Highlands at that time was a terror, and we knew more of him as such, than as of love."[50]

There can be no doubt, however, that Chalmers personally imbibed these catechetical emphases as the basis of the faith that sustained his missionary service. To select but a few examples: writing to Stuart Ross, his Dunedin friend from the furlough visit

---

[50] Chalmers, "Notes for Lizzie," in Hitchen, "Training Tamate," Appendix A, 8.

just three years later, lamenting the death of his wife, Chalmers commented, "God only knows how alone I am, and at times how I feel it. I live the past and sometimes forget it is a past. But, brother, God is Home. In Him through Christ there is all..."[51] Or again three years later again, with thoughts so fundamental only the vernacular Doric could adequately express them, "Let us a' just a wee wee nearer tae Him, and lippen Him wi' a'."[52] But this trust in the living God took very practical expression as he explained his attitude to physical dangers:

> In May, 1878, I began my journeys on New Guinea, in parts hitherto unknown, and amongst tribes supposed to be hostile. I resolved, come what might, to travel unarmed, trusting to Him in whose work I was engaged, and feeling that no harm could come to me while in His care.[53]

What most people saw as bravery, Chalmers admitted could be seen as foolhardiness, but for his catechetically learned confidence in God's moral dependability and active protection.[54]

The second pervading emphasis of the Catechism was that only through the Bible could we know the way to glorify and enjoy God [2]. The special revelation of the written Scriptures was upheld as the only indispensable authority for knowing God aright and for correct behaviour [3]. The possibility of other means of revelation was not altogether excluded. The third commandment forbade "all profaning and abusing of anything whereby God makes himself known." God's works, ordinances, and name were set alongside his Word as worthy of due reverence on that account [54–55]. But how God made himself known in nature and sacraments was developed no further. Christ revealed God's will concerning our salvation

---

[51] Chalmers - Ross, 30 May 1881, cited in Ross, *Tamate: Apostle*, 37.
[52] Chalmers - Ross, 27 March 1884, cited in Ross, *Tamate: Apostle*, 85. At the risk of losing the heart in translation: "Let all of us draw ever nearer to Christ and trust Him fully with everything."
[53] James Chalmers and William Wyatt Gill, *Work and Adventure in New Guinea, 1877-1885* (London: RTS, 1885), 56; cf., 173–74.
[54] Chalmers, "Life in New Guinea," *Sunday at Home* (1887): 582, cf., 457.

through his Word. Through that same Word he shared the benefits of his redemption [24, 88]. The Word of God alone showed what behaviour is acceptable to God [39–40], and what worship pleased him [50–51]. These claims to exclusive religious authority for the Word of God implied a missionary obligation. If the Bible alone revealed the truth about acceptable worship and behaviour, then that biblical message must be proclaimed to all.

Despite this explicit emphasis, the Catechism supported its doctrinal statements by citing selected proof-texts confirming each doctrine in a way that potentially undermined the sole authority of those Scriptures, as we have discussed elsewhere.[55] While challenging this proof-texting use of Scripture, we have endorsed the Catechism's teaching concerning the Bible as the Word of God. Questions 88–90 gave priority to the Word, especially the preached Word, amongst the means for mediating Christ's work to humanity. Question 90 particularly guarded against any superficial or superstitious attitudes to that Word. Chalmers consistently upheld this high view of scriptural authority throughout his missionary service. For one example: when discussing the "much sorrow and suffering" caused by the accepted mission practice of expecting a polygamous convert to put away all but one of his wives before baptism, he complained:

> Surely not the glad tidings of a Father's love through the adorable Son our Redeemer has caused such. No, no, only man's device, a requirement our Lord Jesus has not laid down. Other Missions have required it, it will be said, I answer, not what they have required but what saith the scriptures or what is the spirit of the Gospel.[56]

We trace Chalmers' continuing use and evident respect for Scripture back to this emphasis in the Shorter Catechism, and suggest this

---

[55] Hitchen, "Training Tamate," 216–20.
[56] Chalmers, "Four Years After," 10, enclosed with Chalmers - Thompson, 28 October 1882 (LMS/PL, Box3/2/A, IDC H2123/44), 24; and Ross, *Tamate: Apostle*, 47–48.

commitment contributed to his ready acceptance by his New Zealand colonial hearers in 1877.

A third feature of the Catechism concerns humanity's accountability to God and for one another. The Catechism emphasized human accountability both to our Maker and for each other and linked this accountability to the previous themes by teaching that the presence of the all-seeing and all-knowing God among his people [48] provided the backdrop for human accountability. The levels and implications of such accountability were known only through biblical revelation.

The Godward accountability first implied with the claim that humans have a "chief end," became explicit in our moral duty: "The first commandment requires us to know and acknowledge God... and to worship and glorify him accordingly" [46]. The phrase "God requires" ran as a refrain through the Catechism [3, 39, 85]. Two related questions introduced each of the Ten Commandments: "What is required in the [1st etc.] commandment?" And, "What is forbidden in the [1st etc.] commandment?" This accountability extended as far as God's lordship to embrace all of life. Humans were responsible to God for right worship, reverence, and observance of religious duties; for respect for social structures; for protection of human life; for respect for sex and marriage; for acquisition and use of possessions; for speech and thought; and for our desires and how we expressed them [45–81].

This all-embracing accountability was to a personal God, not vague moral principles. God would require an account before his saviour son on an appointed "last day" [28, 38, 56], with strict justice to be expected [19, 84]. Human accountability was inculcated by the specific language "God requires...," "man's duty is...," and by a range of related terminology such as "obedience," "due to Him...," "bound to keep...," "moral law...," "forbids...," "abusing...," "neglecting of duty...," and so forth. For the Catechism, therefore, sin was seen unequivocally as attitudes and actions towards God. Sin was not merely a personal human weakness or a failure to achieve acceptable social norms: "sin is any want of conformity unto, or transgression of the law of God" [14]. By joining the theocentric emphasis with this all-embracing accountability to a living, personal God, the Catechism taught that the most serious sin was to break the first, not the seventh, commandment.

Accountability to the living God also pervaded the Catechism's teaching on social relationships and the stewardship of our lives, possessions, and socio-economic position. To summarize, the whole moral law required the balance of, "...to love the Lord our God with all our heart... and our neighbour as ourselves" [42]. Thus throughout the discussion of the moral law, "neighbour" or "others" were kept in focus. Humans were to "preserve our own life and the life of others"; to protect our neighbour's as well as our own chastity; to lawfully procure and further "the wealth and outward estate of ourselves and others"; and to be concerned for our neighbour's good name as well as our own [68–78]. "Full contentment with our own condition" must be balanced by "a right and charitable frame of spirit toward our neighbour, and all that is his" [80–81]. The Catechism constantly expanded the application of the moral law, precluding any individualistic or restricted application. For instance, the fifth commandment, "Honour thy father and thy mother," originally focussed on family, is broadened by the Catechism's interpretation to also include duties within the church, community, and political spheres.[57] We may question the understanding of social structures assumed in the Catechism, but we cannot ignore this generalizing tendency which attempted to inculcate the personal duty to maintain worthily the full sweep of social relationships. This accountability for others is also set in a missiological context [102]:

---

[57] It said: "The fifth commandment requires the preserving the honour, and performing the duties, belonging to everyone in their several places and relations, as superiors, inferiors, or equals... [and] forbids the neglecting of or doing anything against, the honour and duty which belongs to everyone in their several places and relations."

In the second petition [of the Lord's Prayer – which is, thy kingdom come] we pray that Satan's Kingdom may be destroyed; and that the Kingdom of grace may be advanced, ourselves and others brought into it, and kept in it; and that the Kingdom of glory may be hastened.

The Catechism, then, called for broad involvement in social and spiritual justice. We suggest these concepts of accountability to God and for our fellow humans were shared by Chalmers and his colonial audiences, and provided key theological assumptions behind Chalmers' appeals for New Zealand Sunday School children and parishioners to share in supporting the Cook Islander missionaries in Papua New Guinea – indeed, behind the whole assumption of missionary obligation to peoples of other cultures and religions which has been a significant focus in discussions of mission history in recent decades and which I have addressed elsewhere.[58]

Fourth, dependence upon Jesus Christ and the Holy Spirit to fulfil God's requirements is a focus of the Catechism. The Catechism built up a progressive case indicating human inability to fulfil the divine requirements apart from the intervention of divine assistance through Christ Jesus. The human race globally was seen as one both in origin and in need before God: "Did all mankind fall in Adam's first transgression?" [16] expected the response: "The covenant being made with Adam not only for himself, but for his posterity; all mankind, descending from him by ordinary generation, sinned in him, and fell with him, in his first transgression." This teaching undercut any ground for racial pride and provided a foundation for mutual equality between different cultures and tribal groups. The "federal headship" of the first humans over the whole

---

[58] Cf., Neill Gunson, *Messengers of Grace: Evangelical Missionaries in the South Seas, 1797-1860* (Melbourne: Oxford University Press, 1978), 33–34, 47–51; S.F. Piggin, "The Social Background and Training of British Protestant Missionaries to India, 1789-1858" (PhD Thesis, University of London, 1974), 57–58; David J. Bosch, *Transforming Mission: Paradigm Shifts in Theology of Mission* (Maryknoll: Orbis, 1991), 5–6; and Hitchen, "Training Tamate," 144–70.

human race also implied a community of need amongst all humans, soon forgotten in the upsurge of individualism of later Protestant thought. Chalmers, however, worked among groups for whom communal accountability and participation in the actions of forebears were central aspects of their own worldview. Furthermore, as a child this doctrine had taught Chalmers that despite the stratification of the class-conscious Inveraray society of his youth, in our standing before God rank, status, and position counted for nothing. When brought to clearer perception by his own later religious experience, this fundamental theological insight accounted, at least in part, for Chalmers' ability to be at home in whatever social setting he found himself: whether in unsophisticated Rarotonga or in the home of the Hon Matthew Holmes in Anderson's Bay, Dunedin;[59] amongst his "savage" friends in Papua New Guinea[60] or dining with George Douglas Campbell, the Eighth Duke of Argyll at Inveraray Castle.[61] The Catechism's emphases levelled and united them all in its social implications.

Because of the "Fall," the Catechism saw all humans in a state of "sin" and "misery" [17]. This sinfulness involved all humans in the guilt of their original father's sin, the loss of their intended right standing before God, a resulting corruption of his or her inner nature [18-19], and thus, actual transgression of God's requirements, for: "No mere man since the fall is able in this life perfectly to keep the commandments of God but daily breaks them

---

[59] The Chalmers met the MP and Mrs Holmes on the boat between Wellington and Dunedin in 1877, immediately struck up a mutual friendship, and were invited as guests to the Holmes' residence in Dunedin. Ross, *Tamate: Apostle*, 9.

[60] Chalmers wrote: "I love savages, not with a sentiment born of philanthropy or Christian zeal, but as the result of experience gained during many years of happy intercourse with them. Although they are unvarnished, and have many dark spots which the arts of civilisation would fain teach them to hide, I prefer real things; and a simple savage, if he seldom has noble traits, is intensely human and capable of sincere and enduring friendship." "Life in New Guinea," *Sunday at Home* 1729 (1887): 328.

[61] See Hitchen, "Training Tamate," 244.

in thought, word, and deed" [82]. This stands in stark contrast to our twentieth century pervasive confidence in the inherent goodness of humanity. But for Chalmers and his 1877 listeners this was basic. Sin was both constitutionally inherent in human nature and explicitly displayed in deliberate transgressions.

After describing human need thus, and elaborating on its "misery" [19],[62] the Catechism proceeded to offer a specific answer. The Lord Jesus Christ came as our redeemer from this sinfulness and misery [20–21]. Christ's divine-human nature and his incarnation were the essential basis for his work in his three "offices" as prophet, priest, and king necessary to redeem the "elect" from their "sinfulness" and "misery." Though clouded somewhat by the vexed question of who were the "elect," the Catechism's emphasis on these "offices" carried an inherent world-wide or missiological concern. As prophet, Christ alone for all the world, declared to us God's will for our salvation [24]. As priest, Christ, and again he alone, satisfied divine justice "in his once offering up himself a sacrifice," and thereby reconciled us to God [25]. As king, Christ continued to work on behalf of his people in the context of spiritual battle [26], where Satan is the opposing ruler [102]. The Catechism taught children to seek their most basic human requirements only in Jesus Christ. He offered right understanding in place of human ignorance, full restoration in place of broken relationships, and enabling power in place of human inability and domineering forces.

Question 29 further endorsed this dependence upon Christ. "How are we made partakers of the redemption purchased by Christ?" The Holy Spirit applied the "purchased redemption" to us by "effectual calling."[63] For the Catechism the sinful state with its

---

[62] See Hitchen, "Training Tamate," 225–26, for a discussion of the way this term "misery" accounts for the oft maligned nineteenth century missionaries' use of terms such as "poor heathen," or the "plight of the savage."

[63] Question 31 explained: "Effectual calling is the work of God's Spirit, whereby, convincing us of our sin and misery, enlightening our minds in the knowledge of Christ, and renewing our wills, he persuades and enables us to embrace Jesus Christ, freely offered to us in the gospel."

"corruption of the whole [human] nature" [18] was such that our conscience and value system, our intellect and powers of reasoning, and our will with its decision making processes, all needed the transforming touch of God himself in the person of his Holy Spirit. Only thus were humans able to receive the new life offered in Christ. Only by a return to face-to-face encounter with, and inward transformation by God himself could the effects of the fall be counteracted. Thus the child was taught to "rest upon Christ alone for salvation" [86]. This belief in the human spiritual state explained the background to Chalmers' LMS application paper responses: "I further believe that man of himself can do nothing to please God, that without the Holy Spirit, the Third Person in the Godhead, working within him he still will persist in his sinful career"; or again, his reference to those he hoped to serve as "my Heathen brethren."[64] Chalmers could safely assume that this sense of need and dependence on Jesus Christ for redemption, which had become central tenets of his own worldview, were shared by his colonial hearers in his after-church evangelistic rallies, and by the children in his Sunday School rallies.

A fifth and final feature is the accepted reality of salvation categories and the overall cosmology of the Catechism. Through the prevailing usage of the Catechism in home and school, religious terminology and religious categories became part and parcel of everyday life for children like Chalmers. Rote learning taught them to regard justification, adoption, sanctification, assurance of God's love, peace of conscience, joy in the Holy Spirit, increase of grace, faith, repentance, and the ordinances as "benefits" for life here and now [32, 36, 85, 88]. Limited though the child's perception of such concepts may have been, their idea and value-forming propensity was still very real.

But, with such salvation categories constantly held before you as desirable ends, if you failed to discover "benefit" in them, then disillusion, rejection, or reinterpretation of the faith must follow. This may be traced in Chalmers' case to his teen-age rejection of

---

[64] Chalmers, 5 June 1862 (LMS/CPQ), Questions 7 and 11.

church and avoidance of his Christian mentors.[65] If instead of, or after, such disillusion a spiritual experience made those categories a personal existential reality, then their personality-integrating effect could become all pervasive. Again, Chalmers was a case in point with his conversion during the 1859 revival in Scotland.[66]

Everyday familiarity with these salvation concepts also led to the free, unabashed use of biblical terms and imagery in nineteenth century home and church life (not to mention novels and literature generally). Theological concepts such as "enlightenment" of the mind by the Spirit and the presumed "darkness" of "ignorance" this inferred [Q31], were commonplace terms for Chalmers from his youth, and he could rightly assume he shared them with New Zealand Sunday School children.

This basic assumed cosmology of the Shorter Catechism took for granted the ontological reality of God and of another realm of created beings transcending the limits of our material, space-time categories. Heaven, hell, and angels were referred to without explanation [28, 19, 103], as were other terms referring to the after-life, like "glory" as a synonym for heaven and participation in the heavenly state [38, 39]. The matter of fact acceptance of another realm beyond ours surfaced again in the "three Kingdoms" concept of Satan ruling the present age, with Christ ruling over the Kingdom of Grace, until he would set up his future Kingdom of glory [102]. Reference to the conflict between God and his enemies [26 and 106] confirmed that the reality of this non-material and invisible order was taken for granted as the context of human experience. The certainty of eternal realities both before and beyond the time-limits of history was stressed by reference to the eternal dimension of God's purpose, will, and action [7, 20, 28, 38], or again with the expected consummation of human history in a "last day" of "resurrection" and "judgement" [28, 37, 38], before believers enjoyed God for all eternity [38].

---

[65] Hitchen, "Training Tamate," 285–93.
[66] Hitchen, "Training Tamate," 318–27.

The overall cosmology assumed in the Catechism, then, took spiritual realities for granted. It regarded God and his purposes as directly controlling and guiding the course of history, the affairs of humanity, and the eternal destiny of created orders of existence. This wider background is again confirmed in the Catechism's matter of fact references to issues such as death [12, 19, 27, 28, 37, 96]. This cosmology was, for Chalmers, his father and his SSPCK teacher, of ontological, not merely mythological, reality. His Rarotongan mission experience had reinforced the relevance of these categories for peoples of other cultures. He maintained this practical ontology throughout his Papua New Guinea service; describing the death of a teacher and his wife at Toaripi, he wrote: "Following in his footsteps, they count not their lives dear; as he went to Calvary, knowing all, so do they, trusting in him, and following his example. Christ shows us how to live, and also how to die, and there are still Calvarys with their grand life ending."[67]

Chalmers' ready rapport with the colonial Christians in Dunedin and the Otago district's Free Kirk colony, and with the Presbyterian and Congregational segments of the 1877 Christchurch Anglican settlement, we suggest, owed much to their embracing the ontological reality of the same set of catechetical assumptions.

Conclusion

The teaching of the Catechism held pride of place among the formative influences of home, school, and sunday school in the world in which Chalmers grew up. It provided the conceptual framework and basic terminology for his theology, cosmology, value system, and life goals, and, when enriched by his later spiritual pilgrimage, proved formative in his motivation and message in his missionary service. Here, we suggest, are five vital worldview components of a typical nineteenth century missionary:

- knowing God as the living Lord of human affairs;

---

[67] Lovett, *Chalmers*, 297.

- accepting the Bible as the basis of all religious authority;
- taking seriously our human accountability to God and for our fellow humans;
- depending on Jesus Christ through the Holy Spirit to enable us to meet God's requirements;
- accepting the everyday, ontological reality of salvation categories, and a cosmology that gives due place to the living God and the spiritual realm.

During Chalmers' youth these worldview commitments were virtually taken for granted in his Scottish community. Home, school, local government, and church – whether "auld Kirk," Free Kirk, or Secession Chapel, Presbyterian or Congregational – intentionally upheld them with few alternative voices. The legal system, accepted community standards, and media all publicly assumed them as the expected and unquestioned moral and religious norm. In embracing these theological and intellectual commitments Chalmers was no different from his peers. His personal rebellion during his teen years was widely recognised in his community as just that, rebellion against the consensus. The five fundamental areas of belief provided a given starting point for further moral development and ethical choice as well as the motivating dynamic for Christian service. This uniform endorsement by the community of the basic tenets of the Catechism would be fragmented and begin to dissolve during Chalmers' later lifetime. But we should give due weight to this contextual confirmation of catechetical values during the 1830s to 1880s in Britain.[68] We are proposing that since this was the same context from which the active Christians of the South Island New Zealand colonies came in the mid-nineteenth century, these same shared catechetical emphases enabled Chalmers to feel so much in

---

[68] Walter Berns, "The Cultivation of Citizenship," in *Public Morality, Civic Virtue, and the Problem of Modern Liberalism* (eds. T. William Boxx and Gary M. Quinlivan; Grand Rapids: Eerdmans, 2000), 1-13, shows how literature and reading primers reinforced similar worldview presuppositions in successive generations of American school children in the eighteenth and nineteenth centuries.

tune with his New Zealand audiences. The missionary deputationist upheld and reinforced these very assumptions in the colonial setting.

Chalmers continued to use the catechetical method in his new phase of service in Papua New Guinea. While based at Port Moresby, Papua, in 1880, Chalmers wrote to his new friend from the 1877 visit, Stuart Ross in Dunedin, "At odd times the [Polynesian] teachers have translated Catechisms, which I am revising, and with new hymns, may soon be able to send to press."[69] Later that year he reported to London, "A catechism finished at the beginning of the year is well known by nearly fifty children."[70] Any adequate analysis of the missionary impact of Chalmers' generation of missionaries in the Pacific needs to give due weight to the influence in their upbringing and ministry of the Shorter Catechism and catechesis generally.

This paper has suggested understanding of colonial New Zealand life in the second half of the nineteenth century could also be enriched by closer attention to the role of the itinerant missionary on deputation amongst New Zealand churches. Moreover, to grasp that influence in any depth, we need to be aware of the nature and pervasive influence of the precepts of the Westminster Shorter Catechism, both in the lives of the itinerant missionaries and of their hearers.

---

[69] Chalmers - Ross, 4 March 1880, in Ross, *Tamate: Apostle*, 30.
[70] Chalmers - Whitehouse, 11 December 1880 (LMS Archives/PL, Box2/4/C, IDC H2123/35), 30. For a later example in 1889 see Lovett, *Chalmers*, 336.

Chapter Two
The foundation of the Bible Training Institute

Peter Lineham

The formation of the Bible Training Institute was an important stage in the development of the interdenominational tradition of evangelical Christianity which became so strong a feature of New Zealand in the twentieth century. For this reason it repays close examination. The story focuses on Joseph Kemp, the pastor in the inter-war years of the largest Baptist Church in New Zealand, the Baptist Tabernacle in Auckland. Kemp had many dreams and plans when he came to New Zealand, and the BTI may not have been high on the list. The stimulus to his action may have been a woman's weekly prayer meeting at the Tabernacle, which began to pray for a school to train Christian workers. This led Kemp to call together a group of businessmen to discuss the venture.[1] Kemp assembled a very interesting group of people inspired by the vision, who were anxious that the venture should not fail. They prayed earnestly that they would make no blunders at their first meeting on 11 July 1921.[2] They also sought carefully to assess the opportunities. They knew how to make a venture succeed in the business world and the decision to recommend the formation to a representative meeting, which was developed a week later, indicated a depth of commitment:

> that we here present having during the past week laid the question of the establishment of a Bible Institute before the Lord in prayer conceive it to be his will that such an institute should be established on similar lines to the Moody Bible Institute in Chicago and the Bible Institute at Los Angeles and that a committee be set up to draw up a constitution to be submitted to an adjourned meeting of 25th inst at 6 30, it being understood that of such Institute the Rev Joseph W. Kemp be

---

[1] "The Importance of the Bible Training Institute," *Reaper* 5 (July 1927): 106.
[2] BTI Minute Book 1 (11 July 1921).

asked to take the position of principal and Mr C.J. Rolls of India that of Superintendent.[3]

The success of the proposal did much to mark out Kemp and his supporters as very significant players in the emergence of evangelicalism. It was, however, one of three different proposals to establish a Bible Training Institute or evangelical seminary. All these ideas have some common roots stemming back to admiration for the work of Dwight L. Moody and his Moody Bible Institute and also the Glasgow Bible Institute, which was a consequence of his great British evangelistic mission of the 1870s. Such was the influence of Moody that we should not be surprised at attempts to emulate his work in New Zealand.

Three other attempts to found a Bible Institute

The first attempt at a Bible Institute in New Zealand came about some ten years before the foundation of Kemp's Institute. It made a brief appearance in April 1912. It was also called the BTI, and was established in Whangareito near Whangarei. The Rev Albert Whalley, the Baptist minister who had founded the Whangarei church in 1904, chose in 1909 to support himself on "faith lines," declining a salary from his church. This marks him out as profoundly influenced by the China Inland Mission. Since the early 1890s missionary support had exploded in New Zealand, and created a demand for training, and Whalley hoped to meet the need. Mrs Francis Verrall, the church secretary, had given him a large house, previously occupied by the Rev F. Robertshaw, and here he decided to establish an Institute, naming the house "En-Hakkore" (Hebrew for "place of retreat"). Among others associated were the Methodist Rev H. Ford and Alfred Galpin, a Baptist home missionary with later links with the China Inland Mission.[4]

---

[3] BTI Minute Book 1 (18 July 1921).
[4] *Northern Advocate* (22 March 1913): 4, mentions both Whalley and Galpin. For Whalley see also *New Zealand Baptist* (August 1911): 160. For the Verrall family at Whangarei see *New Zealand Baptist* (February 1909): 280, *New Zealand Baptist* (August 1911): 160. For Rev Ford and A. Galpin (both

Whalley was very conscious of the example of Bible Institutes in England, Scotland, and America, and claimed to have been in correspondence with them. His key motivation was "to meet the call for missionaries" and he referred in an interview to his particular concern about the need for women missionaries. Elsewhere he described his desire to emphasise the writings of Campbell Morgan and Oswald Chambers, and referred to John R. Mott, who was the notable American founder of the Student Volunteer Movement, although by this time a breach was in fact developing between the SVM and the BTI movement as the divergence between Liberalism and Fundamentalism developed.[5] So he was a man suffused by the new "Keswick" sensibilities which came in the wake of Moody's influence.

What happened to this BTI is not altogether clear. Whalley retired from the church in 1913, and was replaced by Guy Thornton.[6] At his retirement he announced yet another attempt to establish a Bible Training Institute on an interdenominational basis in the vicinity of Auckland, but little seems to have happened. A Mr Vowles graduated from this BTI in 1913 and went to serve in the Baptist church in Wanganui East, but no other graduates are known.[7]

The second attempt to create an institute happened at the same time as Kemp's institute was in planning. Kemp and his committee received an indication from the Rev A.A. Murray and W.R.D.

---

preaching in Methodist and Baptist settings) see *Northern Advocate* (27 January 1912): 1, and *Northern Advocate* (9 April 1912): 5.

[5] "New Zealand Bible Training Institute Opening Ceremony," *Northern Advocate* (6 April 1912): 5. Cutting from unnamed newspapers in Laidlaw College safe: "Training Students for Foreign Missions: Rev A Whalley founds Institute at Whangareito to meet the Clamant Call for Missionaries," n.d. [not traced in *Papers Past*]. See also *New Zealand Baptist* (May 1912): 88.

[6] *New Zealand Baptist* (March 1914): 60. However he was still writing to the *Northern Advocate* in 1918, e.g., 4 June 1918, 3. The *New Zealand Baptist* (May 1916): 98, describes him as supplying the Tauranga church but living in Whangarei.

[7] *Northern Advocate* (12 February 1913): 5; *New Zealand Baptist* (September 1913): 175; *New Zealand Baptist* (October 1913): 200.

Campbell that they were considering a similar venture. This very nearly stymied Kemp's scheme. Alexander Adam Murray (1878-1959) had been the minister of Auckland's First Church, St Andrew's Presbyterian Church, from 1908 to 1920, but had been suspended from the Presbyterian ministry by the General Assembly of 1920 after he had denounced infant baptism. He then founded the United Evangelical Church which met in the Tivoli Theatre. Murray later resigned from the UEC and returned to the Presbyterian Church, but he remained on the fundamentalist end of the spectrum and took a key role in the "Great Bible Demonstration" against the visiting Modernist H.D.A. Major in 1929 although he moved in 1931 to Nova Scotia.[8]

Murray's elaborate scheme seems to have been modelled on Princeton, then the key evangelical seminary in America under B.B. Warfield and others, although just a few years later in 1929 it was split by the Modernist debate and Westminster Seminary became the place of refuge for the conservatives. Murray was evidently interested in a theological academy placing a strong emphasis on the biblical languages and postgraduate study, which was very different from Moody's idea of a body teaching only the English Bible.[9] Murray's proposal never took institutional shape, but he had consulted with the stalwart of Presbyterian conservatism in New Zealand, the Rev P.B. Fraser,[10] another admirer of Princeton who had corresponded extensively with Warfield and Hodge, for his wife's brother-in-law was the Registrar at Princeton. Fraser was the

---

[8] See J.M.R. Simpson, "Joseph W. Kemp and the Impact of American Fundamentalism in New Zealand" (BA Hons Research Exercise, University of Waikato, 1986), 82-91; Presbyterian Church of New Zealand, *Proceedings of General Assembly* (1920), 159-170; *Reaper* 7 (April 1929): 30; *New Zealand Herald* (24 July 1959); *Ashburton Guardian* (7 December 1920): 5. Stuart Lange in his thesis notes that A.A. Murray commanded little respect among evangelical Presbyterians. Stuart M. Lange, "A Rising Tide: The Growth of Evangelicalism and Evangelical Identity among Presbyterians, Anglicans and University Students in New Zealand, 1930-1965" (PhD thesis, University of Otago, 2008), 329.

[9] BTI Minute Book 1 (25 July 1921).

[10] BTI Minute Book 1 (8 August 1921).

publisher of the magazine the *Biblical Recorder* from 1914 to 1935, which was notorious for its sharp criticisms of directions in the Presbyterian Church, notably the teaching of Professor John Dickie at the Theological Hall in Dunedin. Fraser was very willing to use the term "Modernism" of tendencies in the Presbyterian Church. Thus Presbyterian confessionalism was a strand of New Zealand fundamentalism as it was in America.[11] Fraser was very happy to advertise Kemp's Institute in the *Biblical Recorder* and eager to serve the cause, despite his divergent vision (and the vision, perhaps, of most evangelical Presbyterians) of what was needed.[12]

Murray's conception of an Institute was quite different from Kemp's. It was intended as a conservative seminary for the training of ministers. Although it did not only focus on Presbyterians (since Murray was at that time no part of the Presbyterian Church) its vision was shaped by the academic orientation of Presbyterian training, and would never have focused on the needs of those not seeking ordination. There is little surprise that Kemp's proposal was the one with the broader appeal.

The third proposal was much closer to Kemp's vision. About the same time that the BTI was formed, there was also an attempt to found a United Evangelical Bible Institute in Palmerston North. It was planned as a part-time college initially, with rooms in Bryant's Building in Rangitikei Street.[13] It came about through the initiative of the Rev D.B. Forde Carlisle. Forde Carlisle (c1881-1962), the proposed principal, had originally been a Primitive Methodist home missionary, and was ordained in 1911 and was appointed to the Eltham church of that very evangelical denomination. However before the Primitive Methodists merged with the larger Wesleyan Methodist Church, he had resigned and become minister of the Berhampore Baptist Church in 1912 and then the Palmerston

---

[11] Allan K. Davidson, "A Protesting Presbyterian: The Reverend P. B. Fraser and New Zealand Presbyterianism, 1892-1940," *Journal of Religious History* 14 (1986): 214-15.

[12] BTI Minute Book 1 (14 August 1922). Lange, "A Rising Tide," makes very little reference to the impact of Kemp and the BTI.

[13] "Evangelical Bible Institute," *Manawatu Evening Standard* (6 October 1923).

North Baptist Church in 1913. He was a very popular minister initially, and in 1915 published a passionately pre-millennial account of the purposes of God, *Human Failure and Divine Progress*.[14] But in 1918 there was a sharp dispute with members of the congregation over his dispensationalist views and hostility to the Baptist Union, and he and his supporters seceded.

In 1922 Forde Carlisle began what became the United Evangelical Church which met in the Kosy Hall. At this stage Forde Carlisle was a corresponding member of the Auckland BTI Board. He had no involvement in Murray's scheme even though both were ministers in the putative United Evangelical Church. But in 1923 Dr French E. Oliver who had already made an impact in Auckland and Hamilton, was invited to Palmerston North and held large meetings in Everybody's Theatre in Coleman Place near the Square, then transferring to the Empire Theatre and finally to the Opera House. The Palmerston North United Evangelical Church was formally instituted in March 1923.[15] A large group of church people from a range of congregations left their denominations to form the new church. Palmerston North had strong evangelical associations because of the impact of revivalism in the district, linked with the Methodists and the Brethren. Forde Carlisle later fell out with the United Evangelical Church and was suspected of Bullingerist teachings which took dispensationalism one step further. Years later he renounced his ordination, joined the Brethren, and became very active in the International Council of Christian Churches along with Dr William H. Pettit, the former Student Christian Movement missionary to India who had led a secession from that body in reaction to its modernism, and

---

[14] D.B. Forde Carlisle, *Human Failure and Divine Progress* (Wellington: Whitcombe & Tombs, 1915).

[15] G.T. Beilby, *Centennial History of the Palmerston North Central Baptist Church 1894-1994* (Palmerston North: The Church, 1994), 2, 5; Primitive Methodist Church Conference MS Yearbook, pp 233, 226 (Methodist Archives, Christchurch); *1923-1973 United Evangelical Church Princess Street Golden Jubilee* (Palmerston North: The Church, 1973). See *New Zealand Truth* (16 June 1923): 1.

thereafter threw himself exclusively into organisations which defended the fundamental truths of Christianity.[16] No wonder that inter-denominational bodies did not flourish under Forde Carlisle.

Oliver's mission in 1923 and the formation of the United Evangelical Church in the city had given Forde Carlisle a motivation to start an Institute as well in order to make his mark on a wider stage. He had perhaps been poisoned against the Auckland BTI by Oliver's accusation that it was fostering belief in conditional immortality. Oliver ensured that the Palmerston North Institute was on a narrower basis. Oliver gave £100 towards the Institute, which he saw as a guardian against false doctrines in New Zealand.[17] Oliver had been a staff member of the large Bible Institute of Los Angeles, the principal of which was none other than Reuben A. Torrey. Oliver had in fact been suspended by BIOLA after allegations of misconduct, and his visit to New Zealand in 1923 therefore had a somewhat sectarian note to it.[18] For this reason it seems that the Palmerston North Institute never really got under way. For although Kemp's BTI was fundamentalist, it was not sectarian, and its ability to attract people from a number of denominations was critical to its vision. That was quite an achievement in New Zealand in the 1920s.

Kemp's Vision

These three alternative proposals thus indicate some of the pitfalls of proposing an evangelical college. Too academic, too sectarian, too isolated, lacking in breadth of support, all these were perilous for a college. What may surprise is that Joseph Kemp was able to

---

[16] BTI Minute Book 1 (30 November 1921); *Treasury* 64 (1962): 320. For Pettit, see P.J. Lineham, "Pettit, William Haddow," *Dictionary of New Zealand Biography* 3 *1901-1920* (ed. C. Orange; Auckland: Auckland University Press and Department of Internal Affairs, 1996), 398-99.

[17] D. B. Forde Carlisle, Palmerston North, to Bruce Scott, 8 October 1923; E. A. Israel, Palmerston North, to J. W. Kemp, Auckland, 25 September 1923 (Laidlaw College Archives).

[18] Stanley Nicholls, Los Angeles, to Bruce Scott, Auckland, 19 September 1923 (Laidlaw College Archives); BTI Minute Book 1 (19 June 1923).

overcome these handicaps. If he were really as sectarian and aggressive as some portray him, then doubtless it would not have happened. But the portrait by Martin Sutherland of Kemp's cooperation with J.J. North helps to explain why Kemp succeeded.[19]

It was scarcely surprising that Kemp had a vision of founding a Bible Training Institute, for he had already had experience of founding a Bible Training and Missionary Institute during his two years at the New York Metropolitan Tabernacle. It may be that Spurgeon's inspiration was another factor, for Spurgeon's Pastors' College was an influential part of the ministry of his London Metropolitan Tabernacle which had long supplied ministers for the Baptist Tabernacle and other New Zealand Baptist churches. Spurgeon's battle against the Downgrade in the Baptist Union was a sympathy fully shared by Kemp, who would have known about that great English controversy which developed in the 1890s in the early years of his ministry. However the pastors' college was a very different institution from a training institute.

Kemp also had unbounded enthusiasm for teaching young converts. He had emphasized Bible classes in his early pastorates. At his first great pastoral success at Charlotte Chapel in Edinburgh, he began a series of Bible lectures in a School for Bible Study on Sunday afternoons. Charts for the students which summarised the whole Bible were drawn up by Alexander Miller of the CIM. Some 222 students attended these meetings on average in 1906, while other lectures were held on Thursday evenings. From 1907 notes of these were published in a little magazine, the *Record*. In July and August 1907 Kemp visited North America, and visited the Moody Bible Institute, thus confirming his links with this movement.

Another factor was Kemp's Bible Correspondence Course, which developed to provide for those unable to attend the Bible lectures at Charlotte Chapel. He began to send out typewritten notes of the lectures, and gradually people subscribed from far and

---

[19] Martin Sutherland, "Joseph Kemp and the Establishment of the N.Z. Baptist College, 1922-33," *New Zealand Journal of Baptist Research* 8 (2003): 32-51. See also Martin Sutherland, *Conflict & Connection: Baptist Identity in New Zealand* (Auckland: Archer, 2011), 120-21.

wide. He then began to write a column entitled "Back to the Bible" in the Keswick periodical, *The Life of Faith*, in which he used this material. Some 2,500 students enrolled for the material, which was corrected and returned to students. It was one of the earliest forms of extramural instruction, not uncommon among BTIs throughout the world; the best-known was the three volume course written by C.I. Scofield (editor of the dispensationalist *Scofield Bible*) for the Moody Institute in Chicago. Some New Zealanders were among Kemp's distance students. The syllabus consisted of three courses, one on doctrine, one on the Bible and the other on practical Christian work. Kemp brought it with him to New Zealand, and presented it to the Bible Training Institute in June 1923.[20]

The deepest factor was Kemp's rather blunt opinion of regular seminaries. He valued the Glasgow Bible Institute and from it he gained "a certain lurking suspicion of what the higher critics, the modernists, were doing in the regular seminaries." Kemp later commented that Moody's work created a team of voluntary workers who needed training and did not want to be ordained as regular ministers.[21] He saw as the supreme virtue of Bible Institutes that the Bible was the textbook and that "no-one can spend days and nights upon the study of that grand old book without getting to the roots and sources of Christianity, and acquiring discipline of mind and character of heart." He was confident that: "The students of the Bible Training Institutes are kept hard by *the* book."[22] His emphasis on discipline should be noted. He planned to create a tough fighting force, and felt that New Zealanders were not clear and blunt enough in their proclamation of the faith. He saw the BTI as evangelistic, teaching "soul-winning" and supporting world missions:

> What the world needs to-day is a race of preachers – sane, scriptural, sensible and forceful, who know the way to the hearts

---

[20] BTI Minute Book 1 (19 June 1923); Thomas F. Hill, "History of the Auckland Baptist Tabernacle," chapter xxx, *Reaper* 3 (1926): 282-85; *New Zealand Baptist* (August 1920): 121.

[21] J.E. Simpson, "J.J. North," N.Z. Baptist Archives, p. 7; "The Bible Training Institute Idea," *Reaper* 1 (1923): 5.

[22] "The Bible Training Institute Idea," *Reaper* 1 (1923): 5 (emphasis original).

of the people. They may not know how to decline Greek nouns or conjugate Latin verbs; they may fall short by a long way of the standards set up by the colleges and theological halls; but if they can present the gospel of the grace of God in such a fashion as to win the soul to Christ then such are the preachers for whom the world is waiting. The Bible Training Institutes are supplying this want.[23]

Thus in a real sense Kemp's move was radically incompatible with the plans taking shape among New Zealand Baptists at the time of his arrival to found a Baptist Theological College, but as Sutherland has shown, Kemp cooperated with these moves, and provided an early home for the College at the Tabernacle, for his Institute was aimed at an entirely different (and to his mind more urgent) need. As it happened, both were able to succeed.[24]

Unbeknown to Kemp, similar concerns, coupled with problems which the China Inland Mission was experiencing in training its Australian candidates, had led in 1920 to the foundation of the Melbourne Bible Institute by the Rev C.H. Nash, a prominent Anglican minister in that city.[25] For many years the MBI and the BTI were the two premier Bible Colleges in Australasia. Also in 1916 Charles Benson Barnett founded the Sydney Missionary and Bible College. For this was the age in which the new separatist evangelical missions were flourishing as never before, as the fundamentalist controversy spread through the Protestant world.

An Auckland Venture

Kemp's BTI stood a better chance of success than Forde Carlisle's proposal because it was to be based in Auckland. Auckland was a

---

[23] "The Bible Training Institute Idea," *Reaper* 1 (1923): 5.
[24] Sutherland, "Joseph Kemp and the Establishment of the N.Z. Baptist College"; Sutherland, *Conflict & Connection*, 151-54.
[25] Darrell Paproth, "The Melbourne Bible Institute: Its Genesis, Ethos and Purpose," in *The Furtherance of Religious Beliefs: Essays on the History of Theological Education in Australia* (ed. G.R. Treloar; Sydney: Centre for the Study of Australian Christianity, 1997), 124-55.

town with a strong Protestant nonconformist tradition, more so than other New Zealand cities. It also had an evangelical focus, evident for example in the strength of the Auckland auxiliary of the Bible Society. It also had a range of suburban Baptist churches. There certainly was significant theological debate among non-Anglican Protestants, engendered by the influential Lorne Street Hall and subsequently the Unitarian Church. But Protestantism was triumphant. Auckland was the early home of the Orange Lodge and the Reform Party. The Protestant Political Association which excited such intense sectarianism in the years of the First World War, was founded by the minister of the Mount Eden Baptist Church and attracted huge support in the city. Then in 1922 the mayor, the Methodist J.H. Gunson, demanded that Bishop James Liston be charged with sedition for a speech supporting the Irish struggle for independence.[26]

Into this context came Joseph Kemp, appointed pastor of the Tabernacle in 1920. The reasons why the Tabernacle appointed him need not be rehearsed here.[27] But it is important to see him in the context of the ardent Protestantism of the city during that era, which included the formation of the United Evangelical Church. Kemp faced additional friendly competition from May 1924 until 1932 from the Rev Lionel Fletcher an Australian revival preacher who shook up a church with a more liberal tradition, Beresford Street Congregational Church. Fletcher shared Kemp's concern at the decline of the modern church and belief in the need for revival.[28] He saw himself in the Moody tradition although he never

---

[26] Rory Sweetman, *Bishop in the Dock: The Sedition Trial of James Liston* (Auckland: Auckland University Press, 1997), 26-42.

[27] See G.R. Pound, "Reverend J.W. Kemp and the Baptist Tabernacle" (MA Dissertation, University of Auckland, 1978); Douglas B. Ireton, "'O Lord How Long?' A Revival Movement in New Zealand 1920-1933" (MA Thesis, Massey University, 1986); Jane Simpson, "Joseph W. Kemp: Prime Interpreter of American Fundamentalism in New Zealand in the 1920's," in *"Rescue the Perishing": Comparative Perspectives on Evangelism and Revivalism* (ed. Douglas Pratt; Auckland: College Communications 1989), 23-42.

[28] See L.B. Fletcher, "What I Discovered; or a Traveller's Thoughts," *Reaper* 9 (November 1931): 203-205.

used fundamentalist rhetoric. From the first he indicated his sympathy with the BTI, addressed the graduation ceremony of December 1924, and sought the Institute's assistance to provide him with preachers for his out-stations.[29] Thus the convergence of evangelical fervour was striking.

Between the two churches sat Pitt Street Methodist church, the great mother church of Methodism, and not particularly evangelical, but not far away was Howe Street Hall, the central Brethren assembly, which was strongly dedicated to evangelical proclamation. There was a warm evangelical tone in many other Auckland churches, evidenced by the combined tent campaigns of the 1920s and a large united communion service held in the Town Hall on 14 June 1932, with more than 2000 people present.[30] A number of churches beside these particularly supported the Institute. St Stephen's Presbyterian Church in Ponsonby and Grange Road Baptist Church in Mount Eden were among the first to invite Andrew Johnston to conduct a mission in 1929.[31]

Kemp had a larger vision than just leading a city church. Yet equally the Bible Training Institute, while a vital part of Kemp's strategy, did not stand alone. He wanted to gather the Protestant community to work together to defeat the forces of secular modernity. He was certainly strikingly successful in shaping a new alliance of local ministers who welcomed a capable minister who eschewed competition. Evangelical clergy who backed the new Institute also included the Keswick inclined preacher A.S. Wilson who served as secretary of the BTI Board from 1921 to 1927. He became a close associate of Kemp.[32] The Rev T. Russell Cameron,

---

[29] BTI Minute Book 1 (16 December 1924; also 17 February 1925); C.W. Malcolm, *Twelve Hours in the Day: the Life and Work of the Rev Lionel B. Fletcher D.D.* (London: Marshall, Morgan & Scott, 1956), 103-12.

[30] "A Great Communion Service," *Reaper* 10 (July 1932): 89.

[31] Editorial, *Reaper* 10 (February 1933): 229-30.

[32] J. Ayson Clifford, *A Handful of Grain : The Centennial History of the Baptist Union of New Zealand* 2 (Wellington: Baptist Historical Society, 1982), 52, 102-103; G. T. Beilby, *A Handful of Grain* 3 (Wellington: Baptist Historical Society, 1984), 22.

who led an independent evangelical congregation, was another supporter.

Lay support

What is more, Auckland as a commercial city had the resources for what was a classic fundamentalist pattern, a combination of crisp theological conservatism and business-like strategic planning. Kemp's key allies in the formation of the BTI were largely laymen, not ministers. Long term what was emerging was the birth of a new community of religiosity, brokered by a strategic and wealthy group of laity. It is a striking feature of fundamentalism that it combines conservatism in theology with an entrepreneurial spirit. Since this grouping played such a critical role, it deserves some exploration. Russell Stone has indentified a powerful business elite in Auckland.[33] Here I would argue that unlike the Wellington Protestant elite described in *Bible and Society*,[34] it became suffused with evangelicalism.

Inevitably the key figures included many leaders in the large Tabernacle congregation. One was H.R. Jenkins, who, although not a member of the Tabernacle, frequently attended it.[35] Little is known of H. Wilson, perhaps associated with Arthur E. Wilson's Engraving Service which advertised in the *Reaper*, who was an officer and organist at the Tabernacle. Another was H.M. Smeeton, a founder of Smeeton's stores in Manurewa, and a member of the Baptist Tabernacle who was also on the Bible Society Auckland Auxiliary committee and its National Board to 1927 when replaced by Robert Laidlaw. However he resigned before the Institute opened, and served as first chairman of the board of the Baptist

---

[33] R.C.J. Stone, *Makers of Fortune: A Colonial Business Community & its Fall* (Auckland: Oxford University Press, 1973); Stone, *The Making of Russell McVeagh: The First 125 Years of the Practice of Russell McVeagh, 1863-1988* (Auckland: Auckland University Press, 1991).

[34] Peter J. Lineham, *Bible & Society: Sesquicentennial History of the Bible Society in New Zealand* (Wellington: Bible Society in New Zealand & Daphne Brasell Associates, 1996), 177-93.

[35] *Reaper* 4 (March 1926): 2.

College and made his home available in 1928 to enable it to move out of the Tabernacle.[36] Later additions to the BTI Board included Walter J. Lambourne, a home furnishings retailer, officer bearer at the Tabernacle, and Treasurer of the Baptist Union (who resigned in 1925 and also gave generously to the Baptist College) and John Fleming.[37] Samuel Barry (1877-1963), the Queen Street optician and prominent member of the Tabernacle, was invited onto the Board in 1928.[38]

Traditional Presbyterians were an important resource to the Board. The first chairman of the Board was James W. Stewart, a well known Auckland lawyer, of the "old school of believers," a Scottish Presbyterian elder, who died on his way to an extended tour of Europe in 1923.[39] His brother, Robert Leslie Stewart, the general manager of Brown and Stewart, paper merchants, was invited onto the Board on the death of his brother, and immediately appointed to the chair.[40] He served in this role for 20 years, and was a key figure in the foundation of the United Maori Mission, as well as being involved in the Bible Society until his death in 1943. Austere and brusque in manner, he was thoughtful and given to charity to any touching need. He was exceptionally generous to the Institute on a regular basis; he was also shrewd in assessing its expenditure, and would examine its petty cash record with a microscope.[41] The other key Presbyterian was William J. Mains who became a director in 1928 having declined an earlier invitation

---

[36] BTI Minute Book 1 (14 September 1921); G.T. Beilby (ed.), *L.A. North: The Man and His Memoirs* (Wellington: Baptist Historical Society, 1983), 20; *Auckland Star* (8 September 1961); G.H. Scholefield (ed.), *Who's Who in New Zealand and the Western Pacific* (Masterton: G.W. Venables, 1925), 206; E.F. Sherburd and A.L. Silcock, *18,000 Yesterdays* (Auckland: Institute Press, c.1976), 5, 7, 12-13.

[37] BTI Minute Book 1 (30 November 1921).

[38] BTI Minute Book 2 (20 March 1928).

[39] *Reaper* 1 (April 1923): 57. For his denomination see *Reaper* 3 (December 1925): 278.

[40] BTI Minute Book 1 (15 May 1923).

[41] Lineham, *Bible & Society*, 212-13; "In Memoriam," *Reaper* 21 (July 1943): 81; BTI Minute Book 3 (10 June 1943).

in 1921, and later served as honorary Principal. He was highly regarded as a Presbyterian home missionary and conducted many evangelistic missions in many parts of New Zealand.[42]

The Brethren were the other significant source of leadership. One of the owners of Wilson and Horton, proprietors of the *New Zealand Herald*, W.R. Wilson, was perhaps a little uncomfortable with the inter-denominationalism of the BTI, but supported it in various ways.[43] The most notable Brethren supporter was Robert Laidlaw, whose business success took off in 1909 with the formation of the mail-order firm Laidlaw Leeds. He had in 1913 published a little tract, *The Reason Why*, which has been described as "a personal and arguably narrow reflection on the Christian faith. Yet unlike much fundamentalist writing of the time, which was belligerent and sectarian, Laidlaw's tract was irenic in tone."[44] He also had been long devoting half of his profits to worthy causes, and his generosity soon embraced the college. Another Brethren supporter was W.H. Pettit, the well known crusading doctor mentioned above.

All the other Protestant churches except the Church of England also supplied support. From the UEC came Bruce Scott (c1900-1947), a lawyer who resigned abruptly in 1932 but later resumed close links with the Institute and with the Ngaruawahia Convention. He later appealed for the Institute to help found a Bible Institute in Ceylon.[45] From the Congregational Union in 1925 came A.F. Ellis, the very notable phosphate discoverer. J. W. Schakleford of unknown denomination also came onto the Board.[46]

---

[42] BTI Minute Book 1 (9 November and 30 November 1921); BTI Minute Book 2 (19 June and 17 July 1928); *Reaper* 13 (October 1935): 218.

[43] See P. J. Lineham, *There We Found Brethren: A History of Assemblies of Brethren in New Zealand* (Palmerston North: GPH Society, 1977): 117; [Wilson] to Minister of Defence, 8 July 1940 (National Archives AD 227/9/1 vol. 2); BTI Minute Book 1 (30 November 1921).

[44] Graham C. Stoop, "Laidlaw, Robert Alexander Crookston," in *Dictionary of New Zealand Biography* 3 (ed. C. Orange; Auckland: Auckland University Press, 1996): 272.

[45] BTI Minute Book 2 (18 November 1930, 21 June 1932, and 20 July 1937).

[46] BTI Minute Book 1 (17 November 1925).

These men were astute businessmen, members of the commercial elite which developed in the rapid development of Auckland as a commercial centre after the war. The small businessmen who were often strong Protestants and ardent entrepreneurs did well in this decade. Kemp was as astute as any of them, for there had been a deliberateness to his redevelopment of the Baptist Tabernacle, which showed a man who knew his mind, and this perhaps explains why the Tabernacle became the church it did, combining purposefulness with vigorous evangelism.

Staffing the Institute

The final factor which ensured the success of the Institute was the appointment of staff who would inspire confidence in potential students and evangelical churches. However this was the most problematic aspect of the BTI. The BTI's best hope of success was to hang on the coat-tails of Kemp's reputation, but Kemp had much broader interests than managing a small bible school. The board appointed him as Principal and this gave him absolute authority over the institute, but apart from lecturing on Methods of Christian Work he was hardly ever there. Kemp was overseas for a year in 1926, and during this time Laidlaw acted as honorary principal.

In practice the position of Superintendent was a critical role. The first Superintendent was Charles Jubilee Rolls (1887-1986). Kemp approached Rolls very early in the planning, for he had known him twenty years earlier as a brilliant student of his Bible Correspondence Course. In November 1921 Rolls was appointed at £400 per year.[47] Rolls was born in Napier in the year of the royal jubilee (hence his second name). Converted at the age of 14 in 1901, in 1906 he became involved with the Napier Brethren assembly. He went to India as a Brethren missionary in August 1910 and for a period itinerated in the Travancore district among

---

[47] BTI Minute Book 1 (18 July 1921, 15 August 1921, and 30 November 1921).

the so-called "Syrian Christians" of the Mar-Thoma Church.[48] On his return to New Zealand in 1921 he became an itinerant Bible teacher and threw himself into inter-denominational activities. He accepted the superintendency with alacrity but was a little disappointed when he found that in fact the first roll was so low.

Rolls, however, was more a preacher than a systematic teacher, and what system he had was focused on "dispensational truth." While he was popular with students, Rolls' later career indicates some emphases in his interests not unlike those which poisoned the career of Forde Carlisle. After a sabbatical in 1928 he returned to the new role of Dean (for Scott had taken the title of Superintendent in his absence), but he offered his resignation late in 1929, and his subsequent career in the Kansas Bible Institute and the Sydney Missionary and Bible College and as an independent Canadian preacher was somewhat erratic. He became notable as the author of numerous books including *The Indescribable Christ: The Names of Jesus Christ*, issued in five volumes, containing in alphabetical order the biblical names of Jesus and their supposed meanings.[49] Rolls was still writing until his death at the age of 98 in 1986.[50] But his vision after his overseas leave had made him a liability at the Bible Institute. A Board minute on 18 February 1930 recorded their deep gratitude to him and he received a gold purse from his thankful students as a farewell gesture.[51] Nevertheless a

---

[48] L.A. Marsh, *In His Name: A Record of Assembly Missionary Outreach from New Zealand* (Palmerston North: GPH Society, 1974), 172; "Dr Charles Rolls – First Principal of B.T.I. recalls Bible School History," *Challenge* 24 no. 18 (13 May 1966): 6-7.

[49] Charles J. Rolls, *The Indescribable Christ: The Names and Titles of Jesus Christ* (Grand Rapids: Zondervan, 1953).

[50] BTI Minute Book 4 (10 September 1959); "Rev Chas J. Rolls D.D.," *Reaper* 12 (July 1934): 151; *Reaper* 68 (June-July 1986): 16; "Looking Back over 75 Years," Brochure from the Sydney Missionary and Bible College, n.d., (Laidlaw College Archives); "Sydney Bible College," *Reaper* 18 (March 1940): 3; "Dr C. J. Rolls," *Reaper* 19 (September 1941): 151; "Sydney Bible Institute," *Reaper* 20 (August 1942): 113; "Dr C. J. Rolls resigns from Sydney B.T.I.," *Reaper* 27 (April 1949): 45-46.

[51] BTI Minute Book 2 (16 December 1929 and 18 February 1930).

sharp showdown with Kemp and perhaps with the Board about the direction the Institute should take seems to have precipitated his resignation, for a board meeting with staff took place: "at which it was to be given as the considered and unanimous wish of the Board that anything in the nature of date fixing in connection with the Lord's return is not to be taught either in the class-room or privately in the Institute."[52] It is one of several indications that the BTI was as vulnerable as its early rivals to doctrinal debates especially over extremes of eschatological interpretation.

When Rolls submitted his resignation in 1930 Kemp was almost persuaded to resign from the Tabernacle and become full-time Principal. Meanwhile Henry (Harry) Yolland was mooted for the role of Dean. In July 1930 Kemp interviewed Yolland, and he was appointed at a salary of £400 a year. This ensured the teaching stability of the Institute but not its organisation since Yolland despite his business background eschewed practical planning. Consequently J. Oswald Sanders was appointed Superintendent in 1931 and until 1964 this position remained as an alternative authority to that of the Dean and later the Principal. So the Institute was ready when, in March 1933, Kemp suffered a severe stroke and advised the President of the Institute that "the directors could not count on him to render any future service to the BTI."[53] The team of these two men – Yolland a systematic bible teacher and formal traditionalist and Sanders a young and efficient visionary – gave the Institute a basis for its next two decades of growth, although the board felt the need for a nominal principal and W.J. Mains held this role until 1945.

Conclusion

When in 2009 the decision was made to rename what had become the Bible College of New Zealand, the name chosen was Laidlaw College. The implication was that the Brethren layman, Robert

---

[52] BTI Minute Book 2 (18 February 1930).
[53] BTI Minute Book 2 (23 March 1933); "Dr Charles Rolls - First Principal of B.T.I. recalls Bible School History," (1966): 6-7.

Laidlaw, was the principal name associated with the College's history. This paper argues that the Bible Training Institute was always Joseph Kemp's College, at least in vision and conception, and it was this which carried the institute to its singular success, although he certainly needed to harness the support of others from different backgrounds and did so spectacularly well. The need for his institute was created by the combination of evangelism, overseas mission, combative fundamentalism and co-operative struggle against secular modernism which he campaigned for, created, and exemplified. Yet Kemp had not been a success in his New York church and institute, and probably one of the lessons he had learned was that to succeed an educational institute needs to have broad appeal beyond one denomination and one concern. The instructive story of the success of the BTI in the face of some awkward challenges explains that he had learned his lessons well.

Chapter Three
"Baptist and Evangelical": changing perceptions of being evangelical among New Zealand Baptists, 1926-1946

Martin Sutherland

Evangelicalism is an acknowledged phenomenon. The work of Mark Noll (for North America) and David Bebbington (for almost everywhere else) persuasively argues for its significance in post-enlightenment Christianity. Key works like Bebbington's *Evangelicalism in Modern Britain: A History from the 1730s to the 1980s* and Noll's *American Evangelical Christianity: an Introduction* identified antecedents, characteristics, and influences of the movement on a national and regional scale.[1] The ongoing IVP series *A History of Evangelicalism: People, Movements and Ideas in the English Speaking World* (to which Bebbington and Noll contributed the first volumes) seeks to outline its global reach. Given that "evangelicals" themselves have often differed over who can claim the name, careful definition has been crucial to this growing body of historical work. Bebbington has been the most influential here, with his list of key characteristics adopted by nearly all as the "Bebbington quadrilateral." According to this analysis the evangelicalism which Bebbington, Noll, and others present is characterised by a commitment to two theological themes (biblicism and crucicentrism) and two expectations of the Christian life (conversionism and activism).

Bebbington's four-fold lens has enabled the recognition of these common characteristics across the world, allowing valid treatment of the evangelical phenomenon as a single movement. Nevertheless, it remains just as important to acknowledge that the common evangelical elements could take on quite different forms and

---

[1] David Bebbington, *Evangelicalism in Modern Britain: A History from the 1730s to the 1980s* (London: Unwin Hyman, 1989); Mark Noll, *American Evangelical Christianity: An Introduction* (Oxford: Blackwell, 2001).

significance when expressed through denominational identities. This essay examines the New Zealand Baptist story in this regard. New Zealand Baptists were consistently clear that they were "evangelical" and that some other Christian traditions or theological stances were not. It emerges just as strongly, however, that what was meant by the term changed in the middle of the twentieth century, creating uncertainty and division within the denomination.

A contested identity

In the late 1880s what became known as the "Downgrade Controversy" gripped the English Baptist Union. The central character in this drama was Charles Spurgeon, the most famous Baptist in the world. Articulating rising disquiet over historical criticism and its effects on the understanding of the Bible and traditional doctrines, Spurgeon raised the alarm that the Puritan heritage was being eroded. It was on a "down grade," a slippery slope. Spurgeon resigned from the Baptist Union in October 1887. In the following April he challenged his former denomination with the question "Is this Union to have an Evangelical basis or not?"[2] For Spurgeon and his followers it was clear that a well-defined conservatism was fundamental to being "evangelical."

In an example of the close connection between colonial religion and debates at "Home," there was an intriguing parallel to the Downgrade affair among the Baptists of New Zealand. In November 1886 New Zealand Baptists began a controversy which ran for three years and concluded with the only overt action against heresy which the denomination has undertaken. The national conference withdrew funding to the struggling South Island church at Timaru on the basis of its minister's theological position. Rev C.C. Brown had sought to promulgate "conditionalist" views, raising a storm of objection in the fledgling denomination.[3] Brown's case represented an early crisis of identity. Were New Zealand

---

[2] Charles Spurgeon, "Notes," *Sword and Trowel* (April 1888).
[3] "Conditionalist" theology suggested that humans did not by nature possess an immortal soul and that the fate of the unredeemed might be annihilation rather than "Hell" as a place of eternal punishment.

Baptists to adhere to the conservative path mapped out in England by Charles Spurgeon or were they to maintain a more spacious allowance for freedom of conscience? The former position was advocated by the majority, led by Charles Spurgeon's son Thomas, minister in the colony's largest church, the Auckland Tabernacle. Greater toleration was nonetheless sought by some, notably the Christchurch layman Herbert Olney.

> The Union have no right to dictate to a single member as to what he shall believe or teach, when the doctrines held or taught are evangelical, trinitarian, and in accordance with our distinctly denominational views. All minor points must be left to each several church and individual member. To our own Master we are answerable, certainly to no Conference or court of self-constituted judges.[4]

In England, the "resolution" of the Downgrade Controversy was found in the departure from the Baptist Union of the conservative advocate. In New Zealand the opposite outcome resulted. In November 1888 Brown was expelled from the Union. Although the English Baptists had equivocated, the New Zealand Baptists had apparently answered Charles Spurgeon's interrogation "Is this Union to have an Evangelical basis or not?" with a resounding "Yes!"

Yet this is not the whole picture. Personal factors played a part in the small New Zealand Baptist community. More significantly, interdenominational issues were also at play. Baptists were suspicious of the "Life and Advent" movement, regarding it as theologically unsound but also, like the Salvation Army, with sufficient resonances with Baptist themes to be a potential threat to vulnerable Baptist causes. In this regard it is notable that Brown's withdrawal from the Union was sought, not because of doctrinal

---

[4] Letter, H. Olney, *The New Zealand Baptist* [hereafter *NZB*] (December 1886): 186.

heterodoxy, but rather because "he has so far identified himself with another denomination."⁵

It seems New Zealand Baptists were in fact more pragmatic than the Brown controversy at first suggests. They were anxious to preserve their own identity, but, as later events would show, were just as willing to associate themselves with other groups which they could recognise as broadly "evangelical." In a revealing sequel to the expulsion, Brown would be reinstated in 1892, in part because there was now a compelling strategic reason to bring him and his Timaru church back under denominational sway. A local dispute with the Congregational Church was causing tension between the denominations just at the moment when, in England, rumours of union between the two denominations was as common as "roast mutton in the bill of fare of a colonial restaurant."⁶

No union came to pass, either in England or in New Zealand, but such talk was frequent and persistent. In 1902 Presbyterians approached other "evangelical" groups for discussion over the possibility of church union. Those deemed "evangelical" for the purpose were the Presbyterians themselves, plus Methodists and Congregationalists, along with some Anglicans. Baptists were not approached on this occasion and, in any case, made it clear they did not see any chance of union. The meaning of the "evangelical" at this time seems to have orbited around two suns. The first, evangelistic fervour, was common to all parties. Preaching to win souls for Christ was crucial. The second centre of gravity varied. For Presbyterians the word carried the memory of the magisterial reformation, a heritage within which, in different ways, each of its preferred conversation partners could be held to fit but in which Baptists, with their roots in the radical reformation, looked uncomfortable. They might be included as evangelicals, but not for the purposes of union. There was little argument from Baptists themselves. Happy to count themselves as evangelicals, Baptists too knew evangelism alone was not the total picture. For Baptists the

---

[5] Minutes of the Conference of the Baptist Union of New Zealand, Tuesday 13 November 1888, 72. NZ Baptist Archive.

[6] *NZB* (January 1892): 9.

necessary extras were adult conversionism and voluntarism. By these lights all paedobaptists inevitably had ground to make up but, on the evangelism measure, Congregationalists and Methodists (especially Primitive Methodists) ranked well. Presbyterians were a bit suspect but, given the strong voluntarism of the colonial church, they could be accorded the benefit of the doubt. Anglicans on the other hand, with what Baptists rated as merely a territorial approach to salvation, failed to make the cut.[7]

Whilst not blind to doctrinal evangelical emphases, for Baptists the most natural and obvious common ground was the personal challenge with the Gospel. Where doctrine became important, it was more likely to be in denominational distinctives like baptism and church government. Thus, when the Baptist college was set up in the 1920s, its main purpose was to be a training ground for preachers. The obvious person to lead it was John James North. An inspiring preacher and hugely successful and popular minister, North seemed well qualified. He was also the editor of the denominational magazine and had developed a very clear picture of the importance of denominational distinctives.

But was he evangelical?

A focus on evangelism

The first decades of the twentieth century witnessed intense theological controversy among Christians worldwide. Modernism, driven by the very historical-critical questions viewed with misgiving by Charles Spurgeon, was matched by the rise, particularly in the United States, of fundamentalist reactions. The effects were eventually felt in New Zealand. Joseph Kemp, who had encountered the tension first hand in his American ministry, was a determined anti-modernist. North was temperamentally unable to stay away from vigorous debate and as editor of *The New Zealand Baptist* he could hardly avoid comment. During 1926 he made a number of references to the controversy. In June, describing it as "the bitter

---

[7] See the summary of the Baptist response by J.J. North in "The Isolation of the Baptists," *NZB* (February 1903): 25-26.

fight of the day," he criticized the attitudes of both sides. However he made it plain that he felt that new discoveries in science, including "the light on human origins… have one way or another, to be accommodated to the indestructible faith of Christ."[8] This sent disturbing signals to some of his correspondents, who sought a more definite denunciation of modernist error.[9] When North declared his approval of theistic evolution, lingering doubts as to his soundness hardened into outright suspicion.[10]

In January 1927 North, now Principal and emboldened by the promise of a proper home for the college, re-stated his vision for the college in terms not likely to allay the fears of conservative critics.

> The new college must be Baptist to the core, because it must be Christian to the core. We want to make men conversant with the great things of the Faith and we want that faith in its whole extent applied to the whole life of the whole man, and to the whole community. With windows open to all the light which comes from every quarter, and with a fine chivalry, and with an unaffected belief in the sincerity of men who differ from us, we want to see our College fulfill its mission.[11]

North could be as determined a "valiant for truth" as anyone. He was especially hard on any weakness in preaching, lambasting on one occasion "the 'this is how it seems to me' heresy."[12] This was not enough to remove the odour of modernism which would stay with him. At the 1927 Annual Conference a powerful ally came to North's defence. The report of the college debate features an endorsement from none other than Joseph Kemp.

> Rev Joseph W. Kemp made a speech that stirred the conference very deeply. He resented very deeply aspersions that had been made against the "soundness" of Principal North. He declared that if North was a modernist, so in the same sense was he. He did not always agree in details with his friend, but they stood

---

[8] *NZB* (June 1926): 152. See also *NZB* (December 1926): 336-37.
[9] See *NZB* (July 1926): 189; (August 1926): 200.
[10] *NZB* (August 1928): 208-209.
[11] *NZB* (January 1927): 2.
[12] *NZB* (March 1927): 80-81.

together for the great evangelical verities, and he would not hesitate to place anyone for whom he cared under the Principal for theological training.[13]

This boost from such an impeccably conservative source seems only to have blunted objections briefly. During 1928 North was again defending his position in the face of "problems of college."

> We do not believe in a college in which men are taught to repeat the shibboleths of their tutors, and of their sect. We do not believe that orthodoxy can be administered in tabloid forms, and secured with smart little catch cries... We do not allow that the Christian faith is open to serious revision. It is a firm foundation, and it stands sure. We do feel in every fibre of our being the urgent need of relating Christ and the implications of his Gospel to the thoughts and problems of our age.[14]

The college would have to endure a fluctuating but never disappearing reputation for unsoundness. This is evident in the comments made to Ayson Clifford when in 1933 he announced to his friends that he would be going to the Baptist College in the following year. One, a student at Kemp's Bible Training Institute, whilst encouraging Clifford to attend a revivalist mission being held in Dunedin at the time, added

> I can imagine you getting so much on fire that you may even find that your place is in the "B.T.I." instead of the "Bible Banging College". I say, "Come out from among them" & that applies not only to Churches where Modernists preside but also to *all* places where they have any authority at all.[15]

Bible "banging" clearly meant something like Bible "knocking" to this writer. Yet, through all this, no-one, not even those who suspected North of being a "modernist," denied him the label "evangelical." This is because what North had in spades, and what

---

[13] *NZB* (November 1927): 330.

[14] *NZB* (December 1928): 354-55. See also (June 1929): 172-73.

[15] "Bert" to Ayson Clifford, 25 June 1933, f. 4. Clifford Correspondence, NZ Baptist Archive.

Kemp recognised in him, was a total commitment to evangelism and conversionism.

The dominant discourse among Baptists at this time used "evangelical" interchangeably with "evangelistic." Time and again accounts of persons or meetings spoke of "evangelical fervor," "evangelical appeal," "evangelical preaching," "evangelical efforts," "evangelical messages." As late as 1955 Rev Roy Bullen equated "evangelical passion" with "evangelism" and being "missionary minded."[16]

That is not to say, of course, that the two terms were mere synonyms. There was, unquestionably, doctrinal content to "Evangelical Faith." Under that heading, for instance, Laurie Silcock, writing in 1934, declared that "the fundamental facts of our faith are (1) The death and resurrection of Jesus Christ as the means of our salvation; (2) the universal need of salvation, and the efficacy of that salvation when received by personal faith."[17]

Such a definition of evangelical core principles, of course, demonstrates the rule. The central doctrines are the doctrines of "salvation" (mentioned three times) – those beliefs which make the Gospel "good news," which gave you something to preach. In a message entitled "The One Saving Word" (notably, the missionary sermon at the 1937 Annual Assembly) Rev Harold Goring made the connection explicit.

> The implicates of evangelical faith are the spiritual sickness of the soul, its inability to save itself, and the adequacy of Christ alone to meet its need. The revelation of God in Christ is a revelation of God Himself entering into human life in its tragedy and sin with redemptive purpose. For us the supreme

---

[16] Roy Bullen, *NZB* (November 1955): 265.
"WE BELIEVE IN EVANGELISM (Mark 16:12-16)
If we are to justify our existence in the coming decades, then it must be chiefly because of our evangelical passion. Let this grow cold, and the wax-like look of death will be upon our Denomination."
[17] A.L. Silcock, "Believer's Baptism – the defender of the Evangelical Faith," *NZB* (January 1934): 10.

event is Calvary, revealing human insolvency and the salvation of God.[18]

In 1938 A.V. Brown, a convert to Baptist convictions from Plymouth Brethrenism, wrote of one of the attractions of Baptists as "Their spirit of evangelism and Christian love."

> I studied their evangelical position, and found them to be alive to the implications of the Master's words – "Preach the Gospel to every creature." Their message is evangelical, emphasising the great truths of that glorious Gospel in relation to man's sin and need: and to God's provision for that need in the Cross of Christ, and declaring that only through the acceptance of Christ can man be saved.[19]

Between 1931 and 1955 there were 1,010 instances of the word "evangelical" in the pages of *The New Zealand Baptist*. Of these, some 80% could be replaced with "evangelistic" without distorting the meaning.[20] It is this interpenetration of truth and action which formed the common evangelical ground which made it possible for the alleged "modernist" J.J. North to be the preacher at the funeral of his so-called "fundamentalist" friend Joseph Kemp.

A shifting centre

There was, however, a growing alternate discourse which increasingly placed the accent on the *content* of evangelical belief and which allowed a separation, however slight, of the two terms. As early as 1935 the Union evangelist, Rev J. Carlisle, warned

> It is not enough to be evangelical. We must be evangelistic… Evangelical may mean truth on ice; evangelistic means truth on fire. Evangelical may be bomb-proof for defence; evangelistic means an army on the march with every face towards the enemy. Evangelical sings: "Hold the fort, for I am coming"; evangelistic sings: "Storm the fort, for God is leading."

---

[18] H. Goring, *NZB* (December 1937): 385.
[19] A.V. Brown, "Why a Baptist," *NZB* (August 1938): 233.
[20] Source: the Digital Baptist Project, N.Z. Baptist Historical Society, 2011.

> The need of the Church is not Evangelicalism as a thing to fight for, but evangelism as a force to fight with. The evangelical creed merely held and defended becomes a fossil.[21]

Carlisle, the evangelist, was waxing lyrical. The separation was less dramatic than he feared, but it was nonetheless real.

Although, as we have seen, North and Kemp were able to retain a respect for each other's dominant desire to win souls despite theological differences, their successors did not find this so easy. Among New Zealand Baptists, the key figure in the development of the alternate discourse on evangelicalism was E.M. Blaiklock. Blaiklock would become an internationally famous writer of evangelical texts. His Christian commitment began, significantly, under Joseph Kemp. In keeping with Kemp's influence he soon became a popular speaker, especially at evangelistic rallies aimed at young people. Blaiklock's evangelicalism certainly did not lack for evangelistic fervour. Neither was he a fundamentalist. A classics scholar, he was not going to be taken in by the "oddities of interpretation and exegesis" he found in that school.[22] However, his concern at what he saw as a liberal undermining of the authority of the Scripture led him to increasingly vigorous activism. In 1927, by now a lecturer in classics at the University of Auckland, he was a leading figure in setting up an alternative to the Student Christian Movement.[23] Evangelical disenchantment with the SCM worldwide had led to the formation of the Inter-Varsity Fellowship, with which Blaicklock would thereafter be associated.

More pointedly, for the purposes of this study, in 1936 Blaicklock led a conservative reaction against the study materials of the New Zealand Bible Class Union. The Young Men's (and Women's) Bible Class movement had become the principle organisation for Christian young adults. For a number of years a combined syllabus of study had been prepared, aimed at serving all

---

[21] J. Carlisle, "Personal Evangelism," *NZB* (February 1935): 40.

[22] E.M. Blaiklock, *The Bible and I* (London: Marshall, Morgan & Scott: 1983), 24.

[23] Peter J. Lineham, *No Ordinary Union: Centenary History of the Scripture Union in New Zealand* (Wellington: Scripture Union, 1980), 37.

the participating denominations (Presbyterian, Methodist, Church of Christ, and Baptist). Concerns had emerged from early in the decade that the content of the syllabus had moved from central Gospel concerns.[24] The Auckland Baptist Young Men's Bible Class cabinet (of which Blaiklock was Chair) reported in June 1936 that "syllabus has long been a hotly-debated question. We have finally decided that we cannot continue to recommend to our classes an unsatisfactory guide to study."[25] Blaiklock took responsibility for editing an alternative, which within a year was being used by several churches beyond Auckland. By 1938 Blaiklock and his committee were submitting to the national Baptist Bible Class body that it "should put its weight behind one and one only B.C. syllabus & that that syllabus be the one the Auckland Union is producing at present."[26] In November 1938 the Dominion body adopted the Auckland syllabus as its standard and resolved merely to offer the interdenominational one to classes as an alternative.[27]

More and more convinced of the need to defend the doctrines which lay at the core of Christianity, Blaiklock became the leading protagonist for what he termed "informed conservatism." "The Bible ceases to speak, if it is no longer the Word of God... Authority must be objective, not according to the reader's whim or fluctuating choice."[28] In 1942, reviewing the work of his favourite historian, Arnold Toynbee, Blaiklock sounded a cautionary tone. Even as he foresaw a turning to revivalist religion he worried that "the question is whether evangelical Christianity will maintain its purity if ever it is patronised by the powers as a social force."[29] An even harder defensiveness is found in *The New Zealand Baptist* four years later. In 1946 Dr D.S. Milne, writing on behalf of "The Evolution Protest Movement," articulated a key link,

---

[24] See e.g., *NZB* (September 1933): 274; (December 1934): 377.
[25] *NZB* (June 1936): 182.
[26] "Report of the Auckland Y.M.B.C.U. on the Local Syllabus" [1938], NZ Baptist Archive B6/2.
[27] *NZB* (November 1938): 353.
[28] Blaiklock, *The Bible and I*, 28-29.
[29] *NZB* (September 1942): 253.

acknowledging that "there have always been bastions protecting belief in creation and the Creator stoutly defended by evangelical Christians."[30]

Blaiklock was thus merely representative of a growing concern that evangelicalism maintain a doctrinal core first and foremost. In this stream evangelism had to compete with theological soundness. An interesting illustration of this gradual shift in emphasis can be observed in the evolution of advertisements in *The New Zealand Baptist* for the Bible Training Institute, Kemp's college (now Laidlaw College). In its first form (February, 1922) the key descriptors were

Interdenominational
Evangelistic
Missionary and Practical
The Bible is the only Text Book

These advertisements ran for only a short period. A new version appeared in October 1925 in a form in which the masthead now listed the Institute's characteristics as

Evangelical
Interdenominational
Biblical

These categories were given explanations – that for "evangelical" being "stands upon the central supernatural facts of the Gospel of Christ." This suggests a greater doctrinal emphasis, although the use of the adjective "supernatural" connects the statement strongly to both North's and Kemp's writings on revival.

By April 1936 the masthead changed further to

Evangelical
Evangelistic
Missionary

Now, though bound together, the terms are clearly *not* to be regarded as identical. The Bible, previously separately listed, seems wrapped into the "Evangelical" designation. This masthead remained constant into the 1950s.

---

[30] *NZB* (November 1946): 334.

By 1944 concerns were again coming to the fore about the Baptist College. Times and definitions were changing. North, approaching retirement, was becoming perceived as something other than evangelical. Ayson Clifford, appointed as Tutor to assist North, had worked with Blaiklock on material for the Bible Class syllabus and it is likely that Blaiklock was a key member of his selection committee. That he welcomed Clifford's nomination is clear from a letter he wrote soon after the matter was resolved. He first encourages Clifford to undertake serious study in Classical Greek (Blaiklock's own subject) then he makes telling comment on the state of things at the college.

> I hope the I.V.F. will be encouraged by your help. Confidentially I may say that we have lost ground in the denomination lately. A group of ministers (who have never seen the inside of a university) have become evident for S.C.M. (which hasn't a Baptist member) – while in College, J.J. has developed a complex over our doctrine of inspiration. He will attack you on it as soon as he sees you... My position is that you have a work of Christian scholarship to do in Akd. I covet your cooperation.[31]

Bob Thompson (himself a later Principal who would fall foul of Blaiklock), in his first year at the college whilst at the same time taking courses with Blaiklock at the University, also wrote to Clifford.

> Your coming to College will be a great joy to me for one. J.J. is a good old boy, but not particularly sympathetic to E.U. and occasionally fond of having a dig at evangelicals. We have sought to maintain the grand old tradition throughout the year but have found the going a little heavy at times. The College library to my mind is deficient in solid conservative literature but Mr Blaiklock is trying to remedy that. The chaps at Coll. are a fine

---

[31] Letter, E.M. Blaiklock to Ayson Clifford, 6 May 1944. Clifford Correspondence.

crowd but as a whole accept J.J.'s ideas as final truth. You will be a steadying influence I'm sure.³²

In August 1944, J.J. North gave notice that he would conclude as Principal early in 1946. At its meeting in November, the College Committee determined that it needed someone with "experience as Minister of a Church," "evident qualities of leadership," and "satisfactory" academic standing. But above all the second principal for the college was to be "a convinced Baptist and Evangelical."

The nomination eventually fell to Luke Jenkins, a Welshman who had trained at Regent's Park College under Wheeler Robinson. There were, however, immediate clouds over Jenkins' selection. The panel had been alerted to his pacifist convictions. This was a potential problem. A number of New Zealand Baptists held similar views but the majority did not. The committee was aware of Jenkins' position when it endorsed his name but kept it from the wider Union Council. This was clearly a risky strategy. With the likelihood of ex-servicemen being among his students, Jenkins was potentially in a difficult situation. In the event, although some resentment on this score was undoubtedly felt, this question would not be a major factor in Jenkins' principalship. Far more significant was another question raised of his nomination. Blaiklock was a member of the College Committee but he had not been present at the meeting which had decided upon the nomination. It was he who raised the issue "was Luke Jenkins evangelical enough?"

N.R. Wood, as Secretary to the College Committee the person charged to clarify the matter with Jenkins, had been trained under J.J. North and was himself very much of that conversionist school. Thus, to be "evangelical" was for him to be concerned about saving souls. It was on these terms that he addressed Jenkins in a letter in June 1945. "It would help us at Assembly if you could give me a line about any conversions or Baptisms that have taken place lately in your last church."³³ To this Jenkins replied confidently, as he had

---

³² Letter, R.J. Thompson to Ayson Clifford, 18 December 1944. Clifford Correspondence.
³³ Letter, N.R. Wood to Luke Jenkins, 19 June 1945. N.R. Wood Correspondence, NZ Baptist Archive.

had extensive experience in evangelism and missions, with acknowledged results.[34] This was backed up by P.W. Evans, Principal at Spurgeon's College. Here again the understanding of terms was crucial. Wood wrote to Evans asking for comment on Jenkins' "evangelical outlook." He apparently felt no need to explain the term. Evans replied immediately, introducing the pertinent section of his letter "about the evangelistic spirit and activities of Mr Jenkins."[35] Thus it is clear that Wood, Jenkins, and Evans understood the issue alike. To be "evangelical" meant to be "evangelistic." This perception runs through the extensive correspondence between Wood and Jenkins in the second half of 1945.

The problem was that not everyone shared this understanding. What Wood and others did not fully recognize, and Jenkins could not have been expected to appreciate, was that the ground was shifting among New Zealand Baptists. Evangelistic fervour was not waning but theological correctness, especially on biblical authority, was becoming more important. The conservatives, whom Wood's generation tended to dismiss as "Brethrenish" elements – led by such as Blaiklock and fueled by the training many lay activists were receiving at the BTI – were becoming a more vocal and visible factor in denominational life. Amongst this group, the term "evangelical" was finding a new centre of gravity.

The correspondence between Wood and Jenkins cited above was placed before a meeting of the Auckland College Committee in July 1945. This time Blaiklock was present. In his application Jenkins had listed his involvement with the Student Christian Movement. This generated some disquiet and it was agreed Wood should inform Jenkins "that most Baptist students in Auckland are linked with the I.V.F. and that all our college students are linked with that movement." Wood did this in two letters, describing the theological divisions in New Zealand and adding the note "a member of the

---

[34] Letter, L.H. Jenkins to N.R. Wood, 30 June 1945. N.R. Wood Correspondence.
[35] See Letter, N.R. Wood to P.W. Evans, 18 June 1945, and Evans' reply of 2 July 1945. N.R. Wood Correspondence.

college cmte who is Senior Lecturer in Classics at the Varsity takes a leading part in the I.V.F." Jenkins replied that "the S.C.M. has provided me with opportunities of evangelism and fellowship for which I am grateful and which I have found fruitful" and that he sought to avoid theological controversy.[36] These replies were "regarded as satisfactory" by the Auckland Committee at its next meeting. Nevertheless, enough misgiving lingered to provide the seed for later opposition.

Notice of Luke Jenkins' nomination as Principal was given in the August 1945 issue of *The New Zealand Baptist*. Jenkins, readers were assured, "is keenly evangelical, a convinced Baptist, possessed of evident qualities of leadership, and has a brilliant scholastic career." The order of listing is instructive, especially when contrasted to the list of qualifications agreed at the start of the process. In the light of the questions which had been raised about Jenkins' stance it was now considered prudent to place "evangelical" first, "Baptist" second and scholarship last. Local church ministry was mentioned later, merely as information. The appointment was made at the 1945 Assembly although the decision was not unanimous. Some felt there was undue pressure to approve the nomination. The meeting was informed, for instance, that passages for the family had already been booked.[37]

The College now had a new principal but one under a cloud of suspicion. Jenkins' principalship was to prove a personal, family, and denominational disaster. He would never win the confidence of conservatives and his relationship with Blaiklock would descend from coolness to outright hostility. He remained, throughout this time and beyond, a keen and well-received evangelist. But, in Baptist evangelicalism, that was no longer enough.

---

[36] See Letters, N.R. Wood to Luke Jenkins, 24 and 26 July, and Jenkins' replies of 4 August 1945. N.R. Wood Correspondence.

[37] J.A. Clifford, Unpublished Memoirs, File 3, 3. NZ Baptist Archive.

Conclusion

Evangelicalism is a complex phenomenon. What the New Zealand Baptist experience suggests is that, if taken in broad terms, the Bebbington quadrilateral surely does encompass those who claimed themselves to be "evangelicals." But the simplistic use of Bebbington's marks can imply a universal movement – timeless and pure. It would certainly be the case that some within the movement would have wanted to see it that way. Yet this would be to mask the nuances of particular contexts and the shifts of emphasis which are produced, not out of timelessness but by *history*. Changes in circumstances, in perceived threat, or in personnel can alter perceptions, even working definitions. C.C. Brown, Charles Spurgeon, J.J. North, Joseph Kemp, E.M. Blaiklock, and Luke Jenkins might all be termed evangelical. At least, this is an ascription we might apply. Of each other, it is clear, they were not always so sure.

Chapter Four
Spirit and reason: Canon Orange and Professor Blaiklock as contrasting exemplars of evangelical identity in mid-twentieth century New Zealand

Stuart Lange

From the 1930s to the 1960s, two key New Zealand evangelicals were Rev William A. Orange (1889-1966), an Anglican vicar in Christchurch,[1] and Professor E.M. Blaiklock (1903-1983), a university classics scholar in Auckland.[2] Both significantly

---

[1] For previous material about Orange, see Jeremy J. Clark, "Orange, William Alfred, 1869-1966," in *Dictionary of New Zealand Biography* 4 (Auckland: Auckland University Press, 1998), 391-92; Jeremy Clark, "The Evangelical Ministry of William A. Orange, 1930-1945" (BTh Research Essay, Melbourne College of Divinity, 1995); David G.S. Rathgen, "The Church in New Zealand 1890-1920, with Special Reference to W. A. Orange" (LTh thesis, Joint Board of Theological Studies, 1969); "Passing of Canon William Alfred 'Willie' Orange," *Challenge Weekly* 24, 28 (23 July 1966): 6-7; "Further Tributes to Valuable Ministry of Canon Orange," *Challenge Weekly* 24, 30 (6 August 1966): 12; Martin Sullivan, *Watch How you Go* (London: Hodder & Stoughton, 1975), 124-25; L.E. Pfankuch, "The Reverend W.A. Orange, Vicar of Sumner 1930-1945," in *All Saints Church, Sumner Centennial. Parish of Sumner/Redcliffs* (no publisher: n.d.); R.A. Carson, "Some Reflections on the Life of W.A. Orange," *Latimer* 111 (August 1992): 20; P.J. Lineham, *No Ordinary Union: the Story of the Scripture Union, Children's Special Service Mission and Crusader Movement of New Zealand 1880-1980* (Wellington: Scripture Union in New Zealand, 1980); Stuart M. Lange, "A Rising Tide: The Growth of Evangelicalism and Evangelical Identity among Presbyterians, Anglicans and University Students in New Zealand, 1930-1965" (PhD thesis, University of Otago, 2009), especially Chapter Three.

[2] For previous material about Blaiklock, see W.F. Richardson, "Blaiklock, Edward Musgrove: 1903-1983," *Dictionary of New Zealand Biography* 5, 57-58; Trevor Shaw, *E.M. Blaiklock: A Christian Scholar* (London: Hodder Stoughton, 1986); David G. Stewart, "Edward Musgrave Blaiklock," in *Bible Interpreters of the Twentieth Century: A Selection of Evangelical Voices* (eds Walter A. Elwell and J.D. Weaver; Grand Rapids: Baker, 1999): 165-76; P.J. Lineham,

influenced mid-twentieth century New Zealand evangelicalism. Both were highly influential figures in the same small network, that of the university Evangelical Unions and Inter-Varsity Fellowship (NZ). There were numerous points of congruence between Orange and Blaiklock, and also some clear differences. There was a degree of mutual discomfort. It can be suggested that Orange and Blaiklock reflected different tendencies inherent within New Zealand evangelicalism – or at least different aspirations and priorities.

William Orange

From 1930 to 1945, the Rev W.A. Orange was the vicar of Sumner, a quiet seaside suburb on the outskirts of Christchurch. In a diocese which was a mix of low church, broad church, and high church elements, and with no other clergy who were clearly "evangelical," Orange's ministry was distinctive. His emphases were strongly biblicist and "spiritual."

Orange was a devotional Bible expositor of outstanding giftedness. A bachelor, he poured his energies into teaching the Bible to young men. Every Sunday, dozens of them cycled out to Sumner to hear his Bible teaching. They attended his afternoon Bible Class, then stayed on for a prayer meeting, a meal, and more exposition at the evening service. Over the years Orange thus became spiritual mentor and a model in ministry to numerous young evangelical protégés, commonly nicknamed the "Orange Pips." About fifty of them later became Anglican ministers, many also serving as CMS missionaries. Others went into various professions. Through Orange's admirers, a significant post-war evangelical Anglican movement was birthed in New Zealand. That movement began in Christchurch, but its influence gradually

---

"Blaiklock, Edward Musgrove," in *Biographical Dictionary of Evangelicals* (ed. Timothy Larsen; Leicester: IVP, 2003): 55-66; Lange, "A Rising Tide," 76, 81, 104, 106-107, 120, 125-27, 139, 147, 206, 339-42, 351-54, 374-75, 386-87, 398, 402, 413, 476, 496, 502, 537-38, 542.

widened to other dioceses, primarily Nelson (which already had a longstanding evangelical tradition sustained by bishops and clergy from Sydney), and to a lesser extent in Wellington.

Orange was not a flamboyant or forceful preacher. He spoke quietly, with a manner that was gentle and spiritual in tone, never polemical or hectoring. His preaching and teaching generally consisted of deeply evocative meditations on biblical passages. His talks were always meticulously prepared, with every word crafted. His language, according to one Orange Pip, was "golden" like Chrysostom's, conveying the "absolute wonder and beauty of the Gospel."[3] His teaching was exceptionally rich in imagery and typology, with a powerful appeal to the imagination. It was suggestive rather than doctrinaire. He might say, after making some tantalising (but perhaps tenuous) allegorical comment: "You will have your own thoughts. I simply leave you with that suggestion."[4]

Orange had an unusual capacity to captivate his hearers. One of his curates recalled an experience in about 1941:

> I came back early one Sunday night from taking a service at Redcliffs, and as I arrived at the door of the church – which was at the back of the church – along the back seat there was a row of people with their eyes glued on the preacher, and leaning forward, neck outreached, to get every word that fell from his lips. It was exciting to watch, to see the interest that was being maintained. And then when they came out of church, I was standing there still, and I saw these people with their radiant faces, they had a tremendous blessing, it was a real work of the Holy Spirit.[5]

A member of Orange's Bible Class commented that Orange "made the Bible the most interesting book you could possibly want to read," and noted that most of those who went out to hear Orange at Sumner were "fairly academic kids" who found Orange's

---

[3] The Rev R.M.Glen, interview, 27 October 1999, ¶12.
[4] The Rev Dr J. Graham Miller, interview, 23-25 November 1999 [hereafter JGM], ¶236.
[5] The Rev Roger F.N. Thompson, interview, 1 November 1999 [hereafter RT], ¶370.

interpretations intellectually intriguing.⁶ Another Orange Pip recalled Orange's ability to hold youths "spell-bound," even on a book such as Leviticus.⁷ Another, later a classical scholar, was "profoundly influenced" by Orange's "intense respect and interest in every last detail of the text. Every word. That remains with me to this day."⁸ Someone else gained a life-long appreciation of the "wonderful wholeness of Scripture... the New Testament was foreshadowed in the Old, and the Old was fulfilled in the New."⁹ Another recalled that Orange "spoke with authority... [and] had a great and gifted ability of penetrating the scriptures for deeper truths... [and] I was converted at that time." ¹⁰

Graham Miller, an Inter-Varsity Fellowship (IVF) Travelling Secretary who often heard Orange at student conferences recalled that "at any IVF conference, he had them eating out of his hand. I was one of them. You put your pen down. It was sacrilege to go on scribbling your notes." ¹¹ Miller also wrote that "when he [Orange] spoke to students in Dunedin on the book of Esther, our hearts burned within us. It was the voice of the Lord we heard speaking, and our eyes were opened to behold wondrous things."¹²

Orange's charisma was not only evident behind lectern or pulpit; his personality "drew you like a magnet."¹³ At conference mealtimes, students vied to be near him to hear his humorous anecdotes.¹⁴ At Sunday night suppers at Sumner he could tell joke after joke, leaving his audience paralysed with laughter.¹⁵ His own

---

⁶ The Rev Maurice Betteridge, interview, 26 November 1999, ¶32.

⁷ "Passing of Canon... Orange," 6-7.

⁸ Mark Hutchinson, "Professing History II: An Interview with Professor Edwin Judge, 12 September 1990," *Lucas: An Evangelical History Review* 11 (1991): 37.

⁹ Canon R.E. Coulthard, interview by R.M. Glen, 4 February 1990, ¶17.

¹⁰ RT, ¶14.

¹¹ JGM, ¶236.

¹² *The NZ Inter-Varsity News' Bulletin* 1, no. 4 (October 1937): 11.

¹³ RT, ¶26.

¹⁴ JGM, ¶236.

¹⁵ RT, ¶370.

mirth was "infectious."[16] That social aspect – the hilarity and the camaraderie – was a significant dimension in Orange's appeal and helps explain the strength of the group that grew up around him. As in many other evangelical settings, group solidarity was based on more than doctrine alone.

Orange's teaching did not generally address scientific, theological, biblical-critical, or apologetic questions.[17] His frequent allegorising sometimes irritated evangelicals beyond his circle, including those of a more reformed[18] or scholarly approach.[19] When T.C. Hammond was speaking at an IVF Conference, he is alleged to have said "we'll leave the significance of the *third* fig leaf to Canon Orange."[20] Some students joked that when Orange referred to a fig tree, every leaf had a meaning.[21]

Orange's early diaries reveal a lonely, anxiously devout young man. The language of the early diaries reflects diffuse evangelical influences such as revivalism (emphasising repentance and spiritual experience), Keswick spirituality (victory over sinfulness through prayer and submission), and the China Inland Mission (faith and sacrificial discipleship). In 1910 a young Orange was on his knees making what he described as a "full surrender."[22] A few days later he felt his soul "stirring" and that he was "born to do great things"; he imagined himself as a "missioner swaying a multitude of people."[23] He wrote that "my great ambition is that love for Jesus may become

---

[16] Pfankuch, "The Reverend W.A. Orange."

[17] The Rev Rymall Roxburgh, interview, 2-3 November 1999 [hereafter RR], ¶333; R.A. Carson, interview by R.M. Glen, 20 December 1989, ¶12.

[18] Les Gosling was upset by Orange's attempt to give an allegorical meaning to the "four anchors" let out from the ship's stern in Acts 27:29, JGM, ¶236. Also, the Rev G. Morrison Yule, interview, 12-13 August 1999, ¶89.

[19] The Rev Harvey Teulon, interview, 29 September 1999, ¶16: "I had too much of a scientific background… I could not feel that typology had any empirical basis."

[20] Russell Fountain, interview by P.J. Lineham, n.d.

[21] RR, ¶332.

[22] William Orange, diary, 22-29 October 1910.

[23] Orange, diary, 7 November 1910.

the one absorbing passion of my life."[24] He wrote that he was "looking unto Jesus day by day," in the hope of "being so filled with Him that sin finds no place."[25]

At that time Orange was significantly influenced by Plymouth Brethren he met, who amazed and inspired him with their prodigious biblical knowledge.[26] At one of their meetings, he felt over-awed at "plain but spiritually-minded men talking in an animated and cordial way of the sweetest truths."[27] Orange also received with fascination the idea that beneath the "surface" meaning of Scripture there lay another, "under a veil."[28] When a Brethren friend informed him that the Lord would spew the Anglican Church out of his mouth, Orange was disturbed, and came close to leaving the Anglicans for the Brethren.[29] However his vicar dissuaded him, and Orange resolved to continue towards ordination within the Anglican framework.

In Christchurch Orange completed a degree in Greek, Hebrew, and philosophy and then studied theology at College House.[30] He subsequently kept up his biblical languages.[31] He did most of the work for an MA, but failed the Syriac paper. Ordained in 1919, he travelled the world as tutor-friend to a wealthy heir. From 1924 he was a rural vicar at Waikari, where he immersed himself in intense study of Scripture. Orange was an avid reader, with books stored in every room and along both sides of the hallway, and his library eventually contained about 30,000 volumes.[32]

For Orange, the principal threat within his denomination to a living faith was not theological "modernism" or liberalism. For

---

[24] Orange, diary, 29 December 1911.
[25] Orange, diary, 22 July 1911.
[26] Orange, diary, 5 September 1911.
[27] Orange, diary, 10 November 1911.
[28] Orange, diary, 24 April 1912.
[29] Orange, diary, 24 April 1912.
[30] The LTh was the only theological qualification available to College House ordinands at that time.
[31] Orange, diary, 7 July 1935.
[32] Pfankuch, "The Reverend W.A. Orange."

Orange that was a distant threat, quite beyond the pale; as yet College House had scarcely been touched by higher criticism and liberal theology.[33] In Orange's thinking the main foe in the church was "sacerdotalism" or "ritualism," and his attitude was reinforced by Professor Dickson's *Romanism and Ritualism* (published 1912).[34] At College House, Orange reacted strongly against his staunchly Anglo-Catholic Principal, Canon J.R. Wilford.[35] Orange told Wilford that "ritualistic practices" were objectionable and that the preaching of the word mattered much more than the sacrament; Wilford informed Orange he was "very sad" to hear that[36] and that he was "not fit to be ordained."[37] Ritualism, however, was not in Orange's view the worst problem in the church. The key problem in the pews was widespread unregenerate nominalism; for that, the only cure was spiritual conversion.

Orange's spirituality was grounded not only in Scripture but in passionate prayer. He spend countless hours praying, especially on Saturday nights. He always remained anxious that he had not prayed enough. Having read E.M. Bounds's *Purpose in Prayer*, Orange felt convicted of "criminal negligence" in prayer.[38] A spiritual turn-around in the church, Orange wrote in his diary, "shall be accomplished by unceasing prayer and by nothing else."[39] Orange's practice of prayer was closely linked with his intense hunger to see conversions; his diary records: "I must have souls."[40]

---

[33] Those would only gain traction under Principal Stephen Parr (1933-50).

[34] Orange, diary, 23, 27 May 1912. John Dickson, *Shall Ritualism and Romanism Capture New Zealand? Their Ramifications in Protestant Churches* (Dunedin: Otago Daily Times, 1912), 1-66.

[35] John Russell Wilford, *Southern Cross and Evening Star* (London: Martini, 1950), 108-73; Josephine E. Welch, "A Pilgrim on God's High Road: Canon Wilford in New Zealand" (MA thesis, University of Canterbury, 2006). Wilford was Principal from 1913-1933.

[36] E.g., Orange, diary, 6 May 1914.

[37] Wiggins/Glen interview, ¶4.

[38] Orange, diary, 11 July 1924.

[39] Orange, diary, 12 July 1924.

[40] Orange, diary, 29 June, 11 July 1924.

Orange made several visits to Sydney and had close contact there (and later in New Zealand) with leading Anglican evangelicals, including Archbishop Mowll and T.C. Hammond. Mowll was interested in Orange coming to Australia to work among students as an IVF staff person or as Moore College's Vice Principal.[41] Orange was impressed by the zeal and orthodoxy of Sydney Anglicanism, but also had some reservations. He was troubled by the "factional strife, wrangling, and much bitterness," by the driving pace of work expected of clergy, by the low emphasis on the Second Coming, and by what he perceived as a deficiency in Sydney's spiritual tone:

> I realised that there were very many fine evangelical and godly men in Sydney yet I was conscious of a lack on every hand. There are many here who know the Gospel and are able to preach it. They are able to present doctrine also in a masterly manner but what I miss is the fragrance and sweet savour of Christ. The Scriptures are not presented in such a way as to bring out of them what is Christ in them, so that the house is filled with the ointment.[42]

Orange was an individualist, and there was no chance he would ever fit into Sydney's particular way of being Anglican. He did not fit the classic British evangelical mould, either, and did not fit neatly into *any* theological or ecclesiastical template. Orange was, for instance, a moderate in his churchmanship; unlike those committed to the English "Low Church" tradition, Orange habitually wore a stole and saw no need to conduct the eucharist from the "North End." He was Protestant, but better read in the Fathers than in the Reformers.[43] He was broadly reformed, but not closely Calvinistic.[44] He was Anglican, but frequently quoted F.N. Darby, a prominent pioneer of the Plymouth Brethren.[45] Orange emphasised the

---

[41] Orange, diary, 8 July 1935, 22 April 1938.
[42] Orange, diary, 18, 29 July 1935.
[43] RR, ¶333.
[44] Not, at least, by the standards of Graham Miller, a leading Presbyterian evangelical: JGM, ¶236.
[45] Carson, "Some Reflections," 19.

Second Coming, but rejected Brethren dispensationalism.[46] He yearned and prayed for conversions, but was no pulpit-thumping evangelist; he did not give evangelistic "altar calls."[47]

Orange declined to accept the label "fundamentalist," noting that the "label" had become a "libel."[48] In theology and identity, Orange was simply "evangelical." Among friends and followers, he openly embraced that identity.[49] In his diary, writing for himself, Orange used the term repeatedly.[50] He unhesitatingly identified himself with the Evangelical Union (EU), which from the 1930s was helping a clear evangelical identity to re-emerge in New Zealand. After the war, he inspired the formation of the "Evangelical Churchman's Fellowship." Orange wore the identity of "evangelical" ironically, especially when outside his own trusted circle; he was instinctively wary of ostentation or rancour.

Orange's evangelicalism was primarily "spiritual," not doctrinal. His evangelicalism meant prayer, devotion to Christ, and personal holiness. It meant spiritual conversion, not formal religious observance or ritual. It meant profound fascination with Scripture and its words and images, and its awe-filled exposition. Orange's evangelicalism was neither rationalistic nor evidentialist; it richly engaged the intellect and the imagination, but did so above all to nourish the life of the spirit.

---

[46] Maurice Goodall recalled Orange saying about the Second Avent: "No one will turn to his companion, and say 'I told you it would be like this when it happens'." The Right Rev Maurice Goodall, interview, 22 November 2001, ¶11.

[47] The Right Rev Max Wiggins, interview, 2 November 1999 [hereafter MW], ¶75. "I never heard him press for a decision, he just let Scripture loose upon us, let it free to do its own work."

[48] Orange, diary, 7 July 1935.

[49] RT, ¶68-71.

[50] Orange, diary, (excluding references to the Evangelical Unions) e.g., 9, 14, 17, 18, 29 July 1935; 22 April 1938 (twice); 26 April 1938 (four times); 11 May 1938; 14 July 1938 (twice).

E.M. Blaiklock

A rather different New Zealand evangelical style was represented, in Auckland, by Dr E.M. (Edward Musgrove) Blaiklock (1903-1983). The child of a British family emigrating in 1909, Blaiklock did university studies in classics while teaching at a primary school and later Mount Albert Grammar School, gaining two Master of Arts with first class honours (in Latin and French). He was awarded a scholarship for study overseas, but declined that in favour of becoming a Lecturer in Classics at Auckland University College, and took up his position there in 1927. Blaiklock was mentored by the Professor of Classics, A.C. Paterson, and was bitterly disappointed not to succeed him when Paterson died (1933). From 1940 Blaiklock was given responsibility for Greek, and in 1945 he became Professor of Classics. In 1946 he was awarded his Doctor of Literature degree, for a study on Euripides.

Blaiklock was hugely erudite. His writing was elegant and evocative, rich with literary and historical allusions, and showed a mastery of language and metaphor. His public speaking, delivered in a strong clear voice with commanding manner, was fluent, impeccable in choice of words, and seemingly effortless; consciously or otherwise, he emulated the orators of the classical world. He usually prepared thoroughly, then deliberately left his script at home, relying on his "prodigious" memory to replicate it word for word.[51]

At the university, Blaiklock's teaching style was formal and exacting; a shy man, he avoided familiarity with under-graduates. He became prominent in university affairs, serving as Dean of Arts and as University Orator, and often clashing with those of less conservative outlook such as historian Keith Sinclair. Blaiklock became well-known among the reading public, in part because of his weekly newspaper column which he wrote for forty-three years (initially in the national *Weekly News* and later the *New Zealand Herald*) under the thin disguise of his pen name "Grammaticus."[52]

---

[51] Stewart, "Edward Musgrove Blaiklock," 172.
[52] Articles from the *Weekly News* series were later published in E.M. Blaiklock, *Green Shade* (Wellington: A H & A W Reed, c.1967).

He also contributed leading articles to the *Herald*.[53] He gave many radio talks. His reputation was boosted, in the post-war era, by his increasingly prolific output of books. In 1974 he was awarded the OBE for services to scholarship and community.

Blaiklock was also an evangelical Christian. He came from a family which did not attend church much.[54] The young Blaiklock nevertheless imbibed from his father a theistic belief in "the Vast Intelligence" behind the universe.[55] As a child he sometimes went to New Lynn Congregational Church, and acquired a fascination with the Bible.[56] In his youth, reading John's Gospel, he was puzzled by the new birth.[57] He was converted in May 1921, in his first year of university studies. Friends had invited him to a non-denominational fellowship in Blockhouse Bay, and later took him to an evangelistic meeting for young men addressed by the Rev Joseph Kemp, the vigorous new evangelical minister of Auckland's Baptist Tabernacle, and "a fine, clear, dynamic preacher."[58] Kemp "deftly and persuasively brought Christ and God and life together," convincing Blaiklock that faith in Christ was the key to knowing God, and challenging his hearers to take the step of committed faith.[59] Blaiklock pondered Kemp's challenge overnight and the next morning he was a Christian.[60]

Blaiklock was the sort of person for whom it was important to

---

[53] "Goodbye, Grammaticus," *New Zealand Herald* (29 October 1983).

[54] In later years, his parents became closely involved in the church.

[55] E.M. Blaiklock, *Between the Valley and the Sea: A West Auckland Boyhood* (Palmerston North: Dunmore, 1979), 41-42. The phrase was Blaiklock's, not his father's.

[56] E.M. Blaiklock, *The Bible and I* (Minneapolis: Bethany, 1983), 9.

[57] Blaiklock, *The Bible and I*, 8; E.M. Blaiklock, *Still a Christian* (London: Hodder and Stoughton, 1980), 15. Blaiklock had also been troubled by words in the headmaster's daily prayer at Auckland Grammar School: "And while we grow in earthly knowledge, may we also grow in the knowledge of our Lord and Saviour Jesus Christ."

[58] Blaiklock, *Still a Christian*, 15.

[59] E.M. Blaiklock, *Between the Morning and the Afternoon: The Story of a Pupil-Teacher* (Palmerston North: Dunmore, 1980), 16.

[60] Blaiklock, *Between the Morning and the Afternoon*, 17.

have an orderly and purposeful universe, in which beauty, morality and truth cohered, and in which assured knowledge could be found through the revelation of God in Christ and the Scriptures. He longed to know "the Mind" behind all things, and to have a "basis" for his life.[61] Blaiklock's newfound faith offered him a deep "integration" in his thinking.[62] He saw it as embracing reason rather than suspending it,[63] as discovering the truth, as being made "more complete."[64]

Blaiklock claimed his faith "had small emotional content."[65] In matters of faith Blaiklock avowedly put a premium on doctrine, reason, and evidence rather than on emotion. "Whether the purveyors of emotionalism like it or not," he declared, "our faith must have an intellectual basis," by which he meant giving assent to "doctrine objective and clear" and having a readiness "to give a reason for the faith within."[66] Blaiklock did not decry religious experience or emotion,[67] but consistently rejected "emotionalism" as unhelpful – and un-British.[68] Nevertheless, Blaiklock's emotions ran deep, and could sometimes be brittle. When he spoke publically, there was, beneath the measured and cultured manner and the evocative images, an undercurrent of intense feeling. "Sincerity and conviction rang in his words,"[69] and listeners often felt moved.

---

[61] E.M. Blaiklock (ed.), *Why I am Still a Christian* (Grand Rapids: Zondervan, 1971), 12.

[62] Blaiklock, *Between the Morning and the Afternoon*, 18, 21.

[63] Blaiklock, *Between the Morning and the Afternoon*, 42.

[64] Blaiklock, *Still a Christian*, 17.

[65] Blaiklock, *Still a Christian*, 21.

[66] Blaiklock, "A Welcome Manuscript," *New Zealand Baptist* [hereafter *NZB*] (February 1939): 36.

[67] Blaiklock, "A Welcome Manuscript."

[68] E.M. Blaiklock, "Lord, Thou Hast Here thy Ninety and Nine," *NZB* (December 1938): 363. "We are cursed with British phlegm, which makes us hate like the plague the emotional and the dramatic. It is in our blood to hide the inner life away. We hold excessive enthusiasm suspect."

[69] *NZB* (December 1957): 285.

Blaiklock believed in conversion and evangelism.[70] In the 1930s, at Baptist church conventions, special services and Bible class camps, Blaiklock would give an "earnest appeal" for people to respond publicly to Christ.[71] He was instinctively wary, however, especially in the university environment, of revivalist excitement or high-pressure evangelism, which risked making Christians appear irrational.[72] Increasingly, Blaiklock's key emphasis, in his Christian speaking and writing, was to point to the historicity of the New Testament records against the background of ancient history and literature, and thus the credibility of divine revelation. He did so with great conviction and ardour, with his skills and *gravitas* as a scholarly classicist adding weight to his views.

Blaiklock published a total of more than seventy books, often several in one year. There were also numerous booklets. The majority of his publications related to the study of the Scriptures. His titles included various academic and classical studies[73] and new translations of Augustine, Francis of Assisi, and Thomas à Kempis.[74] There were several books of autobiographical

---

[70] For instance, Blaiklock gave a spirited talk in Hawkes Bay on "Why I Believe in Conversion," *NZB* (July 1937): 223. For Blaiklock on evangelism, see: *NZB* (February 1938): 50; *NZB* (December 1938): 363.

[71] For instance, see: "Hastings," *NZB* (July 1938): 223-24; "Auckland Men's Camp – Omana," *NZB* (June 1935): 177. The latter report states that Blaiklock's "fearless revelation of the issue, unclouded by any 'emotionalism', brought twelve fellows to the foot of the Cross in complete surrender."

[72] He counselled the IVF against inviting Dr Howard Guinness back to New Zealand to conduct university missions in 1955. E.M. Blaiklock to Cliff Cocker, February 3 [1952], TSCF C5. Blaiklock was impressed, however, by the 1959 Billy Graham Crusade. *NZB* (May 1959): 120.

[73] E.M. Blaiklock, *The Male Characters of Euripides: A Study in Realism* (Wellington: New Zealand University, 1952); *The Roman and his Trouble: the Significance of Roman History* (Auckland: Whitcombe & Tombs, 1963); *The Romanticism of Catullus* (Auckland: University of Auckland, 1966).

[74] *The Confessions of Saint Augustine* (London: Hodder & Stoughton, 1983); *The Little Flowers of St Francis: The Acts of Saint Francis and his Companions* (London: Hodder & Stoughton, 1985); *The Imitation of Christ* (London: Hodder & Stoughton, 1979).

reflections,[75] all demonstrating Blaiklock's intense, almost mystical reverence for the beauty of creation; he especially loved the majestic kauri-clad hills and lonely seascapes of the Waitakere Ranges.[76] Blaiklock's works of apologetics included such titles as *This Faith or That? Why We Believe in the Existence of God,* [77] *Why I Am Still a Christian,*[78] and *Still a Christian.*[79] He wrote *Who was Jesus? A Classical Scholar Examines the Documentary Evidence for the Man Jesus* (later published as *Man or Myth*)[80] and several books relating the New Testament to its historical context.[81] A common element to all those works was Blaiklock's view that Christian belief is eminently reasonable, and that the Gospel accounts are historically trustworthy and compelling. He wrote a number of books on biblical archaeology, published by major overseas Christian publishers.[82] Scores of Blaiklock titles were biblical commentaries, including a

---

[75] E.g., Blaiklock, *Between the Valley and the Sea; Between the Morning and the Afternoon.*

[76] E.M. Blaiklock, *The Hills of Home* (Wellington: Reed, 1966); *A Love of Trees* (Palmerston North: Dunmore, 1982).

[77] E.M. Blaiklock, *This Faith or That? Why We Believe in the Existence of God* (London: Pickering & Inglis, 1968). Note also E.M. Blaiklock, *No Mists Above: An Examination of the Christian Belief in God* (Auckland: Institute Printing & Publishing, n.d.); *Is it - or Isn't it? Why We Believe in the Existence of God* (Grand Rapids: Zondervan, 1968).

[78] Blaiklock (ed.), *Why I am still a Christian.*

[79] Blaiklock, *Still a Christian.*

[80] E.M. Blaiklock, *Who was Jesus? A Classical Scholar Examines the Documentary Evidence for the Man Jesus* (Chicago: Moody, 1974); E.M. Blaiklock, *Man or Myth* (Homebush West: ANZEA, 1983).

[81] E.M. Blaiklock, *Cities of the New Testament* (London: Pickering & Inglis, 1965); *The Century of the New Testament* (London: InterVarsity, 1962); *Blaiklock's Bible Handbook* (Auckland: Hodder & Stoughton, 1980); *The World of the New Testament* (London: Ark, 1981).

[82] E.M. Blaiklock, *Out of the Earth: The Witness of Archaeology to the New Testament* (London: Paternoster, 1957); *The Archaeology of the New Testament* (Grand Rapids: Zondervan, 1970); E.M. Blaiklock and R.K. Harrison, *The New International Dictionary of Biblical Archaeology* (Grand Rapids: Zondervan, 1983).

historical commentary on Acts published by Tyndale[83] and a one volume Bible commentary.[84] For international Scripture Union, Blaiklock wrote countless Bible-reading *Daily Notes* (eventually covering the entire Bible), and later many study books of Bible characters (later re-published as *Professor Blaiklock's Handbook of Bible People*).[85]

During the late 1960s controversy over the radical theological views of Lloyd Geering (Principal of the Presbyterian Theological Hall and an advocate of the non-supernaturalist, non-revelational "secular Christianity" being promoted overseas by such figures as J.A.T. Robinson), Blaiklock wrote *Layman's Answer: An Examination of the New Theology,* reiterating the evidence for the historicity of the New Testament and the resurrection of Jesus.[86] Blaiklock did not engage in any detail with Geering's views, which he considered merely derivative, but disdainfully surveyed its background in nineteenth century sceptical German theology. He rejected as untenable "double-talk" any attempt to dispense with the central truth claims of Christianity while still claiming to be authentically Christian. He also rejected the contention that modern, post-Enlightenment human beings were essentially different from those in classical and medieval times.

Converted through a Baptist minister, Blaiklock himself became

---

[83] E.M. Blaiklock, *The Acts of the Apostles: An Historical Commentary* (London: Tyndale, 1959; Grand Rapids: Eerdmans, 1959). Also, e.g.: E.M. Blaiklock, *The Pastoral Epistles: A Study Guide to the Epistles of I and II Timothy and Titus* (Grand Rapids: Zondervan, 1972); *The Seven Churches: An Exposition of Revelation, Chapters Two and Three* (Melbourne: S John Bacon, n.d.); *Faith is the Victory: Studies in the First Epistle of John* (London: Paternoster, 1959); *Commentary on the New Testament* (Old Tappan: Revell, 1977).
[84] E.M. Blaiklock, *Blaiklock's Handbook to the Bible* (London: Hodder & Stoughton, 1980).
[85] E.M. Blaiklock, *Professor Blaiklock's Handbook of Bible People* (London: Scripture Union, 1979).
[86] E.M. Blaiklock, *Layman's Answer: An Examination of the New Theology* (London: Hodder & Stoughton, 1968).

(after some years) a Baptist.[87] Conservative in conviction, he appreciated the characteristic Baptist emphasis on biblical authority.[88] He presumably felt comfortable with the moderate ethos of New Zealand Baptists, who were generally given neither to a theological modernism nor to sectarian eccentricities. Despite being a layman, Blaiklock enjoyed extensive opportunities within the Baptist denomination to speak and to have influence. Blaiklock was a member at the Baptist Tabernacle, where he was a Bible Class leader, regular preacher, and elder. He later moved his membership to Mt Albert Baptist, where he was likewise an elder. Blaiklock became very involved in the Young Men's Bible Class Movement, speaking at numerous camps and special events, and was for many years the national vice-president.[89] From the mid 1930s to the mid 1940s Blaiklock edited (and largely wrote) the Baptist's Bible Class syllabus, including Easter Camp studies. Most weeks, Blaiklock was preaching in Baptist pulpits around Auckland, and he preached in Baptist churches all over the country.[90] He had become New Zealand's best-known Baptist lay preacher.[91] By the 1940s, he was writing regularly for the *New Zealand Baptist*, both feature articles[92] and series on Bible problems.[93] Blaiklock served on the council of the Baptist College, where he also taught. In 1971-2 he was President of the Baptist Union.

Blaiklock was not, however, a narrow denominationalist, in either thought or practice.[94] Tellingly, perhaps, his official orations

---

[87] Initially Blaiklock, a loner by nature, was not closely associated with any church.
[88] "A Welcome Manuscript," *NZB* (February 1939): 36.
[89] E.g., *NZB* (May 1932): 141; *NZB* (November 1932): 359; *NZB* (September 1935): 273.
[90] E.g., *NZB* (August 1933): 255; *NZB* (March 1935): 90; *NZB* (April 1936): 124.
[91] *NZB* (April 1968): 5.
[92] E.g., E.M. Blaiklock, "Where Delphi Spoke Truth," *NZB* (June 1942): 171.
[93] E.g., E.M. Blaiklock, "Bible Sidelights," *NZB* (April 1941): 119.
[94] E.M. Blaiklock, *The Answer's in the Bible: One Hundred and One Answers to Familiar Questions* (London: Hodder and Stoughton, 1978): 138-39, 145-47; F.H.L. [Hayes Lloyd], "Dr E.M. Blaiklock," *NZB* (June 1946): 154.

to Baptist denominational gatherings, such as College commencement addresses or his sermon to the Baptist Assembly on becoming President, contained only very rare references to the Baptist denomination and nothing about its distinctives; such speeches of his were not even remotely partisan, and could have been taken as addresses to the whole Western church.[95] Blaiklock had no illusions about his denomination; his own experience of life in Baptist churches may have helped fuel his recurring anxieties about Christian anti-intellectualism, emotionalism, and overbearing evangelism. Beyond the Baptists, Blaiklock was committed to various inter-denominational ministries: he had been recruited by Kemp to teach Greek at the inter-denominational New Zealand Bible Training Institute (later the Bible College of New Zealand and now Laidlaw College), where he also taught John's Gospel for thirty years and served ten years as President; he was a long-time supporter of the Crusader Union and the Evangelical Unions; he spoke at many Keswick-style conventions; he preached in the pulpits of a wide variety of denominations. Across the denominations, Blaiklock became one of New Zealand's most well-known Christians, especially among evangelicals, who admired his learning and felt fortified by the way he lent scholarly credibility to conservative biblical faith. Blaiklock was also sometimes invited to speak in ecumenical circles.[96] He spoke more than once at Britain's venerable Keswick Convention, and preached from the pulpits of leading overseas evangelical churchmen such as Dr Harold J. Ockenga (Congregationalist), Dr Donald G. Barnhouse (Presbyterian), and Dr John Stott (Church of England). When he

---

[95] "Baptist College of New Zealand: Twenty-first Session Commencement Address by Dr E.M. Blaiklock," *NZB* (March 1949): 65; "The Holy War Today," *NZB* (March 1955): 52-53; "The Call to Preach," *NZB* (May 1965): 112-14; "Church Militant," Presidential Address, *NZB* (November 1970): 8-9, (December 1970): 22-24.

[96] Notably, he was one of two laymen selected to speak to the nation (along with six clergy) at a key event in 1944 of the National Council of Churches' "Campaign for Christian Order," *Evening Post* (5 September 1944). The *New Zealand Baptist* saw this as "a great honour." "Some Short Mems [sic]," *NZB* (July 1942): 194.

died, his funeral was held not in a Baptist Church but in the Anglican Cathedral.

As with William Orange, Blaiklock was a revered leader and speaker in IVF circles. Both men completely identified themselves with that movement. From 1927, Blaiklock developed a strong involvement in the small evangelical student group which had broken away from the Student Christian Movement and later became the Evangelical Union (EU). He was a frequent speaker at EU, and every year for over forty years spoke at the "Freshman's Tea" in March. He later wrote that "it was not easy to be identified with a small, intense group… [I] did my best to establish them on a sound basis of common sense and scholarship." There were, he wrote, "over-defensive attitudes which embarrassed me," and he felt responsible for any "folly" they committed.[97] Blaiklock was keenly aware how evangelical Christians were frequently sneered at in university circles, and was anxious for his own reputation. Nevertheless, in the 50s and 60s, and reflecting the widespread post-war resurgence of evangelical Christianity, the EU blossomed, growing to become the largest student club in the University of Auckland. Professor Blaiklock was unquestionably the EU's key mentor, advisor, and luminary. In Christchurch, Orange had likewise become the principal sponsor of the Canterbury EU. Both men would speak at EU meetings and house-parties up and down the country, and both were star attractions at IVF conferences.[98] On more than one occasion they spoke at the same event, such as the 1943 national IVF conference.[99]

As an evangelical Christian, Blaiklock's overriding concern appears to have been the intellectual defence of the Christian faith in the face of modern scepticism. He wrote primarily for lay people,

---

[97] Blaiklock, *Between the Morning and the Afternoon*, 82-83.
[98] In 1937, for instance, Orange was the main speaker at the five-day AUCEU houseparty in 1937, and Blaiklock also spoke. *New Zealand Inter-Varsity News Bulletin* 3, no. 3 (June 1937). In 1939, Orange was invited by all four EUs to speak at their annual house-parties, *New Zealand Inter Varsity Supplement* 3, no. 3 (July 1939).
[99] "Evangelical Students' Conference," *NZB* (August 1943): 185.

to help convince both believers and non-believers that there were solid and persuasive grounds for believing in Christ as divine and the Scriptures as trustworthy. In this he was similar to C.S. Lewis, whom he greatly admired. Earlier figures he admired included James Denney, James Orr, and Gresham Machen. He was also influenced by the conclusions of ancient historians W.M. Ramsay and A.N. Sherwin-White that Luke was a credible historical source.[100] As an academic, Blaiklock wanted to reassure people that Christian belief did not require a narrowing of the mind or of life, and that it was neither un-learned nor "obscurantist."[101] Blaiklock felt considerable indignation at what he saw as the arrogance and poor scholarship of modernist assaults on orthodox Christian faith; he had become a Christian at a time when "a liberal religion which served the Church ill was reducing Christianity to the Golden Rule, Christ to a young Apollo… and the Bible to a sorry farrago of poetry and myth."[102] He was unimpressed by the attempts by such figures as Bultmann to "demythologise" the Christian faith, not least because Blaiklock rejected the presupposition that the New Testament contained "myth," or anything even resembling the myths of the ancient world; for Blaiklock, the New Testament was always a witness to real events.[103] With regard to the theory of evolution, Blaiklock scorned "Darwinism" as a *philosophy*, rejecting its godless faith in implausible chance and its naïve optimism (discredited by the "barbarisms" of the twentieth century) about human progress. On the other hand he appeared quite open to the possibility of some evolutionary process as an intentional part of God's creation,[104] refused to accept that science and religion were enemies, and deplored conservative Christian attempts to refute evolution.[105]

Blaiklock was clearly evangelical – in doctrine, practice, and affiliations. He was a conservative biblical apologist who preached

---

[100] Blaiklock, *The Bible and I*, 31, 68-75.
[101] Blaiklock, *Between the Morning and the Afternoon*, 17-18.
[102] Blaiklock, *The Bible and I*, 17.
[103] Blaiklock, *Who Was Jesus?* 46-56.
[104] E.g. Blaiklock, *The Answer's in the Bible*, 130, 177.
[105] Blaiklock, *The Bible and I*, 22.

for conversion. He was a key figure in self-consciously and explicitly "evangelical" organisations such as the Evangelical Union, the IVF, the Crusader Union, and BTI. In 1946, the *New Zealand Baptist* described him as a "central and evangelical Christian."[106] However Blaikock's usual way of describing his theological position was not as an "evangelical" but as an "informed conservative," a self-designation he adopted after a conversation in 1951 with the British evangelical Dr W.G. Scroggie (whom Blaiklock had got to know when Scroggie spent several months at the Tabernacle in 1933).[107] Blaiklock could thus avoid being misconstrued as either an emotional revivalist or an obscurantist fundamentalist. He may have felt that the term "evangelical" was not self-evident in meaning, and open to misunderstanding (e.g,. as meaning simply "evangelistic").

The principal thing to be conserved by informed conservativism, Blaiklock explained, was belief in an authoritative Bible; but the "informed" aspect of that involved an embracing of true scholarship and its discoveries, and it precluded inappropriate literalism, the defence of indefensible positions, an obsessive "futurist" biblical interpretation, and dogmatism on matters where Christians may legitimately differ.[108] On the one hand Blaiklock rejected "fundamentalism," with its eccentric exegesis, anti-intellectualism, controversialism, intolerance, and separatism.[109] On the other hand he rejected "liberalism" as bankrupt, with its discredited optimism about human nature, its irresponsible scepticism, and its loss of a personal and biblical Gospel.[110] He thought neo-orthodoxy a significant improvement on liberalism, but defective in its lack of an authoritative Bible.[111]

---

[106] "A New Zealand Reavely Glover," *NZB* (June 1946): 154.
[107] "The Task of Educated Leadership: The Presidential Address at the I.V.F. Conference, 1962," NZIVF Christian Codex 4: 5-6.
[108] Blaiklock, *The Bible and I*, 29-30.
[109] Blaiklock, *The Bible and I*, 24.
[110] Blaiklock, *The Bible and I*, 31-35.
[111] Blaiklock, *The Bible and I*, 35-36. Another point of difference would have been Blaiklock's liking for natural theology.

In the 1950s and 60s, Professor Blaiklock was an exponent *par excellence* of evangelical Christian rationalism. In his 1952 IVF Presidential Address, Blaiklock declared that "to deny the validity of reason, is to scorn the image of God within us." "The Christian is the truest rationalist." The world of the Christian alone "makes sense." Christian conviction is "the most truly integrating of all ideas." Faith always involves rationality: "we must accept the reason of man as a legitimate road to God, and must be prepared to submit the tenets and attitudes of religion to its test." "Our faith is a reasonable one." [112] Reason, Blaiklock argued elsewhere, was the first pier in the bridge to faith: "the mind advances to the first pier by reasoned examination of the facts of the natural world" (the second and third piers were revelation and experience).[113] In Blaiklock's emphasis on reason, one can arguably discern echoes not just of Scripture (especially the *Logos* theme in the Johannine prologue), but also of classical philosophy, scholastic theology, and the Enlightenment. There was also his underlying indignation that atheists accused Christians of blind, irrational faith, but were themselves committed to a faith which he considered rationally precarious.[114] Blaiklock reacted against what he saw as a growing "revolt against reason" in Western thought and culture. Blaiklock exhorted IVF students to model "sanity, confidence and scholarship" – in place of irrationality, shallowness, stupidity of exposition, crudity of language, and boisterousness in song-leading.[115] Later, Blaiklock would be moved to rage and despair by the irrationality he perceived in neo-pentecostalism. When a known "charismatic" was appointed as a staff worker by the New Zealand IVF, he sent IVF a curt two-sentence letter: "The sound of hammering on the nails that close the coffin of the IVF is insistent

---

[112] Presidential Address [1952, E.M. Blaiklock], TSCF A1/107. This address was published as E.M. Blaiklock, *Sanity, Confidence and Scholarship* (Wellington: IVF, n.d.).
[113] Blaiklock, *No Mists Above*, 5; *Is It – Or Isn't It?* 9-10.
[114] E.g., Blaiklock, *No Mists Above*, 10-20; *Is It – Or Isn't It?*: 8.
[115] Presidential Address.

in my ears. Lose the intelligent and we lose the lot – and I *do* know universities in four continents."[116]

Orange and Blaiklock: two different types of evangelicals?

Orange and Blaiklock were part of the same emerging movement, mid-twentieth century New Zealand evangelicalism. Both were regarded as among the heroes of that movement. Both had articulated evangelical Christian faith with great conviction and ability. Both stood up for evangelical faith at a time (especially in their younger years) when it was generally unfashionable, against the prevailing views of their professional colleagues (in church and academy respectively). Both had been leading pioneers of the fledgling Evangelical Unions and Inter-Varsity Fellowship, both became honoured elder statesmen of the IVF, and both were among its most celebrated speakers.

At a personal level, there was much that was similar about the two men (and also some significant differences). Both were cultured, bookish, well-read, well-travelled. Both were solitary types, by temperament. Both could be very mystical about nature, and loved to ramble around the countryside. Both were puritanical, and socially conservative. Both were shy and reserved (though Orange could become the life of the party in company where he felt comfortable). Both were very sensitive to criticism. Both had melancholic tendencies. Both had some personal quirks and idiosyncracies (but Blaiklock perhaps less obviously so). Both were profoundy gripped by Scripture (though Orange's primary interest was in the spiritual meaning of Scripture, whereas Blaiklock was preoccupied with its historicity and revelatory trustworthiness). Both were outstandingly gifted public speakers (but Orange spoke only in church and evanglical settings, whereas Blaiklock was a respected speaker in a very wide range of situations both Christian and secular). Both attracted a following (though Orange was perhaps regarded with more affection, and the more austere,

---

[116] Blaiklock to John [McInnes], 3 November [1972], TSCF A3b/17 (emphasis original).

magisterial Blaiklock was perhaps more widely admired). Both had a sense of the significant contribution they were making to the New Zealand church (but Orange, who published nothing, saw his key legacy as his scores of protégés, whereas Blaiklock increasingly saw his main role as writing and publishing).

Unease

Notwithstanding their shared evangelical commitments, Baiklock did not particularly like or respect Orange. It appears Blaiklock thought Orange pretentious, and his scholarship defective. As a professional academic, aware of his own scholarly stature, Blaiklock may have looked down on Orange as a self-taught amateur who did not know his limits. As a classicist, Blaiklock wanted the text read straight, subject to the canons of sound literary and historical criticism, and was deeply averse to "oddities of interpretation and exegesis." [117] Just as Blaiklock rejected as methodologically unsound the typology promoted by Scofield,[118] he rejected Orange's typological tendencies, which he no doubt considered similarly subjective and fanciful.[119] He may have been uncomfortable with Orange's primarily "spiritual" emphasis, as opposed to a more history-based and evidentialist approach; Blaiklock probably felt that, in the sceptical university context, evangelical students needed rather less of the former and a great deal more of the latter. Blaiklock, who saw himself as a public sage, a man of letters speaking wisdom, virtue, and truth into the whole of society through his weekly articles and books, perhaps regretted the inward-looking focus and separatist elements in Orange's teaching; "to influence the world," Blaiklock later wrote, "the Church must infiltrate it."[120] For his role in public life Blaiklock would be later

---

[117] Blaiklock, *The Bible and I*, 24.

[118] Blaiklock, *The Bible and I*, 15-18.

[119] A similar attitude was held by the Rev John Deane, Principal of BTI, who walked out of an address by Orange at a national IVF Conference in the early 1950s when Orange's talk took a typological turn. Telephone conversation with the Rev Ian Kemp, 17 June 2011.

[120] Blaiklock, *The Answer's in the Bible*, 144.

awarded the OBE, whereas Orange would probably have been disturbed by any such worldly acclaim. Blaiklock was probably suspicious of Orange's eschatological views; Blaiklock regarded dispensationalism, millennialism, and the overly-detailed and dogmatic pronouncements of many in the prophetic movement as undermining the credibility of conservative biblical faith.[121]

After Orange spoke at one Auckland houseparty, the EU newsletter eulogised Orange for the "fragrance of a life lived in closest touch with God,"[122] a superlative assessment that Blaiklock would have noted with some disapproval. Blaiklock felt the adulation Orange received in IVF circles was undeserved. He harboured a private suspicion that Orange was some sort of plagiarising charlatan, lifting his addresses directly from (dubious) books. Consequently, Blaiklock did his best to block invitations for Orange to speak in the Auckland EU. In the late 1940s there was some temporary inter-evangelical conflict, after the relationship soured between Orange and L.B. Miller, the Brethren financier of Tyndale House, an evangelical conference and study centre on the hills above Christchurch. The conflict eventually pulled in many others, including leading IVF figures and the BTI Principal, John Deane, and Blaiklock's view of Orange disconcerted IVF leaders.

Contrasts

Orange's influence inspired a whole new evangelical movement within New Zealand Anglicanism; but Blaiklock, while reinforcing the conservative tendencies in the mid-twentieth century Baptist

---

[121] Blaiklock, *The Answer's in the Bible*, 19-22. Blaiklock's views on such matters may have been consolidated by his involvement as a defence witness in a 1943 defamation lawsuit brought against the Baptist Union by several individuals who, on the basis of alleged numeric codes in the Bible (including the 153 fish in John 21) had specified 17 July 1944 as the date of the Second Coming. They had taken offence when the *New Zealand Baptist* called them "impudent prophets and bounders." "The Libel Case," *NZB* (July 1943): 150-51; *Evening Post* (27 May 1943): 5.

[122] *The NZ Inter-Varsity News Bulletin* 1, no.1 (July 1936); *The New Zealand Inter Varsity Supplement* 5, no.3 (November 1941).

movement in New Zealand, was responsible for no significant new denominational development. Orange's influence was largely within one denomination, but Blaiklock's Christian influence was much more inter-denominational. Orange was a humble parish vicar, seeking to work inconspicuously; however Blaiklock always had a much more prestigious and public platform from which to exert influence. Orange had his greatest personal impact in the 1930s and 40s, but Blaiklock's peak period of influence coincided with the post-war evangelical renaissance. Orange's influence was almost entirely within New Zealand (and then largely within the upper South Island), but, through his role among Baptists and through his writings, Blaiklock's influence was nationwide and to some extent international.

Conclusion

Blaiklock's unease with Orange was in part a matter of a younger and better-qualified man bridling against what he saw as undue student veneration towards Orange. It also highlighted the contrast between his own rationalistic, evidentialist caste of thought, and the more spiritualising tone of Orange and his Christchurch circle. Likewise, it demonstrated the differences between the more defensive, intellectually isolated, and separatistic flavour of Orange's evangelicalism (reflecting both the influence of the Brethren and an earlier, more hostile context) and the more expansive, confident, and intellectually defensible evangelicalism of Professor Blaiklock. It would be saying far too much to suggest that the differences and tensions between the two revealed any rift in New Zealand evangelicalism, or two clearly-identifiable separate evangelical strands. It did illustrate, however, the existence of perceptibly different aspirations and apprehensions within New Zealand's mid-twentieth century evangelical movement, within a greater evangelical oneness.

Chapter Five
Evangelicals equipping Melanesian men and women: an interpretation of the training ministries of the Christian Leaders' Training College of Papua New Guinea, 1965-2010

John M. Hitchen

The Christian Leaders' Training College (CLTC) of Papua New Guinea (PNG), an evangelical, interdenominational Bible and Theological College, commenced teaching at Banz in the Western Highlands Province (now Jiwaka Province) of PNG in 1965. Since then, the College has served the evangelical and mainline churches of PNG by equipping men and women for Christian ministry and service in Melanesian society. This essay offers an emic interpretation of the focus and development of CLTC's educational programmes over its first forty-five years of ministry. The author served successively in the roles of Lecturer, Dean of Studies, and Principal of CLTC during its first fifteen years and has been involved as a member the College Council or Academic Advisory Board for the last twenty years of the period under review. He willingly admits his resultant bias. The reader must judge the extent to which that involvement may have been an advantage or hindrance for the purpose of this chapter.

What follows addresses the following topics: the founding and focus of CLTC; the educational programme developments of CLTC; the principles and issues in developing the CLTC curriculum to express evangelical identity; and aspects of CLTC's contribution to South West Pacific evangelical identity. Throughout the essay we attempt to address missiological issues and insights inherent in the CLTC story.

The founding and focus of CLTC
The College's beginnings can be traced to an initiative of George Sexton, the Field Leader of the then Unevangelised Fields Mission

(later Asia Pacific Christian Mission and now Pioneers). Following a UFM field leaders' discussion, Sexton circulated to other evangelical mission leaders in March 1959, a letter giving reasons for the suggestion: "would it not be possible for the evangelical missions to get together and establish a 'Central Bible Training School'?"[1] He proposed discussing this at the next Government-Missions Conference the following year. Whereas the letter drew little response, the conference discussion in 1960 revealed several of the missions had been considering higher level biblical training programmes, but had taken no action because of the assumed costs.[2] Sensing they were being challenged to take a cooperative step, they agreed to approach the Council of the Melbourne Bible Institute (later Bible College of Victoria, now Melbourne School of Theology), asking MBI to establish a Bible College in Papua New

---

[1] The full text is given in J. Oswald Sanders, *Planting Men in Melanesia* (Mt Hagen: Christian Leaders Training College, 1978), 26–28.

[2] The core group of evangelical missions (and in brackets the national churches they would establish within a decade) cooperating in the commencement of CLTC were the Australian Baptist Missionary Society (Baptist Union of PNG); the Unevangelised Fields Mission (Evangelical Church of Papua [later, of PNG]); The South Sea Evangelical Mission (South Sea Evangelical Church), both in the Sepik Province of PNG and in the Solomon Islands; The Australian Churches of Christ Mission (Melanesian Evangelical Churches of Christ); Christian Missions in Many Lands (Christian Brethren Churches); and Manus Evangelical Mission (Manus Evangelical Church). From the start students from other, smaller evangelical missions and churches joined the student body, such as the Evangelical Bible Mission, Christian Union Mission, and Kwato Extension Association. Within a few years the major Pentecostal missions, Assemblies of God Mission, Apostolic Christian Mission, and the Wesleyan and other Holiness Mission groups like the Church of the Nazarene Mission, also sent students. The Southern Highlands Region of the Methodist Overseas Mission (United Church of PNG and the Solomon Islands) also regularly sent students. Other United Church Regions did likewise once control passed into national hands. Over the years, CLTC's student body has reflected almost exactly the membership of the Evangelical Alliance of the South Pacific Islands, with occasional students coming from virtually all the main-line denominations and some para-church service agencies.

Guinea as a missionary outreach. The MBI Council accepted the challenge and set up a sub-committee to explore the possibility.

Their first task was to identify a suitable person to head up such a venture. One of those in the original UFM field discussions, Charles Horne, while on furlough playing golf in Sydney, shared the College concept with a former Baptist missionary colleague, Rev Gilbert McArthur, who quickly warmed to the idea. By 1963 the MBI Council had appointed McArthur as principal-elect of the new college. He took over the preliminary work Leonard Buck, the committee chairperson, had already achieved towards finding a suitable physical location and consulting with the cooperating missions. One morning in February 1964, almost at wits' end over frustrations and delays in securing a site in the Wahgi Valley near Banz in the Western Highlands District of PNG, McArthur sensed the Lord confirming the Giramben property as the right location. In his mind's eye a vision formed of how the various aspects of the programme could be laid out on this block of land.[3] From that point confirming the land lease, recruiting workers and future missionary staff from Australia, New Zealand, and PNG, accessing the property, and initiating the building programme all moved with heaven-directed alacrity.

Thus in February 1965 the first group of eighteen students arrived at the College. These men came with considerable pastoral and evangelistic experience and represented the best of evangelical mission education at that time, having attained the English entry requirement – the equivalent of completing primary schooling.

In 1973 the Melbourne Bible Institute CLTC Committee transferred full governing responsibility for the College to a properly constituted Papua New Guinea-based council incorporated under the Associations Ordinance of PNG. Membership of the self-perpetuating council was made up of a number of evangelical church leaders (mostly graduates of the College) recognised for their evangelical leadership in their communities; representatives of the churches the College serves; and a small number of expatriates

---

[3] See Sanders, *Planting Men in Melanesia*, 35–39.

representing mission agencies and the Australian and New Zealand groups who had shared in founding the College. Advisory Councils with fundraising and staff recruiting but no governing responsibilities were set up in Australia and New Zealand. By the early 1970s steady progress was being made in "localising" staff positions, both in the support and teaching programmes. A significant number of expatriates have, however, continued to serve in key roles throughout the College's first forty-five years.

The original student group presented the College its basic challenge: to develop a higher level English language biblical/theological curriculum to equip Melanesians for church and community leadership. From 1965 a pattern of consultation was initiated with evangelical mission leaders in PNG on curriculum development.[4] The key components were established early:

- Biblical and theological study at the centre of the curriculum, as the prime requirement for young evangelical churches growing from the then-dominant missions.

- Using English as the language of instruction: both to utilise the one common language uniting students from across the nation and to equip students with the language and literacy skills to bridge into the wider Christian world.[5] Neo-Melanesian, Tok Pisin, was used for pastoral care amongst students and in College outreach ministries.

- Keeping a practical and holistic perspective: equipping leaders both for church and community leadership, but also for agricultural, mechanical, and building ministries – and, in the original plan even teacher training.[6]

---

[4] The CLTC Consultative Committee served from 1965 until 1973 when its functions were absorbed into the PNG-based Governing Council. More recently, an Academic Advisory Board, as a sub-Committee of the College Council, has assumed responsibility for guiding curriculum development.

[5] The rationale for using English is set out in the early Staff Orientation Paper, J.M. Hitchen, *Why English as the Medium of Instruction at CLTC?* (Unpublished duplicated paper, CLTC, 1967).

[6] Plans for a Teacher Education "arm" of CLTC never eventuated. The UFM's strong involvement in education and the clear vision of some of their

- Rooted in Melanesia with a strong self-support commitment: seen at first in developing the money-earning capacity of the property, but increasingly worked out in the curriculum in terms of contextualization – making the teaching relevant to the cultural settings of Melanesia.

The educational programme developments of CLTC[7]

Certificate, Diploma, Bachelor, and Masters developments, and associated initiatives

The initial four year Certificate of Church Leadership course used controlled English vocabulary and sentence structures in its teaching materials and class-room procedures. Lecturers developed detailed notes as an ongoing resource to enable students to bridge into existing English biblical study materials. Up to a quarter of their study focused on improving their English and general education. Daily routines fostered a strong communal living experience. Vacation "commando" outreach missions built team-work and gave vital practical application for the class-room input. After a decade the Certificate course was reduced to three years. Practical internships of up to six months back with the home church partway through the course, less general education, and more ministry-related subjects have been some of the adaptations in later years. These days the College encourages the churches they serve to develop their own certificate level programmes and offers support and opportunities for students from such programmes to move into higher level study at CLTC.

---

educational missionaries, particularly Alwyn Neuendorf, always favoured a separate, UFM/APCM-run Teachers' College to serve the Evangelical Alliance constituency – which eventuated with the establishment of Dauli Teachers' College in the Southern Highlands growing out of UFM's earlier work at Awaba in the Western Province.

[7] The curriculum details are gleaned from the writer's own papers and confirmed from CLTC reports presented to Annual Council Meetings, and the associated minutes, held in the archives of Laidlaw College, Auckland.

Lack of accommodation when teaching began in 1965, meant the wives of the first student group could not join their husbands until the second year. The instruction of wives in Pidgin literacy, home-craft, discipleship, and Christian marriage, plus selected biblical and practical ministry subjects quickly established a pattern that has continued. Where wives' previous education warranted it they have studied in the English programmes.

The evident value of the Certificate programme led to calls for mature church workers not yet at the Standard 6 English level to be able to enrol. The early experience, however, suggested the standard set was a necessary minimum to benefit from the programme. So, with the help of Wycliffe Bible Translators' Summer Institute of Linguistics staff and experienced literacy teachers from other missions, a "Special English Course" was devised to prepare selected groups of potential students through an accelerated English literacy course, conducted first at Lapolama in the Sau Enga area, and later at Koroba in the Southern Highlands (now Hela) Province. These programmes were only ever intended as a stop-gap measure, but opened the door into higher level education for a significant group of Christian servants.[8]

By the College's fourth year of teaching, 1968, a one year Christian Education course had been grafted on to the Church Leadership Certificate. This offered teachers, youth, or children's workers a shorter, more focused pathway into a range of ministries supplementing their vocational commitments. This option only ever attracted small numbers of students, but it formed the content of the discipleship training given to technical trainees in the early years and would become the basis of the Single Women's course.

By 1968 the College was also drawing heavily on the advice of an inter-church and mission Consultative Committee which that year made two further proposals to the Annual Council meetings.

---

[8] By Al Pence, the then Director of Wycliffe Bible Translators/Summer Institute of Linguistics in PNG, becoming involved in the planning and running of this 1969 Special English Course. WBT/SIL were taking early steps towards national Bible translator training which would lead later to the founding of the Bible Translators' Association of PNG.

They endorsed plans to commence a higher level Diploma of Theology course in 1969, and recommended considering a Single Women's course from 1970, both of which eventuated as planned, despite warnings from some expatriate missionaries that a single women's course on the same campus as courses for men would prove a recipe for moral disaster – which, we are glad to note, did not eventuate. The positive tone and impact of the Single Women's programme over the years can be attributed to the godly lives and pastoral wisdom of a succession of influential Deans of Women and women lecturers at the College.[9] The Single Women's course also produced many who have contributed much to Melanesia as wives of CLTC staff and other National leaders.[10]

The Diploma of Theology course also attracted only small numbers of students in its early years – but all were significant people of real potential. By 1977 the Diploma curriculum was re-evaluated and re-structured so as to introduce a Bachelor of Theology degree programme from 1978. After the first three years of the diploma, including six months practical internship, a student could either complete the final fourth year of the diploma or go on to a fourth and fifth year for the degree. Alternatively those with an existing diploma level qualification could enrol for the two final years to complete the degree.

Thus within fifteen years of commencing the lecture programme a series of inter-related biblical courses were in place to fulfil the original vision. The most recent higher step was in 1997 when a proposal was presented to Council to commence a Masters level course, along with a report of an initial pilot Masters course already in progress. After two further pilot courses, from 2008 a regular taught Master of Theology programme has been instituted. Comprising normally six taught courses and a 20,000 word dissertation, the major assignments of these courses have been

---

[9] Such as Julie Martin, Jill Gordon, Dorothy Tweddell, Basanuc Zurenuo, Berris Clarke, Hazel Nate, Kathleen Wilson, Eunice Marua, Alison Palmer, and Bev Sundgren.

[10] Connie Taruna and Mone Daimoi would head any list of such influential graduates.

moderated by scholars of standing in the Australasian theological education scene to ensure realistic comparability of achievement standards in this CLTC programme. The Master of Theology was one of the programmes included in the process of accreditation of CLTC through the Office of Higher Education in 2008–2010.

Multi-stage programmes

The series of "stair-cased" biblical and theological programmes from certificate to degree we have just outlined were primarily geared for people sensing a call into Christian service as a vocation. For most these courses were pre-service training and education. CLTC soon began serving other groups as well.

Once the first CLTC graduates returned home to take up their ministries, it became evident their higher levels of English language training could easily cause problems. Many of the older, mature, but comparatively less educated church leaders found the arrival of these better educated younger men and women a real challenge. CLTC realised they needed to help upgrade the qualifications of the older senior pastors. So from 1973 a series of six-month courses were conducted in which selected older, experienced men of God came to CLTC for special studies on the nature of the changes going on in the church and world and the importance of their mature roles during the transitions that were taking place. By bringing them onto the campus and ensuring they mixed with the younger trainees the misunderstandings could be transformed into mutual respect and appreciation of the inter-dependence of their respective contributions to the life of the church. The first group included several Solomon Islanders with a wealth of experience of new religious movements – several had been involved in the Masinga Rule movement – and of the Holy Spirit working in revival. These men had a significant influence as they moved around Papua New Guinean churches sharing their experiences and seeing the Holy Spirit move in outbreaks of revival as they ministered.[11] Such

---

[11] The full significance of the visit of these senior pastors still awaits adequate historical study. Various aspects of their influence are referred to in Sanders, *Planting Men in Melanesia*, 113–20; John Garrett, *Where Nets Were Cast:*

courses were held every second or third year through the 1970s. In the 1980s they were re-oriented to serve Pidgin-speaking pastors, with similarly beneficial results.

The College has also developed a range of graduate refresher programmes over the years. Regional conferences and seminars, itinerant visits by College staff, the late Bafi Womenaso's short (10 week) courses for graduates at the Banz campus, and a graduate magazine, *Servant*, are a few of the methods utilized.

Multi-mode and multi-site

Alongside the core residential programmes CLTC has developed alternative modes for delivering their educational ministry. In 1970 the then Dean of the College was deeply impressed by reading of the impact of the Theological Education by Extension movement in Latin America.[12] A staff study paper was duly prepared on the nature of TEE and how it could supplement the College's residential ministries.[13] Two years later, 1972, the College presented the challenge of extension theological education as a topic for consideration at the annual meetings of the Evangelical Alliance. No significant developments took place, however, until 1975, when the first TEE pilot course in English was conducted in the first half of the year in Mt Hagen and then repeated in Port Moresby and other centres in the second half, with a second pilot of a new course

---

Christianity in Oceania Since World War II (Suva and Geneva: Institute of Pacific Studies, University of the South Pacific in association with World Council of Churches, 1997), 336–38, 363; Joan Kale, "The Religious Movement among the Kyaka Enga," in *New Religious Movements in Melanesia* (eds Carl Loeliger and Garry Trompf; Suva: IPS, USP & UPNG, 1985), 45–74; Joel Robins, *Becoming Sinners: Christianity and Moral Torment in a Papua New Guinea Society* (Berkeley: University of California Press, 2004); John M. Hitchen, "Dreams in Traditional Thought and in the Encounter with Christianity in Melanesia," *Melanesian Journal of Theology* 27 (2011): 35–36.

[12] As reported in Ralph D. Winter (ed.), *Theological Education by Extension* (Pasadena: William Carey Library, 1969).

[13] John M. Hitchen, "The Concept of Theological Education by Extension and its Relevance for Melanesia" (unpublished CLTC Study Paper, June 1970).

continuing in Mt Hagen. New staff member Ian Malins conducted the second pilot and from that point took responsibility for the development of a TEE programme to extend the ministry of the College around the country. The number of students, courses, and extension centres expanded rapidly each year, and the programme, now called Distance Theological Education, continues to prove a very significant part of the work of CLTC.

The College's first President, Leonard Buck, had close ties with the evangelistic ministry, Everyman's Hut, in the nation's capital, Port Moresby. Thus from the beginning he impressed upon staff the challenge the urban centres held for the future of the church. The College's first foray into Port Moresby, the national capital, was in December of 1973 when Rev Francis Foulkes, then of Bible College of New Zealand, and Dr Ted Gibson, Principal of Queensland Baptist College, joined CLTC staff Berris Clarke and John Hitchen to run a three week Vacation Bible Course on the university campus for students and Christian professionals. Keen participants, like Joe Taruna and William Longgar, would later become national staff of the College. When Dr Bruce Nichols of the World Evangelical Fellowship Theological Commission visited the College in 1980 he stressed the importance of developing an effective ministry in the nation's urban centres. He sowed seeds that would mature over the next few years so that in 1983 proposals were brought to the annual Council meetings for CLTC centres to be established the following year in both Port Moresby and Lae, the two largest cities in the country. With Bob and Doseena Fergie appointed as the dynamic first leaders of the Port Moresby programme, it soon developed an Urban Ministry Internship course in both English and Pidgin that has equipped a steady stream of key lay and pastoral leaders in the nation's capital. The task in Lae has been harder going, with different shorter courses being offered. Regular Diploma of Theology courses are also now on offer through the regional centres, with plans to trial higher level courses in the near future.

The central Bible teaching ministries of the College have thus developed to embrace many levels, to serve people at every stage of involvement in Christian service, and to do so through various modes of delivery in several locations across the nation.

The integrally associated programmes

To round out the story it is necessary to add to these focused Bible teaching programmes the closely associated vocational training programmes which also characterized the CLTC vision.

Agricultural Training: From the first intake of Farm Management Course students in 1966 the College struggled with ways to prepare young men to develop farming and agricultural understanding and skills suited to influence the direction of economic development at the grass roots as the nation headed towards independence. Attempts at developing a model farm, introducing "intermediate technology," applying globally proven "development" processes, and trying our own creative approaches have met with differing levels of success. Cultural problems in changing traditional decision-making and farming procedures, and difficulties in developing sustainable supply lines, creating regular market outlets, and handling unreliable (or non-existent) transportation systems could be listed as some of the issues and problems encountered. Although in more recent years the agricultural training has been discontinued, then re-born as a rice-growing training programme, and now potentially expanding back into some of the earlier areas of project training, we have no cause for shame in the effort made, the lives influenced, and the skills imparted that have been an important part of the nationwide struggle to determine how best to integrate the old and the new in a young nation's economy.

Initial mechanical–technical and later apprenticeship training: Similarly the original vision of a strong technical training arm in building and mechanical trades did not develop as fully as at first expected. But, again, the people who have had doorways opened to ongoing usefulness in such trades and the mission and church programmes that have benefited in some measure from these efforts are not insignificant.

Support programmes in agriculture, timber, and transport: To build the College facilities in a highland valley 500 kilometres from the coastal port of Lae required the College to develop its own transportation services and supply lines. From the outset, the vision had also been to make the College self-supporting as far as practicable through agricultural programmes developed within the economy of PNG. Thus poultry programmes, dairy and beef cattle programmes, pig breeding, fruit and vegetable production, and various other smaller projects have over the years provided the College's food supplies and significant funding for the theological education operations and capital development. A significant transport business (serving church and mission agencies and local communities) and timber milling operations (needed to produce building materials) were developed to the point where a separate body, Alliance Training Association (ATA), operated them for many years with varying economic success. These support programmes have been an important aspect of the College's holistic vision and commitment to a Melanesian based educational programme. They have modelled responsible stewardship, provided channels for a massive contribution by expatriate volunteers, trained a stream of national workers, and contributed to the developing economy of the young nation through their various business ventures.

Principles and issues in developing the CLTC curriculum to express evangelical identity

The College faced a number of challenges in establishing its distinctive curriculum emphases and ministry. Implicit in these challenges have been demands to clarify the College's identity as an evangelical theological college, and to address strategic missiological issues in mission-church-academy relationships particularly.

Problems and potential of an "extraction" model of theological education

In its early years CLTC was often accused by the missionary fraternity of introducing to PNG an unhealthy "extraction" model of biblical training by taking students from their own villages and vernacular language areas to a central and more sophisticated setting for their education. The expectation was that they would thereby be "spoiled" for ministry back in their home areas after graduation. The College took this criticism seriously, and acknowledged its potential validity. A response was developed at several levels. The first was to stress that future ministry effectiveness depended on the local church being involved in the selection and sending of students to the College. Thus as its normal procedure CLTC would only accept as students those who came with endorsement and some level of support from a local church. A second emphasis was placed on theological education as a partnership between the local church and the College. Thus by November 1966 College faculty presented to the CLTC Consultative Committee a paper entitled: "The Place of Vacation Ministries – and the role of the missionary in such ministries – in the overall training of CLTC Students." The paper stressed the importance of students returning to their home areas during holidays for re-integration, practical ministry, re-establishing links with village, church, and mission leaders in their home area, and actively to explore and evaluate their readiness for various kinds of future ministry.[14] The philosophy behind these first two responses was articulated in a paper Gilbert McArthur presented to a regional government seminar in 1967.[15] A further response to this criticism was to explore and highlight biblical precedents for "extracting" key leaders from their own culture for important phases of their preparation and education, as in a paper presented at a Melanesian Association of Theological Schools Study Institute held at CLTC in January 1976 entitled, "Some Biblical Patterns of Ministerial Training and their Relevance for Melanesia Today."[16]

---

[14] John M. Hitchen, "The Place of Vacation Ministries - And the Role of the Missionary in Such Ministries – In the Overall Training of CLTC Students" (CLTC Paper presented to Consultative Committee Meeting, CLTC, 15 November 1966).

[15] G.J. McArthur and J.M. Hitchen, "Leadership in Rural Communities in Melanesia" (Unpublished paper, CLTC, March 1967).

[16] Subsequently published in *Point* 1 (1976): 85–121. This paper interestingly anticipates by two decades key aspects of the biblical material in Robert Banks,

At a later stage of CLTC's curriculum development, internships were built into the diploma and degree structures to further address the need for their training to be earthed in live, local settings.

Melanesian integrity and contextualization issues

As first planned the theological curriculum was composed of and brought together in the way common in Australasian bible colleges of the 1960s. But after even the first year of lectures, the teaching staff were already convinced significant changes were necessary. Melanesian students were not at home with the abstract approach to theological concepts, nor with selection of biblical passages based on Western systematic frameworks. From the second year the College began to focus the teaching around selected core courses. One, originally called "Bible Backgrounds and Old Testament Message," sought to lead the student chronologically through the successive stages of God's dealings with his people, highlighting the progressions in this divine-human encounter. Some decades before the concepts of "narrative theology" and "theo-drama" became buzz words in Western theological circles, we were finding the importance of these concepts for a Melanesian approach to biblical study. Likewise in structuring the basic course on the theology of God, humanity and sin, we found the biblical sequence of creation, cumulative revelation of God's nature through concrete historical events (like the Exodus, construction of the tabernacle, etc.), and historic experiences in which God disclosed himself, offered unexpected teaching tools. By rooting the theology in the historical events and the concrete experiences, and by giving attention to the significance of names and metaphors as means of God's self-revelation, we found Melanesians could steadily gather the building blocks for theological insight, reflection, and discussion, which did not happen using the Western abstract ideas approach with which we had commenced. It would be some years before we could step

---

Reenvisioning Theological Education: Exploring a Missional Alternative to Current Models (Grand Rapids: Eerdmans, 1999).

back, summarise, and theorise about what we had been doing, but the process had begun from early days.[17]

When CLTC shared in the initial accreditation processes of the Melanesian Association of Theological Schools (MATS) in 1968 one of the accreditation requirements was to demonstrate the Melanesian orientation of the College's curriculum. This further stimulated the inclusion of courses in cultural anthropology and translation principles in which the practical steps of taking English learning and re-expressing it in vernacular and trade languages were developed.

In the mid 1970s Dorothy Tweddell (Harris), the first CLTC staff member sent overseas to do doctoral level study, and David Price, who would later become Principal and soon followed her, both grappled with applying contextualization insights to the College's curriculum. Tweddell wrote a series of papers, one entitled "Burn it Down or Contextualize," challenging the College to address the local relevance of each course much more seriously.[18] Price's work on biblical and Protestant understandings of conversion,[19] together with his earlier participation with Joshua Daimoi, another later Principal, in the seminal Lausanne Congress of 1974, brought both biblical depth and fresh awareness of global trends in theological thinking to bear on curriculum development.

---

[17] John M. Hitchen, "The Place of the Bible in Curriculum Design for CLTC Residential and Extension Courses" (unpublished CLTC Faculty Discussion Paper, CLTC, July 1979); See letter, John M. Hitchen to Marilyn Rowsome, 8 July 1981, articulating the philosophy behind the structure of the Introductory Theology course; John M. Hitchen, "Culture and the Bible - The Question of Contextualization" (paper presented at the South Pacific Association of Bible Colleges' Biennial Conference, Adelaide, 1–5 July 1991), reprinted in *Melanesian Journal of Theology* 8 (1992): 30–52.

[18] Dorothy Tweddell (Harris), "Burn it Down or Contextualize: Some Guidelines for Contextualization at the Christian Leaders' Training College, Banz, Western Highlands District, Papua New Guinea" (Term Paper, Contextual Theology Class, Wheaton College, 1976).

[19] David J. Price, "The Protestant Understanding of Conversion and Its Implications for Missionary Obedience" (DMiss dissertation, Fuller School of World Mission, 1979).

Since that time the importance of such contextualization has been a regular focus of curriculum planning, though none of the faculty would claim full satisfaction with the extent to which the concerns have been addressed. When the new wave of charismatic renewal swept across PNG churches from overseas influences in the late 1980s and early 1990s, superficial links were made between the charismatic emphasis on demonic activity and the often only partially addressed primal religious assumptions in Melanesian culture. But despite this apparent relevance the overall effect of the movement was to disregard a more serious concern for culturally relevant application of biblical teaching and a sad reversal of earlier contextualization progress.

While CLTC has made some valuable contributions to the development of Melanesian Theology, not the least Joshua Daimoi's Doctoral thesis, again, there is still much that can and needs to be done in this area.[20]

Commitment to an ecclesiology embracing the equal importance and dignity of different levels of education and training for Christian ministry and service in the nation

CLTC has shown that the church and nation need – and value – leaders at a wide range of levels of training and competence: from certificate to postgraduate educational levels; from voluntary, to part-time, to full-time involvement in ministry; and for vocational, lay, and ordained forms of service. In societies which have often been hierarchical and stratified in terms of prestige accrual, the College has declared that respect belongs to every Christian worker no matter how supposedly humble or exalted their training and work in human eyes. This is basic to a healthy understanding of leadership in Melanesian churches and for a sense of positive

---

[20] Joshua Kurung Daimoi, "An Exploratory Missiological Study of Melanesian Ancestral Heritage From An Indigenous Evangelical Perspective" (PhD thesis, School of Studies in Religion, University of Sydney, 2004). For a survey including CLTC faculty and graduate contributions to Melanesian Theology, see John M. Hitchen, "Steps Towards a Melanesian Christian Theology," (unpublished Laidlaw College Class Notes, 2008).

national well-being. It also reflects CLTC's strong evangelical commitment to the priesthood of all believers and an ecclesiology that respects diversity of gifts and ministries as equally important and valuable in the church of Jesus Christ. A strong theology undergirding these emphases was articulated in the 1970 paper introducing TEE,[21] and again in 1983 following a visit of Bobby Clinton of Fuller Seminary to the College.

Professional enrichment and localisation amongst National staff

In his final report to the Council in 1970, Gilbert McArthur referred to the priority of training, equipping, and transferring responsibility to local Papua New Guinean staff members. Appended to his report that year was a "Localisation Plan" for all the key faculty and staff positions in the College, to be achieved within fifteen years. This concern had been stirred up particularly by a visit the year before of Bishop Alfred Stanway from the Church Missionary Society Anglican work in East Africa. He warned that however hard we worked at localisation from that point, it would be seen later to be too little, too late. Various forms of in-service training, study leave provisions, and support for achieving higher qualifications have been used in virtually every section of the College's work. We learned early that we needed to plan for more than one potential person to fill specific roles; that wider experience beyond College would often be a necessary step before a trainee could be expected to work permanently at CLTC; that obligations

---

[21] Hitchen, "Theological Education by Extension… for Melanesia." On a personal note, I recall the visit around 1966–67 of a delegation of mission leaders from the Australian Council of Churches to CLTC. Its leader published a report in an Australian Methodist paper in which he faintly praised CLTC's work before condemning it for a "lack of any real ecclesiology" or words to that effect. His comment spurred me to want to say that our ecclesiology was there – but it did not endorse the hierarchical assumptions that the leader in question apparently regarded as the only acceptable mark of a "real" ecclesiology. The 1970 TEE paper spelt out some ecclesiological reflections following that visit.

to family and "wantoks"[22] would often jeopardize continuity of service at CLTC; and, since we did not have an independent pool for recruiting staff, that to employ top quality persons we were dependent on the grace and mercy of the churches we serve – and those qualities are not necessarily the first that young churches cultivate. Nevertheless we thank God for the progress made over the years, faltering and partial as it has been.

Personal spiritual formation has been at the heart of the curriculum

Even a cursory reading of the annual Council reports shows the high priority every Principal, Vice-Principal and College Dean has placed on the personal spiritual and relational growth of students. Processes and structures for discipling, regularity of quality spiritual input, communal attention to failures and to forgiveness and restoration, concern to sustain the College's prayer life, evident sorrow and heart-searching when discipline or dismissal were necessary are all found regularly in the official documents. "Proclaiming, teaching, warning with all wisdom to present every student mature…" (Col 1:28), these are well-known processes in the training methods of the College.

So we could continue to comment on other curriculum-related developments and issues. Preparation of resource materials deserves space to enlarge on things like *Sing His Praise*, the controlled English hymn book collated and edited at CLTC and used widely for more than three decades across churches, schools, and colleges of the nation. Or the continuing use of evangelistic booklets prepared initially for the Ralph Bell Crusade in 1973 as follow-up material. Or again, the way both regular College teaching materials and particularly TEE materials have been published and used, both within Melanesia, and in the case of Ian Malins' original TEE notes, widely in other parts of the world as part of Malin's Discipleship Ministry. Or yet again we would need to consider the importance of Bob Fergie's *On Target* Youth Resources, produced first for the EA youth workers, then further developed under

---

[22] Literally: those speaking the same language, neo-Melanesian for the extended family and relatives who share mutual expectations and obligations.

Fergie's guidance for the National Youth Council in the 1980s. Often in collaboration with Christian Books Melanesia, the CLTC contribution to Christian literature has been significant. And we have not even mentioned the College's contributions to the ministries of Christian Broadcasting Service/Kristen Redio, or Gospel Recordings/Language Recordings/Kristen Kaset, or the Bible School of the Air, each of which deserves serious evaluation.

But we have tried to indicate some of the emphases and issues that developing an evangelical theological education programme in Melanesia has highlighted, and to give hints regarding the way they have been addressed.

Aspects of CLTC's contribution to South West Pacific evangelical identity

In a range of ways CLTC, especially through its teaching programmes and the ministry of its graduates, has brought a wider testimony and contribution to Melanesia generally and PNG particularly. We have just mentioned its media ministries. We could have expanded on its conference ministries, like the "Keswick Conventions" for encouraging and strengthening the spiritual lives of missionaries and church leaders in the early days; or "Crossroads" Easter camps and "Launch Out Mission" camps for youth and tertiary students; or the role of College faculty in promoting the 1975 nationwide conference on evangelism. But instead, we need to refer to some more directly evangelical identity-related issues:

Commitment to an inclusive rather than exclusive evangelicalism

Throughout its ministry, certainly up until the mid 1990s, CLTC has sought to serve the full spectrum of evangelical churches in PNG – at least as fully as such groups would themselves allow.[23] Thus a range of more conservative to mainline churches has

---

[23] The focus of this paper is on CLTC's development in its early years as an expression of Australasian evangelical mission. Since the early 1990s increasing North American evangelical input to faculty has brought some changes in emphasis that may not be reflected adequately in this paper.

regularly been represented in the student body. Pentecostal and charismatic, as well as non-charismatic churches have welcomed and utilized the College's ministry. But this inclusive evangelicalism has not always been easy to maintain.

An important test came at the 1973 Council meetings. Questions had been raised by some in our constituency as to whether we should accept students from Pentecostal and charismatic churches and whether that would cause divisions within the student body. The Australasian Council members had come from Australian and New Zealand settings where there had been significant divisions over charismatic issues. It became evident in the meetings that, particularly in the light of the fact that this meeting was due to hand over responsibility to a PNG based Council, a hard line should be taken against any potentially disruptive influences in the College. But the issues regarding the working and manifestations of the Holy Spirit were importantly different in the Melanesian cultural setting. Many if not most evangelical churches regularly saw miraculous events like healings and demonstrations of Christ's victory over demonic forces. Such activities were accepted as normal for those who follow Christ in cultures still often all too well aware of the powers of evil surrounding them. College faculty were concerned that a hard line on such matters could be more divisive and undermine evangelical unity in the nation at a more serious level than any potential problems arising from having Pentecostal and non-charismatic students studying together at CLTC. So faculty representatives worked overnight to draft a positively worded statement of what the College does believe about the person and work of the Holy Spirit as a possible basis for continuing to include the full range of evangelical believers within the College's constituency. When the inclusive statement was presented to Council the next day, the then Principal, J. Oswald Sanders, retracted his previously declared hard-line intentions and admitted the value of the proposed inclusive approach. Through his humility and wisdom other Council members were persuaded, and CLTC's commitment to stand for what it is for as an evangelical college won the day, rather than becoming known for what it is against.²⁴ Such an inclusive stance, of course, needs to be re-affirmed regularly as various other fresh issues threaten the unity of the evangelical cause in a nation like PNG.

The College's contribution to standards and credibility within the tertiary theological education sector

Through helping establish the Melanesian Association of Theological Schools,²⁵ CLTC has contributed to establishing and maintaining the credibility of our sector's work in the eyes of other tertiary education programmes. College staff and students have contributed regularly to MATS student conferences and staff consultations and have taken their turn editing the *Melanesian Journal of Theology*. With a number of previous MATS members, including CLTC, recently moving to their own forms of accreditation through government recognition as separate tertiary education institutions, the future of MATS as a credible accreditation body is currently under review. But efforts in 2010 to re-establish the Association for purposes of mutual encouragement and to stimulate Melanesian theological reflection and writing, suggest MATS will move into a new phase of cooperative service to theological education in the region.

Fostering the development of the Evangelical Alliance and a healthy evangelical ecumenism contributing to holistic National development

CLTC played a major role in fostering the development of the Evangelical Alliance of the South Pacific Islands, and particularly in

---

[24] The CLTC 1973 "Statement on The Person and Work of The Holy Spirit" has continued as a guide to faculty in this doctrinal area, and was revised slightly in 1990. A copy is available from the author of this paper. J.O. Sanders' PNG experience led him to revise sections of his previously published and widely circulated books on the Holy Spirit.

[25] CLTC staff wrote the Constitution so as to ensure the ongoing theological integrity of each member, providing a basis for participatory ecumenism which in no way compromised evangelical commitments.

its transition from being an organisation of largely expatriate missionaries to a significant forum for national church leaders.[26] Through, and on behalf of, EA, CLTC has brought church leaders together to cooperate, to discuss, and to relate in Melanesian ways. Students at College have regularly discovered traditional enemies to be brothers and sisters in Christ, and lasting relationships and friendships have been cultivated across tribal, regional and denominational divisions. The College helped ensure positive, open relationships between EA and other groups such as the Melanesian Council of Churches.[27] To help find appropriate ways to refresh these cooperative relations between evangelical groups is one of the current challenges facing the College.

The positive form of evangelical ecumenism has been particularly evidenced in the College's contribution to national education, youth and welfare programmes of the Government. CLTC faculty played a key role in developing the Christian Education Syllabus for the national education system in the 1960s.[28] Likewise Port Moresby–based CLTC faculty made major contributions to the Government's National Youth Movement programme, notably its resources development, and to the National

---

[26] Formed in May 1964 the Evangelical Alliance of the South Pacific Islands ante-dated CLTC by a few months, but from 1965 CLTC took a major responsibility for its meetings, ministries, administration, and creative thinking. This is helpfully documented in chapter three of Bob Fergie's thesis referred to in the next footnote.

[27] Robert D. Fergie, "A Study of Church/Government Relations in Papua New Guinea with particular reference to the Evangelical Alliance of the South Pacific Islands and its involvement in the Government's National Youth Movement Program during the 1980s" (ThD thesis, Australian College of Theology, 2000), 71–84.

[28] When the Government convened an inter-church Conference in Lae, 5–12 September 1966, and challenged the churches to produce an agreed syllabus of Christian Education for Government Schools, a paper prepared by the CLTC delegate entitled, "A Biblical-Thematic Approach to a Christian Education in Schools Curriculum for the Territory of Papua and New Guinea," provided the theological and educational philosophy upon which the Conference agreed to work together for the Syllabus.

Youth Council from 1983.[29] They were also influential in developing the Government's 1990s National Non-Government Organizations Policy.[30] College staff were also involved in EA and MCC groups such as the Churches' Council for Media Coordination and its radio and literature development work as well as in its role preparing the way for the introduction of nationwide television standards and ethics procedures. As Fergie's thesis demonstrates, CLTC played a key role ensuring evangelicalism in PNG during the period 1965-1990s was moving ahead of the wider international evangelical recapturing of a holistic commitment to social involvement in its constituent communities.[31]

The social and political involvement of College faculty is matched and exceeded by the College's role in equipping graduates for nationwide influence in public, community, and political arenas. Several graduates have served as elected members of the House of Assembly.[32] Others, like George Euling and Kirine Yandit, have successfully challenged major overseas corporations and brought social justice for their people in dealings with mining companies. Some, like faculty members, Joe and Connie Taruna and other Bougainville graduates, have played key roles in re-building their communities after major societal disruptions.[33]

Stimulating awareness of global mission contributions

Through the Prayer Warrior Movement, and Joshua Daimoi's, Walo Ani's, and Marilyn Rowsome's in-depth contributions to

---

[29] Fergie, "A Study of Church/Government Relations," 148–81. Bob Fergie served on the National Youth Council Executive from 1983-89.

[30] Fergie, "A Study of Church/Government Relations," 215–33.

[31] Fergie, "A Study of Church/Government Relations," 59–84. Fergie's thesis focuses on the EA generally, but his text, diagrams, and appendices document CLTC's contribution for those who recognize the names of its faculty and students recurring throughout.

[32] Traimya Kambipi (Lumusa, WHP), Glaimi Warena (Kauapena, SHD), Wesani Iwoksim (Telefomin, ESP), Judah Akesim (Brugam, ESP), to name some of the first group.

[33] John Garrett, *Where Nets Were Cast*, 351.

fostering global mission awareness and commitment, a new spirit blows across PNG today in comparison with the early days. The nation that had always thought of itself as a mission-receiving region has become a significant mission-sending country. One time CLTC faculty member and Parliamentarian from the Solomon Islands, Michael Maeliau has stimulated a Prayer Conference movement which in its early days at least, revitalized churches and had a wide missional impact across the Pacific.[34]

Demonstrating the holistic inter-dependence of the body in developing a ministry for God, and in influencing the ethical tone of society
The way people with so many diverse gifts, talents, and contributions have been necessary for CLTC to fulfil its ministry, and the way so many practical, professional, and vocational skills have been integrated together into making the College what it has become have been noted by successive generations of students and stakeholders in the nation. This has been a significant object lesson, seldom seen so evidently in modern mission. The College has particularly shown the inter-relationship of the teaching and support programmes, and the significant contribution of each to national life. The inter-dependence of the material and spiritual ministries in the total College has highlighted the place of practical vocations in the Kingdom of God. The impact CLTC/ATA has had on business practice and ethics in the poultry and transportation industries has helped shape the economy of the nation.

But above all the evangelical "people-development" focus of the College's ministry is seen in the continuing ministries of those who have lived and studied at CLTC. Primarily this is evident in the ministries of the CLTC graduates. Over 1,100 CLTC graduates are found across every level of church life in PNG, the Solomon Islands, and in other Pacific nations:[35] as unheralded itinerant

---

[34] We are too close historically to Michael Maeliau's more recent prophetic, breakaway movement, to evaluate the nature of its long-term influence on Melanesian churches.
[35] Students have come to CLTC from the Solomon Islands, Vanuatu, Fiji, Samoa, and Tonga, as well as most, if not all, of the districts of PNG.

evangelists in previously un-reached pockets of PNG; as steady, long-serving village congregation pastors, serving as community rallying points in their own tribal areas; as pastors of urban congregations struggling to address the pressures of post-modern city living; as teachers and administrators in every kind of vernacular, neo-Melanesian or English-speaking Bible school across the nation; as chaplains to the military and police forces; as translators, literacy teachers, and literature and audio-visual producers for multiple language groups; as heads of denominations and members of regional and national councils of churches; as cross-cultural missionaries in significantly different cultural groups in their own country; and as missionaries in foreign nations. Add to these church-related ministries the work of graduates serving with para-church agencies: in evangelism; discipling programmes; radio and literature ministries; development and aid projects; social welfare, student, and educational service of various kinds. Several graduates have gone on to other professions, especially education and medicine, and to a range of entrepreneurial and business vocations. We have already referred to those entering the political sphere. This diversity may be illustrated by one example.

Siosifa Lokotui had completed training in Tonga for the Wesleyan Methodist ministry and had also completed two years at the Fiji Bible College of Evangelism before coming to CLTC in 1981 to undertake the two year BTh programme. He pastored Methodist Church congregations in Tonga for six years after graduating from CLTC. In 1989 he moved to Victoria, Australia where he completed an Australian College of Theology MA programme through Bible College of Victoria. Then followed ten years of Wesleyan Methodist Church pastoral ministry amongst migrant Tongans, and other Australians, in Melbourne. He also lectured from 1995-2001 at the Wesleyan Kingsley Bible College. In March 2002 he was awarded the Doctor of Ministry degree from the Pacific International University, Missouri, USA. In 2002 Lokotui joined the academic staff of Bible College of New Zealand to head up its Tongan language Ministry Internship programmes. While in New Zealand Lokotui was instrumental in commencing more than four Wesleyan Methodist congregations. Most recently he has returned to suburban Brisbane to develop a new Wesleyan congregation amongst migrant Tongans. Pastor, church-planter, teacher, mentor, and servant of Christ, Lokotui has shown himself available for re-deployment at the Master's will, serving significant church communities at their points of need and growth.

Lokotui is just one example of what CLTC is – a link in the ministry formation and Christian service education chain. But, perhaps surprisingly, there is another vital contribution CLTC has made to Australasian and indeed, global, evangelicalism. That is the College's contribution to the development of expatriate staff. Ex-CLTC faculty and staff have enriched theological education in Australasia and farther afield. We only need mention David and Margaret Price, Adrian and Margaret Rickard, and Bob and Doseena Fergie at Bible College of Victoria (now Melbourne School of Theology); Garth and Ruth Morgan, John and Ann Hitchen, Margaret Motion, Alison Weymouth (Palmer), Denise James (Drake), and Russell and Pearl Thorp at Bible College of New Zealand (now Laidlaw College), and Pathways College of Bible and Mission, Auckland, to make our point. Add to that Dorothy Harris's (Tweddell) itinerant teaching ministry; Ian and Diane Malins and John Fuller's Discipleship Training Ministry; Margaret Motion's contribution to Baptist theological education in Bangladesh; Tubu and Layan Padan in East Malaysia; Isaac and Grace Ababio in Ghana; and Philip and Gillian Tait's ministry at the ECWA Seminary in Jos, Nigeria, and the influence becomes broader. At another level the way Barry and Beverley McWha, Norm and Pat Bartlett, Brian and Elaine Brandon, Ivan and Fran Shepherd, Brian Andrews, and Graham Read (and the list is not complete) have gone on from their support roles at CLTC to ordained church ministries shows another formative role CLTC has played. It is, indeed, humbling to pause and consider the changes in direction, the enrichment in continuing vocations, and the character and spiritual growth all these can trace back to their CLTC days.

Conclusion

Our CLTC story, then, has surveyed the components and development of the College's theological and associated education and training programmes. We have commented on issues rising in that development that are common missiological and ecclesiological concerns globally: whether the theology of theological education applied; the extent of the integrity of contextualization achieved; the way unity and diversity are integrated in a guiding ecclesiology; and the development both professionally and spiritually of students and faculty.

We have also explored the College's not inconsiderable contribution to evangelical identity in our region of the globe: cultivating features including inclusiveness and the priority of mission; fostering evangelical unity expressed in holistic evangelistic, social and societal involvement; demonstrating the value of an interdependence in the church and its ministry that transcends the secular-sacred dichotomy common in Western evangelicalism; while upholding the central importance of people formation at the heart of theological education. The story narrates a creative, effective, unfinished, and challenging chapter in Australasian evangelical mission. To God alone be the glory.

Chapter Six
The role of the Evangelical Unions and Inter-Varsity Fellowship in defining evangelical identity in mid-twentieth century New Zealand

Stuart Lange

In the period from the 1930s through to the 1960s, many New Zealand evangelicals became much more defined and self-aware in their evangelical beliefs and identity. It can be shown that a crucial factor in the sharpening of evangelical self-identity was the influence of the Evangelical Unions and Inter-Varsity Fellowship on university students and graduates, a significant leadership group. There was a strong new sense of belonging to a movement which transcended denominational, regional, and national identities. In the postwar era, the EU/IVF brand of evangelicalism stimulated the formation of new, explicitly "evangelical" movements within New Zealand's two largest Protestant denominations, the Anglicans and Presbyterians.

Earlier New Zealand understandings of "evangelical"

Among Anglicans in New Zealand in the earlier twentieth century, the identity of "evangelical" had fallen into widespread disrepair. There was some residual historical awareness of the term "evangelical": in connection with the Reformation, or the eighteenth century revivals, or the nineteenth century Evangelical party back home in the Church of England (and such figures as Lord Shaftesbury and Bishop Ryle), or the early Church Missionary Society missionaries among the Maori. There were some individuals, often those who had come from England and especially Ireland, who had definite evangelical or Low Church sympathies. Both of those tendencies were common in the Diocese of Nelson, which maintained significant informal links with the Diocese of Sydney. A few New Zealand Anglicans had been influenced by the English Keswick movement, or by service with the China Inland Mission. However from the latter nineteenth century the church in

New Zealand had gradually settled into a broad and theologically-undifferentiated Anglicanism, significantly influenced by successive high church movements back in England. Of all the New Zealand churches, the Anglican denomination was the one least influenced by revivalism, and the denomination had no organised evangelical movement. The only identity that generally mattered was simply being "Anglican." The term "evangelical" was thus neither well defined nor commonly used. Some, such as a youthful William Orange, seemed to regard the term "evangelical" as meaning "low church," and used it as an antonym for "sacerdotalist."[1] Others understood the word to mean "evangelistic."[2]

Among New Zealand Presbyterians, the historic ethos was more evangelical in flavour, and the word itself was more commonly used. Among Presbyterians settling in New Zealand there were memories of Scottish revivals, the 1843 Disruption, and the campaigns of D.L. Moody. Many colonial Presbyterians were brought up on sabbatarianism and daily family devotions. In 1901 the visit of American Presbyterian evangelist R.A. Torrey had a high impact on many Presbyterians. By the early twentieth century there was widespread experience, among younger Presbyterians, of participating in Christian Endeavour and Bible Class. Between 1918 and 1934 revivalist missions were conducted in a large number of Presbyterian parishes by the official Assembly Evangelist, John Bissett. New Zealand Presbyterians were often characterised by a broad evangelical piety and biblically-grounded moral conservatism. However, most Presbyterians in New Zealand did not usually define themselves as "evangelical," or by any other label; their identity was simply "Presbyterian."

Since about 1910, when John Dickie began teaching at the Theological Hall, there had been a liberalising trend among younger Presbyterian ministers, strongly reinforced by the influence of the Student Christian Movement (SCM), which was increasingly given to theological exploration and a rejection of credal boundaries.

---

[1] William Orange, diary, 6 November 1911, Latimer Fellowship, Christchurch.
[2] Minutes of Annual Meeting, Minute Book, Summer Parish, 21 April 1937, Diocese of Christchurch Archives.

The word "evangelical" continued to be used by Presbyterians in various ways. A survey of the Presbyterian Church's weekly paper in 1930-31 shows that the meaning of the word "evangelical" had become extremely diffuse. Sometimes it meant "Protestant" or "Reformed."[3] Sometimes it meant "non-conformist" (i.e. "non-Anglican").[4] Sometimes it meant "evangelistic."[5] It might mean a broad enthusiasm about recruiting people to serve God.[6] The term did not necessarily imply theological conservatism, and H.E. Fosdick the prominent American modernist was described as a leader of "modern evangelical Christianity."[7] Karl Barth – although retaining a critical view of the Scriptures – was acclaimed as "thoroughly evangelical."[8] It was clear that the word "evangelical" had acquired a multiplicity of meanings, that it was used by those of various theological perspectives, including those of liberal or neo-orthodox views, and that the word was regarded by all as a positive and reassuring word. In New Zealand Presbyterianism, the term "evangelical" had yet to be claimed as a distinct mark of identity by those who were both biblically conservative and evangelistically active.

Catalyst for a sharper New Zealand evangelical identity

The key catalyst in the growth of a clearer (and narrower) evangelical identity in New Zealand appears to have been the influence of the British Inter-Varsity Fellowship (IVF), formed in 1928, which in 1930 inspired the establishment in New Zealand of the first university Evangelical Union (EU) and in 1936 the IVFEU(NZ). The EU/IVF movement had a profound influence on many university and theological students, including those who

---

[3] E.g., *Outlook* (6 October 1930): 5.
[4] E.g., *Outlook* (22 June 1931): 6.
[5] E.g., New Zealand Bible Training Institute advertisement, *Outlook* (1 December 1930): 36.
[6] *Outlook* (7 July 1930): 3.
[7] *Outlook* (22 December 1930): 6.
[8] J.V.T. Steele, "The Theology of Karl Barth," *Outlook* (25 May 1931): 20.

would later launch explicitly "evangelical" movements within the post-war Anglican and Presbyterian denominations.[9]

The movement was brought to New Zealand with flamboyant missionary zeal by IVF enthusiast Dr Howard Guinness, who introduced the IVF to Canada and Australia and then spent six frenetic weeks in New Zealand. Guinness' visit took place against the backdrop of widespread disaffection among biblical conservatives with the modernist directions of the SCM. In the later 1920s some conservatives had already defected from the SCM, and groups of conservative students were already meeting in Otago and Auckland for separate Bible Study. The idea of university Evangelical Unions under the umbrella of a new, internationally-affiliated organisation greatly appealed to a number of theologically conservative figures in various New Zealand denominations, and in Guinness' wake an EU was formed in the University of Otago, and later in the other three university colleges (Canterbury, Auckland, and Victoria). Guinness also inspired a vigorous feeder movement in the high schools, the Crusaders. In Otago, a dutiful attempt had been made to form an Evangelical Union as a separate group within the SCM's Christian Union. Predictably, permission was declined, and the conservatives then felt free in their conscience to begin a new movement, in Otago and elsewhere. This new movement would play a critical part in establishing the ethos and identity of New Zealand evangelicalism, helping it become a cohesive and confident trans-denominational movement that would become especially strong in the post-war era.

The EU/IVF movement blended evangelical piety and evangelistic zeal with a strengthened intellectual defence of biblical conservatism. The IVF in the United Kingdom regarded itself as in the classic British evangelical tradition, and looked back to what it saw as the heyday of student evangelicalism in the late nineteenth century prior to the deeper inroads of sceptical biblical scholarship

---

[9] See Stuart M. Lange, "A Rising Tide: The Growth of Evangelicalism and Evangelical Identity among Presbyterians, Anglicans and University Students in New Zealand, 1930-1965" (PhD thesis, University of Otago, 2009). A book based on this study is forthcoming with Otago University Press in 2012.

and theological modernism. In Britain, Canada, Australia, and New Zealand, the IVF implicitly defined itself by its self-differentiation from the SCM, which the IVF regarded as doctrinally adrift. The SCM was committed to theological openness, but the IVF was committed to faithful orthodoxy, to biblical "soundness."

A doctrinal basis for evangelical identity

Through the Doctrinal Basis, to which all EU leaders and speakers were required to adhere, the EU/IVF movement took a firm line on a number of matters where conservatives and liberals tended to differ, such as biblical infallibility, substitutionary atonement, the divinity (and bodily resurrection) of Christ, and the necessity of personal spiritual regeneration. The Doctrinal Basis was by no means extreme. It avoided narrow definitions and second-order issues such as evolution and eschatological schema. The IVF's "Official Interpretation" of the Doctrinal Basis, *Evangelical Belief*,[10] contained careful explanations which appear intended to protect the Evangelical Unions both from excessive conservatism within the movement and from misrepresentation beyond. In connection with Scripture, for instance, *Evangelical Belief* stated that inspiration involved "the whole personality of the individual" and was not "mechanical." It avoided the term "inerrancy," often favoured in conservative American contexts, and instead explained that biblical "infallibility" meant that the Scriptures, rightly understood, "will never lead astray."[11] Curiously, *Evangelical Belief* did not comment on the word "evangelical," but the implication of the whole book was that the beliefs it expounded constituted the indispensable marks of true evangelical faith.

The EU/IVF version of evangelical Christianity was also buttressed by a growing number of IVF publications, which dealt not just with doctrinal and apologetic issues but also with devotional disciplines and lifestyle. These included T.C. Hammond's *In*

---

[10] Inter-Varsity Fellowship of Evangelical Unions, *Evangelical Belief: the Official Interpretation of the Doctrinal Basis of the I.V.F.* (Compiled by the Advisory Committee; London: Inter-Varsity Papers, n.d. [1935]).
[11] *Evangelical Belief*, 7-9.

Understanding Be Men (a doctrinal handbook), H.E. Guillebaud's *Why the Cross?* (a defence of substitutionary atonement), *Search the Scriptures* (a Bible study manual), *The Quiet Time* (reinforcing the devotional discipline expected of all evangelicals), and Howard Guinness' *Sacrifice* (a call to earnest personal discipleship).[12]

It was the growth of a confident, new, university-based evangelicalism that was the key contribution of the Evangelical Unions. It was an identity that was understandable and readily communicable. In the Evangelical Unions large numbers of younger New Zealanders would became familiar with the term "evangelical," and adopted it as their own theological and ecclesiastical identity.[13] Many would later take that understanding and identity into various leadership roles.

Support for IVF-style evangelicalism from within the churches

The IVF vision of evangelical Christianity was eagerly embraced in New Zealand by a number of influential church figures, who saw the Evangelical Union as an ideal alternative to the SCM. Instead of the university students in their congregations going off to university and being influenced by the SCM towards theological modernism, such students could be channeled into a movement that was highly intentional about strengthening their faith both spiritually and intellectually. The EU was seen as a very useful adjunct to the church's own work among youth. In Dunedin, the EU at Otago University was actively supported by such people as

---

[12] T.C. Hammond, *In Understanding Be Men. A Handbook on Christian Doctrine For Non-Theological Students* (London: IVF, 1936); H.E. Guillebaud, *Why the Cross?* (London: IVF, 1937); G.T. Manley (ed.), *Search the Scriptures* (London: IVF, 1934); Frank Houghton (ed.), *The Quiet Time* (London: InterVarsity Fellowship of Evangelical Unions, 1933); Howard Guinness, *Sacrifice: A Challenge to Christian Youth* (London: IVF, 1936).

[13] In the research which lies behind this chapter, numerous interviewees were asked when they first become aware of the term "evangelical." Almost all (except for two who came from unusually theologically-aware homes and one who had attended the New Zealand Bible Training Institute) indicated that it was through the Evangelical Union.

R.S. Cree Brown, an Open Brethren engineer who had been leading the evangelical Bible study group, and by the Rev Thomas Miller, the minister of St Stephen's Presbyterian Church near the university. Miller had a strong preaching and Bible-teaching ministry, especially among young adults, and he became a key supporter of the EU/IVF movement both locally and nationally. In Christchurch, the key figure in the EU at Canterbury University College was the Anglican minister at Sumner, Rev William Orange. Many members of Canterbury EU were devotees of Orange, who ran a remarkable Sunday afternoon Bible class at Sumner, drawing large numbers of earnest young men to hear Orange expound Scripture. Orange was also a frequent speaker at EU, and later at national IVF conferences. Many Open Brethren people also became strong EU supporters. In Auckland, the leaders of several inner city conservative evangelical churches (Baptist, Presbyterian, and Brethren) gave strong support to the EU. Within the university itself, the young EU was sponsored (and kept in line) by the highly erudite E.M. Blaiklock, who taught classics. In Wellington, in what may have been the most secularized of the four main centres, the relative weakness of the EU at Victoria University College possibly reflected the absence of a strong base of evangelical churches in Wellington at that time.

A moderate evangelicalism, not fundamentalism

The new sense of evangelical identity being forged by the EU and IVF was biblically and theologically conservative, but not narrowly or militantly so. The IVF's theological differences with the SCM always fostered a defensiveness in the IVF outlook. Nevertheless restraint and moderation were prominent values within the IVF. The IVF reflected the relatively temperate tone of the British evangelical tradition, and derived little or nothing from the more strident tones of American fundamentalism. Taking their cue from the IVF in Britain, IVF leaders in New Zealand explicitly rejected both the label and the perceived attitudes of American fundamentalism. In 1939, for example, EU leader Max Wiggins warned that:

> One of the difficulties under which the Evangelical movement

labours is its association in the minds of many with the extremes and extravagances of American Fundamentalism. It is the opportunity of the Evangelical Unions... to counteract this impression.[14]

EU members did not usually identify themselves as "fundamentalists." In part that was because it was a foreign, North American term, whereas the assumptions, influences, and identity that shaped the Evangelical Unions were overwhelmingly British rather than North American. The word "evangelical" seemed sufficient to EU people. It was enshrined in the name of their movement, and had long been part of the British theological and ecclesiastical scene. IVF evangelicals in New Zealand freely identified with what they saw as the earlier and more positive meaning of "fundamentalist," that is of being faithful to the "fundamental" beliefs of orthodox Christianity.[15] By the 1930s, however, they were realising that "fundamentalist" was becoming a negative, pejorative term,[16] denoting extremism, militancy, anti-intellectualism and separatism.

However the evangelicalism fostered by the EU/IVF movement encouraged neither extremism nor militancy. Eager for acceptance and respectability in both church and university, the emerging new evangelical movement placed a very high value on moderation and restraint. That moderation was conscious and deliberate, and pervaded the IVF culture. The atmosphere at EU and IVF meetings was not one of polemics or emotionalism, but a "spiritual" one, with the key activity being the careful, devotional exposition of Scripture, preceded and followed by prayer. Sectarian emphases and eccentricities were avoided. Leading figures such as Orange, Blaiklock and John Laird strongly disapproved of any evangelical student behaviour which could be regarded as ignorant, fanatical, or

---

[14] Max Wiggins, IVFEU TSPU [Theological Students' Prayer Union] circular, April 1939, TSCF I1/035.

[15] Rev Rymall Roxburgh, interview, 2-3 November 1999 [hereafter RR], ¶364.

[16] Rev Dr J. Graham Miller, interview, 23-25 November 1999 [hereafter JGM], ¶495-96, ¶512; Rev Maurice Betteridge, interview, 26 November 1999, ¶84, ¶327.

impolite. They warmly believed in personal evangelism, but deplored evangelistic campaigns conducted with excessive pressure or emotional intensity.

Like British IVF leaders, Laird was uncomfortable with the militancy of American fundamentalism, and he always appeared eager that the growing evangelical movement in New Zealand should be distinguished from it.[17] When he returned in 1933 from a trip that included a visit to the USA, he warned a group of EU and Crusader supporters that some American evangelicals were "too hard-line," and that they needed "fundamentalism plus love."[18] What distinguished evangelicalism from fundamentalism, Wiggins implied, was that "God has given us the spirit of a sound mind," by which he meant "sobriety and balance"; significantly, it was precisely in the context of contrasting [British] evangelicalism and American fundamentalism that Wiggins extolled those values of restraint.[19]

Neither was the new evangelical movement being shaped by EU and IVF anti-intellectual. On the contrary, a key part of the EU/IVF *raison d'être* was the intellectual defence – in a university context and beyond – of biblical faith. The relationships of faith to reason and evidence were constant preoccupations. The EU would always value faith above scepticism, but there is no evidence that its members were any less intellectual than their SCM counterparts. What differed were the focus and the constraints of IVF-style intellectualism; rather than favouring the speculative exploration of faith or its accommodation to the latest winds of contemporary human thought, the IVF valued above all a well-informed, faithful understanding of orthodox Christianity. A high premium was laid on instructional reading and teaching. The basic EU text, *In Understanding Be Men*, was an attempt to have EU students thinking, studying, and well-informed, at least to the same level as their university studies. In its earlier days, the IVF struggled to catch up against the predominant liberal biblical scholarship and theology, but by the 1960s it was clear that a recovery of evangelical

---

[17] RR, ¶358.
[18] RR, ¶338-42.
[19] Wiggins, IVFEU TSPU circular.

scholarship was well under way in Britain, with IVF people deeply involved; with that recovery, evangelicals would grow in confidence and become a little less intellectually defensive.

The emerging new evangelicalism was not inherently separatist. In its first few decades, however, the EU/IVF movement was profoundly shaped by the fact that it had its origins in a rift with the SCM. That schism had come about precisely because, from the perspective of evangelical conservatives, the SCM's expansive policy of doctrinal inclusiveness had led to serious doctrinal slippage. Against that background, the IVF movement was utterly determined to safeguard its doctrinal purity, and consistently refused to co-operate with the SCM, or with anyone not accepting its Doctrinal Basis. Nevertheless, the EU/IVF movement was never *ecclesiastically* separatist, and strongly urged evangelicals to be loyal to their own denominations and active in their local churches. Instead of leaving denominations which were theologically straying, evangelicals were encouraged to stay within them and to work for their spiritual and theological renewal. Ecclesiastical schism and fragmentation played no part in the new evangelical model being built by the IVF.

The expansion of the IVF-style evangelical identity

From the 1930s, the IVF style of evangelical Christianity was imparted to successive generations of New Zealand students, in the university colleges, and soon in other tertiary training contexts (including theological colleges and teachers' colleges), and also Nurses' Fellowships. In every local union or fellowship, as in the SCM, the movement transcended denominational boundaries. For many students and graduates, their sharpened theological identity as evangelicals became more profoundly important to them than their continuing denominational affiliation. Many former members of the EU could have echoed the view that EU was "one of the greatest influences in my life, helping me to formulate and... crystallize my basic theology and providing me with ongoing fellowship of like-minded people."[20]

From 1936 onwards, the annual IVF National Conferences played a key role in strengthening many evangelical students in their sense of belonging to a movement that was trans-denominational, national, and international. The conferences assisted the New Zealand evangelical movement to become nationally cohesive, in a way that it had never been before. Young evangelicals – future evangelical leaders – were brought together from across the whole country, and from across the denominations (especially Anglicans, Presbyterians, Brethren, and Baptists). The conferences acquainted members of the Dunedin (Presbyterian) evangelical movement centred on Thomas Miller with the Christchurch (Anglican/Brethren) evangelical movement centred on William Orange, and forged links between those Otago and Canterbury networks and the more Baptistic-Brethren evangelical community of Auckland. The conferences also brought together evangelicals of the same denomination but from different parts of the country, thus helping lay the foundations of future denominational evangelical movements.

The impact on different denominations

The effect of the EU/IVF movement on various New Zealand denominations was mixed. It had no effect on those churches barely represented in the university setting at that time, such as the various Pentecostal groups. It had minimal effect on Methodists; Methodist students were more likely to remain loyal to the SCM movement. It had some effect on the Baptists, but it may be that internal factors were more important in shaping the distinctive Baptist evangelical flavour and identity. The EU/IVF movement had a significant effect on those Open Brethren who joined it, chiefly in encouraging Brethren inter-denominational engagement, especially in evangelical para-church organisations.

The greatest impact of the EU/IVF movement was on the two Protestant denominations which were the most heavily represented

---

[20] RR, ¶28.

among the university student populations, the Anglicans and Presbyterians. Most Anglican and Presbyterian students who were active enough in their faith to join a student Christian society would stay with the SCM, but a growing minority of youth from both denominations chose the EU (and, by the 1960s, a majority). For such Anglican and Presbyterian students, participation in EU and IVF was often very significant. The EU/IVF movement strongly reinforced the embryonic evangelical network growing up in Christchurch around William Orange, drew in isolated evangelically-minded Anglicans from across the country (but especially in Nelson and Wellington), made the developing Anglican evangelical movement much more aware that it was part of something much larger than just Orange or Anglicanism, and provided a basis on which it could expand. For theologically conservative Presbyterians, the EU/IVF movement offered what they saw as the ideal alternative to the corrupting liberal influences of the SCM, and furnished a reconstructed evangelical language and the identity around which they could build a new "evangelical Presbyterian" movement.

It was those Anglican and Presbyterian graduates who had come up through the EU and IVF in the 1930s and 40s who would construct and lead evangelical movements in their own denominations in the 1950s and 60s. The identity "evangelical" was at the core of both organisations, an identity that was a direct result of the defining influence of the EU and IVF. Numerous protégés of William Orange entered the Anglican ministry through the Dioceses of Christchurch and Nelson, and in 1945 founded the Evangelical Churchman's Fellowship (ECF). Although the ECF also drew in many businessmen and other lay people who were not university graduates, the ministers who founded and led it had all been closely associated with the EU at Canterbury University College.[21]

---

[21] Roger Thompson, a key ECF leader in the 1950s and 60s, was not a university student but nevertheless a regular EU attender. Rev Roger Thompson, interview, 1 November 1999, ¶22, ¶49, ¶137, ¶181, ¶185.

In 1950 a group of young Presbyterian ministers and theological students in Dunedin had established the Westminster Fellowship (WF), which defined itself (in its by-line) as "A fellowship of evangelical Presbyterians in New Zealand" and named its periodical the *Evangelical Presbyterian*.[22] The Westminster Fellowship founders and Executive members had in varying degrees all been influenced by the Dunedin ministry of the Rev Thomas Miller. Even more significantly, they had all been very active in the Otago University Evangelical Union. In some ways the ECF and the WF were an expression of the desire to recreate in a denominational setting the sort of safe evangelical haven that their founders had already experienced in the EU. It was also a different (and more practicable) application of the IVF concepts of a Graduate Fellowship and its sub-section the Evangelical Ministers' Fellowship. In New Zealand both existed, but once they left the university setting most graduates had little interest in such bodies; ministers in particular saw more immediate value in evangelical fellowships in their own denominations than in a less focused interdenominational grouping.

Both the ECF and the WF conspicuously professed allegiance to their denominations' historic confessional standards, the Thirty Nine Articles and the Westminster Confession of Faith; they could scarcely have done otherwise, given the yearning of both groups to be recognised as the most faithful of all Anglicans and Presbyterians. The ECF and WF also regarded the historic standards as excellent bulwarks against doctrinal declension. Nevertheless, it may well be that for most ordained leaders within the ECF and the WF, the operative credal standard, invisible but ever present, was the IVF Doctrinal Basis. ECF and WF leaders might sometimes demur on some of the emphases and fine print of

---

[22] See Lange, "A Rising Tide," Chapters 6 and 9; also Stuart Lange, "Westminster Fellowship Evangelicals and the History of Presbyterianism in New Zealand," in *The Spirit of the Past: Essays on Christianity in New Zealand History* (eds Hugh Morrison and Geoff Troughton; Wellington: Victoria University Press, 2011), 184-96.

the historic confessional documents, but they would never take a doctrinal position contrary to that enshrined in the IVF Doctrinal Basis. At the inaugural meeting of the WF, there had been considerable support for adopting the IVF Doctrinal Basis,[23] but it was then decided to choose the Westminster Confession.

As minority groups who rejected the prevailing directions in their denominations, the ECF and WF were viewed with suspicion. Church leaders with a strong SCM background were well aware that the ECF and WF were led by those who had been prominent in the EU, which they regarded as obscurantist, separatist and trouble-making. The SCM/EU schism of the 1930s had left deep scars, which were constantly renewed by the EU groups refusing SCM requests for "co-operation." Those church leaders nurtured in the SCM were pressing for church union; those who had come through the EU usually rejected the ecumenical dream (because of the fear of doctrinal indifferentism).[24] Notwithstanding the theological establishment's suspicions of the ECF and WF, both organisations in fact followed the lead of the IVF and emphasised denominational loyalty. They disavowed any schismatic intentions. "We are not out to divide the Church," the WF insisted, "but to revive it."[25]

Likewise, the ECF and WF generally maintained the restrained tone that was characteristic of the IVF. The pages of the *ECF Review* and the *Evangelical Presbyterian* exhibited strong and clear evangelical conviction, but generally avoided being denunciatory or shrill; the aim was not to hector from the margins but to take the high ground, to strengthen evangelical faith, and to woo others to the cause. When, in the midst of the torrid church union debates of the mid-1960s, the *Evangelical Presbyterian* adopted a more polemical approach there was a negative reaction by a number of theological students with strong IVF connections.

Following the lead of the IVF, the ECF and WF had no interest

---

[23] Anon., ¶165.

[24] In the 1960s, however, the ECF became cautiously open to church union, while the WF became increasingly resistant.

[25] Editorial, *Evangelical Presbyterian* (April 1951): 1.

in being identified with American "fundamentalism." They did, however, identify in principle with the sense of defending orthodoxy. [26] Neither group had any time for the rancorous separatist fundamentalism of Rev Dr Carl McIntire in America, who in 1948 founded the International Council of Christian Churches as an ultra-conservative alternative to the World Council of Churches. Following the IVF, the ECF and WF felt an affinity not with the ICCC but with the much more moderate and constructive tone of the National Association of Evangelicals, the voice of the emerging American neo-evangelical movement in the United States, and associated with such figures as Carl Henry and Billy Graham. The ICCC's New Zealand magazine lashed out at the WF, which resolved to avoid all contact with the ICCC. [27]

Other influences shaping evangelical identity

The EU/IVF movement was by no means alone in defining mid-twentieth century New Zealand evangelicalism. Other voices and forces were also at work. Through its graduates and its magazine the *Reaper*, the New Zealand Bible Training Institute (founded in 1922) had a growing nationwide influence; it modelled a moderate biblical conservatism and emphases on evangelism and overseas mission. The Keswick-style conventions, at places such as Pounawea and Ngaruawahia, inculcated a spirituality of consecration. Inter-denominational missionary societies and their missionaries promoted a culture of Gospel, costly service, and prayer. The Crusader Unions worked to win and disciple youth in high schools. The Scripture Union kept promoting Bible reading. The Brethren, characteristically biblicist and conservative, fostered a particular style of evangelical piety and personal evangelism, as did in their own way the Baptists, along with numerous smaller conservative groups such as the Church of Christ (Life and Advent) and the fledgling Pentecostal denominations. Across the

---

[26] E.g., [A.G. Gunn?], "What is the Westminster Fellowship?" *Evangelical Presbyterian* (September 1963): 260-61.
[27] Minute Book of the Westminster Fellowship, 1950-61: 20 September 1955, 5 August 1957.

denominations, evangelists and revivalists regularly reinforced the importance of conversion and good living. In the latter 1950s, Billy Graham publicly authenticated conservative evangelical theology and praxis with his effective crusades in the northern hemisphere and then in New Zealand. All these things played their part.

Conclusion

However, it can be argued that, more than anything else, it was the Evangelical Unions which effectively defined and thus re-launched New Zealand evangelicalism in the mid-twentieth century. Through their work among university students, a key elite whose influence would be much greater than their numbers, the Evangelical Unions and IVF provided for New Zealand evangelicalism a clear name, doctrinal ethos, and identity. That clarified identity would be a key factor in the emergence of explicitly evangelical movements in New Zealand's two largest denominations, but would also sharpen the identity of some evangelicals in other denominations, and would give many evangelicals a clear sense of belonging to a movement whose identity was trans-denominational.

Chapter Seven
Does a rose by any other name still smell the same?

Kevin Ward

For most of my life my journey in the Christian community has been within the evangelical stream, and it is still the heritage with which I would basically identify. My denominational belonging for most of that time has been with a church clearly identified with evangelicalism, the Baptist Church. After a number of years as a minister in that church I then spent a considerable period as a lecturer at the Bible College of New Zealand,[1] another unmistakably evangelical institution. Over recent years however a variety of experiences, giving me fresh insight into how others view us, has made me more reluctant to wear the label too prominently.

Two incidents about a decade ago, both in the same year, illustrate this. The first occurred on a world trip I undertook to a variety of countries, including some in the Middle East, Lebanon and Israel among others. At the time I was employed both as a lecturer at Bible College and on the pastoral staff of a Baptist church, so could use a variety of occupational identities. Clearly in the Middle East I did not want to identify myself as a minister of religion so said I was a lecturer. Having left that part of my journey I flew into Los Angeles to begin the North American leg and was called over by a heavily uniformed immigration official, who also happened to be black. The second question he asked me was, "What is your work?" Thinking it would be a safe occupation in the United States I replied "a minister of religion." "What kind?" he asked. "Baptist," I replied. "The worst kind" was his immediate response. It led to an interesting discussion of the supposed differences between Baptists in New Zealand and the United States. The discussion did have the benefit of meaning there was no further investigation of what suspected contraband I might be carrying.

---

[1] Now renamed as Laidlaw College.

The second incident occurred while I was researching congregations for my doctoral dissertation. I had indentified one particular mainline Protestant congregation as a good subject for one of my case studies, so contacted the minister and arranged to meet. I began these initial meetings by being upfront about who I was, where I belonged, and what the hypothesis was that was framing my research. After the discussion had been going for some time, and had traversed a variety of topics, the minister confessed to me that they were very surprised about some of my views as they had assumed certain things about me because I was Baptist and Bible College and therefore evangelical. In light of that they were surprised to discover I didn't vote for the Christian Heritage Party, was supportive of many feminist concerns, was in favour of the decriminalisation of homosexuality, did not support Israel's policy in the Middle East nor believe that creationism should be taught in schools, and admired both Helen Clark and Bill Clinton.

These are just two examples of many incidents I have experienced as I have travelled extensively and moved and worked widely among sectors of the church and academia outside of the "evangelical ghetto," which have given me a very different perception of what the label "evangelical" points to outside of "our own community." This has been increased since I moved from the Baptist to the Presbyterian denomination and from working for the Bible College of New Zealand to the Presbyterian theological centre based at Knox College. The Presbyterian Church in New Zealand, while having a very strong evangelical stream, embraces a breadth of theological perspectives while Knox College over recent decades had a, generally deserved, reputation as a liberal institution, scorned by most evangelicals.

One thing the postmodern critique has shown is that words have no intrinsic meaning in themselves, but rather have the meanings that are assigned to them by readers or hearers. Therefore, if we wish to communicate, that is what is important rather than, as Humpty Dumpty put it in *Alice In Wonderland*, "when I use a word it means just what 'I' choose it to mean—neither more nor less." My argument here is that what the meaning of the word "evangelical" points to for those outside of the movement is now considerably different from what it may have been for much of the history of the movement and that, therefore, it may be time for those of us who still identify with the heritage the movement has represented to drop the name itself as an identity marker. If it is widely misunderstood is it of any further use? The question for many, of course, is "Does a rose by any other name still smell the same?"

Defining evangelicalism

Of course defining evangelicalism is "notoriously difficult," as Mark Noll acknowledges.[2] John Stott in his sort of swansong, *Evangelical Truth*,[3] quoted one report suggesting there were 57 varieties of evangelicalism and another from Clive Calver identifying twelve tribes. From an Australasian perspective, Rowland Croucher as far back as 1986 identified sixteen different groups.[4] More simple is Gabriel Fackre's 1993 grouping of six different categories.[5] Of course part of the challenge is that not all of these groups recognise the others as being "true" bearers of the label. This led Stott to bemoan the "tendency to fragment" and a group of 108 evangelical leaders in the United Sates in 2002 to issue a largely ignored call "to resist attempts to propagate rigid definitions of evangelicalism that result in unnecessary alienation and exclusion."[6]

There have been several recent attempts to define evangelicalism, perhaps the most widely referred to being those by David Bebbington[7] and Alister McGrath.[8] To indicate where I

---

[2] M. Noll, "The Future of Protestantism: Evangelicalism," in *The Blackwell Companion to Protestantism* (eds A. McGrath and D. Marks; Oxford: Blackwell, 2004), 421.
[3] J. Stott, *Evangelical Truth: A Personal Plea for Unity* (Leicester: IVP, 1999).
[4] R. Croucher, *Recent Trends among Evangelicals: Biblical Agendas, Justice and Spirituality* (Heathmont: John Mark Ministries, 1986), 1.
[5] G. Fackre, *Ecumenical Faith in Evangelical Perspective* (Grand Rapids: Eerdmans, 1993).
[6] "The Word Made Fresh," [cited 10 August 2006]. Online: http://jmm.aaa.net.au/articles/14234.htm.
[7] A stress on conversion, activism, biblical authority, centrality of the cross. D.W. Bebbington, "Evangelicalism in Modern Britain and America: A

might be seen as standing I prefer Roger Olson's identification of four characteristics.⁹
- The Bible as the supreme norm of truth for Christian belief and practice.
- A supernatural world-view that is centred in a transcendent personal God who interacts with and intervenes in creation.
- A focus on the forgiving and transforming grace of God through Jesus Christ in the experience called conversion as the centre of authentic Christian experience.
- Seeing the primary task of Christian theology as to serve the church's mission of bringing God's grace to the whole world through proclamation and service.

I would also place myself along with those who follow Stanley Grenz in arguing for a "spirituality based identity" rather than a "creed based identity,"¹⁰ and suggest that this has been historically where evangelical identity grew from, the "heart strangely warmed" of Charles Wesley.

Evangelicalism and the development of Christianity in New Zealand

The Protestant Church arrived in New Zealand with a basically evangelical ethos. The church first arrived in missionary form with Anglicans in the Church Missionary Society and Methodists with the Wesleyan Missionary Society. Both were products of the eighteenth century evangelical revival. While Presbyterianism

---

Comparison," in *Amazing Grace: Evangelicalism in Australia, Britain, Canada and the United States* (eds G. Rawlyk and M. Noll; Grand Rapids: Baker, 1993), 366.

[8] Focus on person and death of Christ; Scripture as the ultimate authority; emphasis on conversion; concern for sharing the faith. A. McGrath, *Evangelicalism and the Future of Christianity* (London: Hodder & Stoughton, 1993), 22.

[9] R. Olson, "The Future of Evangelical Theology," *Christianity Today* (9 February 1998): 40–50.

[10] S. Grenz, *Revisioning Evangelical Theology: A Fresh Agenda for the 21ˢᵗ Century* (Downers Grove: IVP, 1993).

arrived somewhat later as a settler church and the minister of the first church was of the established Church of Scotland, its "evangelical strength" has been noted, [11] a character furthered by the dominance of settlers from the Free Church in following years. These were followed by Baptists, Brethren, and Salvation Army. Keeping with the Protestant mainline churches it appears true to say that by and large through until at least the 1960s they were broadly evangelical in ethos, with difference being between a more conservative evangelical stream and a more liberally inclined group. This difference was seen in whether they identified with the Inter-Varsity Fellowship or Student Christian Movement respectively. The word "evangelical" was seen as a good word, a fact I have found in discussing this with a number of elder statesmen in these churches who would now be identified as liberal. This sense lay behind the proposal passed by the General Assembly of the Presbyterian Church in 1902, for an evangelical Protestant Union of New Zealand, made up of Presbyterians, Methodists, and Congregationalists. I was also somewhat surprised in my congregational studies of a Presbyterian and an Anglican Church, both of which would be seen as liberal, to find that in 1960 when my period of study commenced, they were both essentially evangelical in ethos, although would probably not have been given the label. An indication of this was seen in their very strong involvement in and commitment to the Billy Graham Crusade of 1959.

The essentially evangelical character of Protestantism in New Zealand can be seen in the very broad support for and participation in the Graham Crusade by the Protestant churches and the warm commendations and gratefulness expressed for the responses and commitments it led to. Another expression of this essential character can be seen in the Methodist "Crusade for Christ and His Kingdom" commencing in 1948 and the "Presbyterian New Life Movement" in 1949, aiming among other things for a "re-vitalising

---

[11] P. Matheson "1840 to 1870: The Settler Church," in *Presbyterians in Aotearoa 1840 to 1990* (ed. D. McEldowney; Wellington: Presbyterian Church, 1990), 21.

of the inner life of the Church, through aggressive congregational evangelism." Bryan Gilling in an article on the failure of militant fundamentalism in New Zealand in the mid twentieth century gives as a major reason the role of evangelical leaders, including the principals of Bible College of New Zealand and spokespersons such as E.M. Blaiklok, R.A. Laidlaw, and J.O. Sanders, for whom "evangelism and a winsome lifestyle took precedence in practice over doctrinal controversy and an irenic, co-operative spirit over a combative, separatist one."[12]

Where America goes we go

So what changed? I want to suggest that among other things one explanation may be found in the fact that up until the 1960s the major influence on New Zealand evangelicalism was from Great Britain, but from that time on increasingly the influence has come from the United States.[13] David Bebbington has argued that these two movements coming from common stock gradually diverged and grew in different directions. "Fundamentalism became the dominant force in American evangelicalism, whereas in Britain it was contained... the United States adopted a more idealistic, clear-cut, crusading style."[14] To some extent this difference can be seen in the suspicion that a number of evangelicals in the United States have held towards at least some of the broader views held by some evangelicals from Britain, such as James Dunn and John Stott, or Canada, such as Stanley Grenz and Clark Pinnock.[15]

---

[12] B. Gilling, "Contending for the Faith: The 'Contender' and Militant Fundamentalism in Mid-Twentieth Century New Zealand," in *"Be Ye Separate": Fundamentalism and the New Zealand Experience* (ed. B. Gilling; Hamilton: Colcom, 1992), 63.

[13] The heading at the start of this section plays on Prime Minister Michael Savage's famous line, in declaring New Zealand's support for Britain in the declaration of War in 1939, "Where she goes we go, where she stands we stand."

[14] Bebbington, "Evangelicalism in Modern Britain and American," 212.

[15] See, for example, Donald Carson in *The Gagging of God: Christianity Confronts Pluralism* (Grand Rapids: Zondervan, 1996), 285–97, 481, 518–33.

In the United States Robert Wuthnow in *The Restructuring of American Religion* argues that there has been a religious realignment which has transcended denominational divisions and has lined up along a conservative/liberal axis.[16] This has moved churches from religious pluralism to religious polarisation, and alliances along these lines are now more important structures than denominations themselves. Wade Clark Roof and William McKinney in *American Mainline Religion,* in examining the legacy of the sixties find a flourishing of religious fringes to the right and left but a "collapse of the middle."[17] One expression of this realignment has been the emergence of such groups in the 1980s as the Moral Majority in what is commonly referred to as the New Christian Right. John Evans argues that a similar restructuring has occurred in New Zealand religion.[18] He argues that the problem conservatives faced was the "liberal acquiescence in the advance of the 'permissive society' and the erosion of Christian principles." The conservative stance had been that the church should not be involved in politics and focussed on personal piety, but "when the church failed to press the state to maintain certain moral stances, such as the sanction of the criminal law against male homosexual acts" they felt forced to act.[19] Thus liberal Christianity, often described as "humanistic liberalism," became as much the enemy as the permissive society, controlled by what was described as "secular humanism." Out of this emerged a plethora of conservative groups including the Society for the Protection of Community Standards, Society for the Protection of the Unborn Child, and Coalition of Concerned Citizens. Links to similar organisations in the United States have been well

---

Clark Pinnock was accused of heresy by some evangelicals in the US and in 2002 a number, led by Norman Geisler, endeavoured to have him expelled from the Evangelical Theological Society.

[16] R. Wuthnow, *The Restructuring of American Religion* (Princeton: Princeton University Press, 1988).

[17] W.C. Roof and W. McKinney, *American Mainline Religion: Its Changing Shape and Future* (New Brunswick: Rutgers University Press, 1987).

[18] J. Evans, "The New Christian Right in New Zealand," in *"Be Ye Separate",* 69–106.

[19] Evans, "New Christian Right," 71–72.

documented, including the visit there in 1985 of John Massam, editor of *Challenge Weekly*, the main media voice of these groups, to meet with groups within the New Christian Right, including the Moral Majority. Ultimately it led to the Christian Heritage Party and other Christian political parties since including the Christian Democrats, Future New Zealand, United Future, Family Party, and Destiny. Viv Grigg in a recent University of Auckland PhD claims, "The evangelical mindset in New Zealand includes a perception of disempowerment, a sense of shock at the rapid breakdown of social structure, a quiet rage at their sense of the loss of legitimacy and morality of the established church, then anger at the 'benign' governments."[20]

To return to the theme of increasing influence from the United States on evangelical Christianity in New Zealand, it was not only in this sense of political activism and crusading spirit. One of the themes that emerged in my study of churches in New Zealand between 1960 and 2000 was this very shift inside the churches themselves. It was seen in the influence of the church growth and church management movements, signs and wonders, New Zealand Pentecostals being influenced less by the British stock from which they arrived and more by North American Pentecostalism, the influence of churches such as Willow Creek, Saddleback, and Vineyard, and organisations such as Navigators, Campus Crusade, and the creation science movement.[21] In the 1960s, even in the Baptist Church, it was of no consequence whether one believed in evolution or not. Increasingly New Zealand evangelicals have looked to United States seminaries for further education rather than British Universities.

---

[20] V. Grigg, "The Spirit of Christ and the Postmodern City" (PhD thesis, University of Auckland, 2006), 93. This was written during the third term of the Labour Government led by Helen Clark, regarded as pursuing a liberal secular humanist agenda.

[21] While this is a fairly broad movement, it also embraces a number of organisations, including the Creation Research Society and Institute for Creation Research.

I had an interesting discussion with American Baptist sociologist Nancy Ammerman and a British Baptist doctoral student studying under her at Boston University, about changes in the ethos of Baptist churches in the three countries. I was making the point to her that I believed New Zealand has become considerably more conservative than that in which I grew up and commenced my ministry, partly because New Zealand Baptists had previously looked primarily to British Baptists, but from the 1960s increasingly to the Southern Baptists. Reflecting on that she talked about her father, a very fundamentalist Baptist minister visiting New Zealand in a Crusade in the 1960s, along with a large number of other Southern Baptist ministers. This Crusade in 1965 had a significant impact on Baptist churches here and led to a growing number of ongoing visits and connections between Baptists in the two countries.[22] As well as this increasing influence Southern Baptists themselves have become increasingly conservative and fundamentalist, as has been well documented in the United States leading to many of the faculty in seminaries losing their position and high profile members such as Jimmy Carter resigning membership.[23] The Baptist Church I was involved with as a student had Bob Thompson as Principal of the Theological College, Angus MacLeod as Secretary of the National Council of Churches, Bruce Albertson as Director of Social Services, and counted Labour stalwart J.K. Archer as one of its heroes. None of these, I suggest, would find a place of leadership there today.

On the broader cultural landscape this thesis of a growing American influence is also suggested by James Belich in his history of New Zealand where he finds a growing re-colonisation of New

---

[22] In 1965 a number of Southern Baptist ministers visited New Zealand as part of a "Trans Pacific Crusade" organised by the Baptist Union of New Zealand. I remember this well as at the appeal at one of these services I made my first "public acceptance of Christ."
[23] An excellent account of this is in Nancy Ammerman, *Baptist Battles: Social Change and Religious Conflict in the Southern Baptist Convention* (New Brunswick: Rutgers University Press, 1992).

Zealand culture by the United States.[24] Writing on Australian evangelical Anglicanism, Brian Dickey finds similarly increasing influences from the United States rather than England since the 1950s: "Australian Anglican Evangelicalism has changed substantially in the last thirty years as this new wave of ideas and practices has reached Australia across the Pacific, not the Atlantic."[25]

Who's in and who's out: embracing new boundary markers

I would argue, then, that these changes have led to changes in evangelical identity in New Zealand. As Bebbington has suggested, evangelicalism in the United States has been dominated by fundamentalism with its crusading and separatist tendencies. The difference between fundamentalism and evangelicalism is of course a rather murky issue, more grey than black and white, despite the Archbishop of Sydney's claim in an address in Christchurch in 2007 to New Zealand evangelical Anglicans that he is "not prepared to wear the label 'fundamentalist'"[26] and John Stott's attempt in *Evangelical Truth* to set out clearly the differences between the two. I found his arguments somewhat tenuous. What some have referred to as the "new evangelicalism" of course emerged from fundamentalism after World War II, and Stott acknowledges that originally "fundamentalist" was an acceptable synonym for "evangelical." Billy Graham who was the flag bearer of evangelicalism for much of the post-war period was himself of fundamentalist background and when asked if he was a fundamentalist, while not willing to accept the label in terms of certain behavioural traits such as bigotry and prejudice, said in terms

---

[24] J. Belich, *Paradise Reforged: A History of the New Zealanders from the 1880s to the Year 2000* (London: Allen Lane Penguin, 2001).

[25] B. Dickey, "Evangelical Anglicans Compared: Australia and Britain," in Rawlyk, *Amazing Grace*, 239.

[26] This in response to the book by Muriel Porter, *The New Puritanism: The Rise of Fundamentalism in the Anglican Church* (Melbourne: Melbourne University Publishing, 2006).

of essential beliefs "I am a fundamentalist."[27] George Marsden argues these new evangelicals "while maintaining the essential core of fundamentalist belief, were much more moderate in their application of principle. They continue to oppose liberalism in theology, but dropped militancy as a primary aspect of their identity."[28] In other words a difference of style rather than substance. It follows then that if evangelicalism has become increasingly militant, both in the United States and New Zealand, then trying to distinguish evangelicalism from fundamentalism becomes an increasingly difficult task. The statement by 108 evangelical leaders in the United States referred to earlier identifies that evangelical actions have "repeatedly led to militant, separatistic habits of mind and heart from which evangelicals in the mid-twentieth century struggled to free the movement. We are concerned that some claimants to the evangelical heritage appear to be falling back into some of the more onerous attitudes of fundamentalism."[29]

Along with this increasingly crusading and defensive spirit has gone a preoccupation with certain social and cultural issues. These are particularly to do with issues of personal sexuality, and a defence of what they define as the Christian or "traditional" family, although sociologists would label these as "modern" rather than traditional. Traditional families were much more diverse in form, and the pattern of family life that they enshrine as Christian, the nuclear family of mum, dad, and two or more children, as presented in this understanding, is in fact the product of the industrialisation and urbanisation of modernity itself, rather than of tradition or Scripture.[30] The focus on this is seen in the political arena as the

---

[27] Quoted in B. Gilling, "Mass Evangelism in Mid Twentieth Century New Zealand," in *Rescue the Perishing: Comparative Perspectives on Evangelicalism and Revival* (ed. D. Pratt; Waikato Studies in Religion 1.; Hamilton: Colcom, 1989), 1.

[28] G. Marsden, *Understanding Fundamentalism and Evangelicalism* (Grand Rapids: Eerdmans, 1991), 128–29.

[29] "The Word Made Fresh."

[30] See, for example, Mary Stewart van Leeuwen, *Gender and Grace* (Leicester: IVP, 1990), 168–71.

equation of "Christian values" with "family values," "God, family and country" (seen so strongly in the labelling of the most recent expression of a Christian political party in New Zealand as "The Family Party," which stood in the 2008 election but is now defunct), a reductionism which cannot in any way be justified either biblically, theologically or out of our tradition. An example of this rhetoric can be found in Grigg's work where he writes about the "social engineering" and "imposition of… strong feminist/lesbian/ homosexual agendas" of the current government.[31]

I was interested to read for review the recent book by Tom Oden, *Turning Around the Mainline*.[32] The book examines how renewal or confessing movements, made up of evangelicals who have remained in rather than left mainline Protestant denominations, have been turning around the slide into liberalism of these denominations and moved them toward more orthodox positions – a subject I have much interest in. I was somewhat surprised in reading the statements of faith or confessions of these groups how much they had in them about expressions of sexuality and the "traditional" family, a preoccupation with issues that if one reads the historic expressions of evangelicalism are not at the core of evangelical identity. Being aware of a similar preoccupation in similar groups in New Zealand mainline denominations it should not have surprised me. Along with these trends is the continuing threat of such groups to leave or separate, a sure sign of a fundamentalist spirit as identified in the title given by Bryan Gilling to a collection of articles on fundamentalism in New Zealand, *"Be Ye Separate"*.[33]

If one adds to this excursions into the public domain by groups such as Destiny Church, petitions against the civil unions bill, prostitution law reform, and anti-smacking legislation by evangelical groups, and the pushing in the church and public arena of creation science (now often renamed intelligent design), then it is

---

[31] Grigg, "The Spirit of Christ," 95.
[32] T. Oden, *Turning Around the Mainline: How Renewal Movements are Changing the Church* (Grand Rapids: Baker, 2006).
[33] Gilling (ed.), *"Be Ye Separate"*.

clear that in the public and wider church domain an "evangelical" identity has been captured by those for whom these are the primary concern, rather than those central concerns which preoccupied those who gave birth to and carried the movement through its early centuries. Linked with this conservative social and cultural package is also a conservative, or more correctly free market, economic orientation, demonstrated during the 2005 election campaign by the Exclusive Brethren funding of National Party marketing and a previous leader of the Baptist church in New Zealand calling on Baptists to vote for National instead of Labour. Research in the United States shows how the two party system in the church mirrors the two party system in politics, with conservatives voting for Republicans and liberals for Democrats. I suggest that research would lead to similar findings here. This is ironic given the heritage of the evangelical movement in working for the working classes in eighteenth and nineteenth centuries Britain. Where would that great saint of evangelical heritage William Wilberforce fit?

Noll identifies two of the dangers for evangelicalism as running off into "political extremism" and "polemical science," a warning that may be too late. He writes that "It has recently become customary to define all religious movements that combine militancy with adherence to traditional religion as 'fundamentalistic'."[34] The Archbishop then may refuse to wear the label, but he may have no choice if it has already been so widely given that it remains permanently attached. A statement by the British Evangelical Alliance acknowledges that the term evangelical now is "in danger of conveying nothing… except the generally negative view held by the press" and so many "are now wary of using it themselves."[35]

Who wants to be an evangelical today?

What I am arguing then is that while within the movement many of us may want to make a distinction between evangelicalism and fundamentalism, because of the actions of many who are evangelical

---

[34] Noll, "The Future of Protestantism," 434, 423.
[35] [Cited 30 July 2009]. Online: http://www.worldevangelicals.org.

both within their churches and in the wider society, most who are outside of the movement in both the church and society, do not see the difference, and simply describe it all as fundamentalism. Alan Jamieson, in his research and writing on church leavers, popularised the phrase EPC churches as a block identity for evangelical, Pentecostal and charismatic churches bearing similar characteristics.[36] Steve Taylor picked up this identity in his PhD research on Cityside.[37] John Drane, referring to it in both of these works, asked me if it was a commonly used identification unique to New Zealand as he had not come across it anywhere else. While Jamieson had helpfully used it in a well nuanced way in his research, I had some reservations about its growth into a more widely undefined, and often pejorative, label in New Zealand. However over time I have come to see that from an outside perspective there is much truth in it, perhaps partly brought about by the "charismaticisation" of much of evangelicalism in New Zealand and the blurring of distinctions between Pentecostalism and the charismatic movement. This widespread influence of the charismatic movement and Pentecostalism in evangelicalism in New Zealand is one of the distinctive characteristics of the movement here. It is certainly something that makes us different from evangelicalism in Australia, which has a strongly reformed and often anti-charismatic sector. Most of the writing in the New Zealand media identifies Pentecostal and evangelical Christian movements and churches as fundamentalist, or sometimes a "new fundamentalism." There is that and mainstream Christianity, going back to Wuthnow's two party system. The older irenic, cooperative spirit of pre 1960s New Zealand evangelicalism seems to have well disappeared to be replaced by the latest expression of the church militant, and the sign of "evangelical" Christians dressed in black and marching in unison down Wellington streets on Parliament is

---

[36] A. Jamieson, *A Churchless Faith* (Wellington: Philip Garside, 2000). Based on a Canterbury University PhD thesis.

[37] S. Taylor, "A New Way of Being Church," (PhD thesis, University of Otago, 2004).

an image seared on the minds of many New Zealanders that takes more than refusal to wear a label to erase.[38]

This makes it increasingly difficult for many of us who still identify with the historic ethos and concerns evangelicalism has stood for, and who still see ourselves as standing within that stream of the church. Brian McLaren, for example, writes of being listed in Robert Webber's book *The Younger Evangelicals* as the key leader of this group. He says he was asked by a friend if he felt offended by his inclusion. His friend explained "I thought you wouldn't want to be associated with that label… with all its negative connotations." He comments "my friend is right," and goes on to list some of those negatives, but he is reluctant to give up the name,[39] although perhaps Don Carson has made the decision easy for him in his attack on McLaren's evangelical credentials in his *Becoming Conversant with the Emerging Church*, a title which is rather ironic since he wrote the book without having one conversation with an emerging church leader.[40] This is a theme I find increasingly among young leaders who belong to evangelical mainline churches. As one on the pastoral staff of a leading Presbyterian evangelical church put it to me recently, "I feel really uncomfortable about being identified with this term." It is seen also in the way in which younger Christian leaders are not flocking to keep going to clearly evangelical ginger groups and organisations. Likewise it shows up in the smaller percentages of younger people than older in the Church Life Survey New Zealand identifying themselves as evangelical.[41]

---

[38] This referred to a street demonstration by members of Destiny Church in Wellington in 2006 against the "Civil Unions Bill," which gave same sex relationship the same legal status as marriage. I was reminded of how much this image remains when, while I was working on a final revision of this chapter, it was brought up the by influential New Zealand broadcaster Chris Laidlaw in a conversation with him. This was over five years later.
[39] B. McLaren, *A Generous Orthodoxy* (Grand Rapids: Zondervan, 2004), 115–17.
[40] D.A. Carson, *Becoming Conversant with the Emerging Church* (Grand Rapids: Zondervan, 2005).
[41] Data from the National Church Life Survey, 2001, 2007.

To return to where I began then, whatever we within the movement might like to define an evangelical as, and however much we may try and distance ourselves from fundamentalists and Pentecostals, the reality is that the meaning attached to words by hearers is more significant than what we might think they mean. They identify EPC as one group. For many of us in New Zealand who feel we identify with and stand within that rich and important evangelical tradition, and would like to further the ethos, values, and involvements it has carried, the label itself may well have passed its use-by date. Despite the call by various groups and reports I have referred to, to reinvest the label with a meaning truer to its historical trajectory, I would suggest it has become too associated with other less desirable qualities, for many inside as well as almost all outside the church, for it to carry any significant value as an identity marker nowadays except in our own self talk. For myself I find the most helpful self identity marker to use to place myself within the Christian perspective is as simply "orthodox." The question many would raise is of course, "does a rose by any other name smell the same?"

Part Two
Theological

Introduction to part two

Derek Tidball

Looking back on the notes I made at the end of the second Evangelical Identities Conference in Auckland, New Zealand, which focused on theological issues, I see I jotted down the comment, "evangelical scholarship is alive and well." And so it was. The conference was an impressive and stimulating experience for the participants and I am glad that some of its papers are now being published for a wider audience. [1]

The four hallmarks that were evident in the conference are also evident in these papers. The first hallmark was that they are *evangelical*. While there is an absence of sectarian spirit and the scholarly integrity of the writers is beyond question, they all share a commitment to the evangelical faith with its characteristic convictions about a high view of the Bible, the importance of doctrine, and mission. Two papers bring the doctrine of the church, often considered to be neglected by evangelicals, centre-stage. Murray Rae's paper discusses how to correct the tendency of evangelicals to capitulate to individualism, while Andrew Burgess explores the concept of "witness" as a potentially fruitful way of considering the churches' present responsibilities while living "between times." Concern for the way we read Scripture is uppermost in the paper by Tim Meadowcroft. Meadowcroft's paper led to the invitation to him to write a fuller work, *The Message of the Word of God*, in IVP's Bible Speaks Today Themes Series (IVP, 2011), which has recently been published. His chapter in this volume is a clear introduction to the way he approaches the task of hermeneutics. Systematic papers by Myk Habets on T.F. Torrance's

---

[1] Editors' note: for a fuller exploration of the landscape of contemporary evangelicalism, which captures the essence of the longer paper offered by Tidball at the colloquium, see his subsequently published "Post-war Evangelical Theology: A Generational Perspective," *Evangelical Quarterly* 80 (2009): 145–60.

approach to Scripture and Brian Harris' excellent discussion of Stanley Grenz's revisioning of evangelical theology both demonstrate a quest for evangelical fidelity. The choice of topics and the approach to them ensures this is an exercise in evangelical theology.

Secondly, all the papers are *contextual*. Theology cannot help but be contextual. Those who deny this in search of some contextless form of propositions are, in reality, often championing (or opposing) theology that arose in earlier historical contexts. Two contexts are particularly evident in these papers. The first is the global context of postmodernity which has affected all culture but particularly that of the academy. The second is the more specific New Zealand context (and perhaps the wider Australasian context as well). While the former context impacts virtually all the papers, the latter comes into sharp focus in Martin Sutherland's discussion of the limits and opportunities of a specifically New Zealand approach to theology.

Thirdly, these papers are *creative*. No paper suffers from the bane of academic conferences in which noted and overworked scholars repeat ill-prepared and well-worn positions. Each of these papers makes a fresh contribution to discussion and some do so in remarkably creative ways. In this regard Judith Brown's chapter on music, in which she expands the boundary of classical theology and considers whether music is not a vehicle of general revelation reflecting people's bearing of the image of Christ, deserves special mention. Also worthy of special mention is Martin Sutherland's consideration of the possibility of "Kiwi" theology which is marked by a breadth of understanding about New Zealand history, literary and artistic culture, and, equally, by judicious discernment.

Fourthly, these papers are *courageous*. Some evangelicals are nervous of stepping out of line and feel compelled to shelter within familiar and well-defined territory. But scholarship advances on the sort of open enquiry that is evident here. What, perhaps, the papers cannot betray is the quality of relationships and trust that was evident in the conference, which released this spirit of enquiry from fear, although I hope this does come through in this book. As a visitor, I was perhaps blissfully ignorant of political issues and nuances. But it did not seem that anyone was seeking to "tick the right boxes," or looking over their shoulder to ask what negative reaction they might provoke if they ventured this or that proposition. Their willingness to listen to one another and be supportive, without being gullible or uncritical, was a model of how evangelical scholarship should conduct itself.

In all such discussions the base note that beats incessantly underneath all the other melodies is the question of the identity of evangelicalism. Wisely no great energy was expended in seeking to nail the precise definition. Attempts to do so can prove arid while exciting applications of evangelical theology lie gasping for breath, like a fish that has jumped out of the fish tank. The fish needs to breathe in the water, not necessarily to be able to discuss its chemical composition. Here, evangelical theologians show healthy signs of life and the freedom to swim in the nourishing waters of evangelicalism.

Evangelical theology is a precarious exercise. It is like walking a high wire tightrope, easy to fall off one side or the other. Falling off one side plunges one into obscurantism and fundamentalism that merely parrots the past. Falling off the other plunges one into an equally fatal liberalism that allows culture alone to be sovereign and dictate what it is credible to believe. Walking the rope requires the keeping of a balance between revealed truth and contemporary culture. These papers show skilled evangelical theological acrobats in action, not for the entertainment of us all but for the instruction of us all. Thank you for the enrichment they will bring to our being faithful disciples today.

Chapter Eight
Locating the church in evangelical theology

Murray Rae

Laments about a lack of ecclesiology in evangelical theology have become commonplace in recent years. Donald Bloesch, for example, complains of the "apalling neglect" of ecclesiology in evangelicalism.[1] Clark Pinnock, likewise, considers evangelicalism to have neglected "the ecclesial nature of Christianity,"[2] and Donald Carson notes that "evangelicalism as a movement is much more defined by Christology, soteriology and bibliology than by ecclesiology."[3] This would seem to be borne out by David Bebbington's identification of biblicism, conversionism, activism, and crucicentrism as the principal marks of evangelical identity.[4] Chief among the reasons to overcome the neglect of ecclesiology, however, is that Christology, soteriology, and bibliology, to use Carson's categories, are themselves impoverished if not informed by

---

[1] Donald G. Bloesch, *The Future of Evangelical Christianity* (Garden City: Doubleday, 1983), 127. Bloesch himself has recently contributed to the overcoming of that neglect through publication of his book, *The Church: Sacraments, Worship, Ministry and Mission* (Downers Grove: IVP, 2002).

[2] Clark H. Pinnock and Delwin Brown, *Theological Crossfire: An Evangelical-Liberal Dialogue* (Grand Rapids: Zondervan, 1990), 198.

[3] Donald A. Carson, "Evangelicals, Ecumenism and the Church," in *Evangelical Affirmations* (ed. Kenneth S. Kantzer and Carl F.H. Henry; Grand Rapids: Zondervan, 1990), 355. There are others, too, who concur with the view that evangelicalism has neglected ecclesiology. For a brief survey of similar sentiments, see Stanley J. Grenz, *Revisioning Evangelical Theology: A Fresh Agenda for the 21st Century* (Downers Grove: IVP, 1993), 163–69.

[4] David W. Bebbington, *Evangelicalism in Modern Britain: A History from the 1730s to the 1980s* (London: Unwin Hyman, 1989), 2–17. Conforming to the same general pattern, David F. Wells and John D. Woodbridge included no discussion of the church in their edited collection, *The Evangelicals: What They Believe, Who They Are, Where They are Changing* (Nashville: Abingdon, 1975).

the biblical insistence that salvation involves incorporation into the new community of the body of Christ, and by considerations of how the Bible itself is both formed by, and informs the people called to live as the community of God's people.

I will proceed in this paper, first, by considering briefly some of the reasons for the neglect of ecclesiology, and will attempt, secondly, to identify what ought to be key features of an evangelical understanding of the church. Along the way I will consider some efforts recently made to formulate an evangelical ecclesiology, and will identify sources from beyond the evangelical strand of Christian faith from which evangelicalism could helpfully learn.

Historical roots

It is not my intention in this paper to settle the question of why the doctrine of the church has not received the attention in evangelical theology that is due to it. My concern rather is to establish some bearings for journeying forward. Yet some attention to the influences upon evangelicalism that might have led to this neglect will be helpful. In his book, *Evangelicalism and the Future of Christianity*, Alister McGrath sets out the generally agreed view that evangelicalism may be traced back to three major sources, the Protestant Reformation, Puritanism, and Pietism. It was at the time of the Reformation, of course, that the quadruplet of "solas" emerged, *sola scriptura, sola gratia, solus Christus,* and *sola fide.* Commitment to these principles continues to be a defining feature of the evangelical movement,[5] a commitment it shares of course, with other strands of the church deriving from the Reformation.

Behind the affirmation of these principles in the Reformation, and gathering momentum through the Reformation itself, was a growing ferment of discontent in European culture with those structures and institutions of the medieval world that purported to mediate between God and the people but that served, it was

---

[5] These principles constituted the essential content of the declaration of the Alliance of Confessing Evangelicals, Cambridge, Massachusetts, 1996.

increasingly believed, merely to protect the privileges of a ruling class and to deny to ordinary people access to God, to knowledge and truth, and to effective power. Luther's challenge to traditional authorities appealed to a yet more ancient source, that of the Christian Scriptures, and as his protests against the corruption of the church continued he determined that every Christian should have access to the truth and authority of the Bible for him/herself. The course of the controversy eventually led Luther to declare his allegiance to God and to Scripture in opposition to the contemporary dictates of the church. It is common, and understandable, though nonetheless mistaken, to suppose on the basis of this history that allegiance to the ecclesia was of secondary importance to Luther and indeed, that it was dispensable as a mark of the true Christian. Michael Horton notes that Luther has often been interpreted as setting individual rights and conscience over against the community, and is made to sing a duet with Frank Sinatra: "I did it my way."[6]

As Horton goes on to point out, however, Luther, and Calvin too in due course, renounce all individualistic or solitary conceptions of authentic Christian life. Both were profoundly committed to the importance of the ecclesial community and sought, not to dispense with the church, but to recover a true and biblically grounded form of ecclesial life.[7] Under the pervasive influence of modern

---

[6] Michael S. Horton, "Recovering the Plumb Line," in *The Coming Evangelical Crisis* (eds John H. Armstrong *et al.*; Chicago: Moody Press, 1996), 246. Horton goes on to say (p. 248), "It is absolutely vital to understand that the Reformation did not set the individual against the church, as evangelicals often have in this century."

[7] Luther writes, "He who wants to find Christ, must first find the church. How would one know Christ and faith in him if one did not know where they are who believe in him? He who would know something concerning Christ, must neither trust in himself nor build his bridge into heaven by means of his own reason, but he should go to the church; he should attend it and ask his questions there." *Luther's Works* (ed. Hans J. Hilerbrand; Philadelphia: Fortress, 1974), 52:39. Calvin concurs, titling the first chapter of Book 4 of the *Institutes of the Christian Religion* (trans. John Allen; Philadelphia: Presbyterian Board of

individualism, however, many Christians, evangelicals among them, have been slow to recognise that Luther's plea for a faithfully Christian understanding of salvation was equally, and inseparably, a plea for the reformation and not the marginalisation of the church in the life of the believer. Indeed the split with the Church of Rome was not an outcome that Luther himself sought. To the notion that we could dispense with the church in matters of biblical interpretation, for example, Luther caustically remarked: "That would mean that each man would go to hell in his own way."[8] Evangelicalism's solid grounding in the Reformation is central to its continuing vitality and faithfulness, not least in its emphasis on the sole sufficiency of Christ for salvation as witnessed to in Scripture, but as some evangelical theologians remind us, we must take more care in our reading of Reformation history and theology in order to recover a less individualistic conception of what it means to follow in the way of Christ.

A second key historical influence upon evangelicalism is Puritanism. From Puritanism, evangelicalism has inherited the conviction that conversion to new life in Christ requires a transformation not only of one's basic beliefs, and of the orientation of one's thinking, but also of one's moral life. As Alister McGrath points out, evangelicalism's emphasis on a "religion of the heart" also has roots in Puritan thought. This emphasis as it emerged in Puritanism was a mixed blessing, however. On the one hand, the evidence of individual conversion and the inward experience of God's grace helped to overcome the uncertainty bequeathed by Calvinism about whether one belonged to the elect or not. Further, it helped to recover a proper emphasis on the need for personal decision and commitment in response to Christ's invitation that we should follow him. On the other hand, this emphasis on a subjective mark of salvation encouraged a turn inwards and the elevation of

---

Christian Education, 1936), "The True Church, and the Necessity of Our Union with Her, Being the Mother of All the Pious."
[8] Cited by Horton, "Recovering the Plumb Line," 247.

personal experience as the touchstone of truth and of authentic Christian faith.

That same emphasis was central to pietism in the late seventeenth century and to the evangelical revivals of the eighteenth century. Both found a positive place for personal experience in testifying to the truth of Christian faith. The accumulated tradition of church doctrine was thus relativised and took second place to the experience and personal judgements of the individual. Pietism and the evangelical awakening did not have to lead in this direction, as John Wesley's strict regime of ecclesial disciplines makes clear, but under pressure from a surrounding individualistic culture the convictions arising from personal experience easily assume a greater authority than those of a church, or indeed of any external authority.

A further feature of evangelicalism's somewhat patchy attention to ecclesiology is a rather disputatious and schismatic history. It is somewhat ironic that evangelicalism's clear-sighted understanding of the pervasiveness of human sinfulness should have been accompanied on a number of occasions with perfectionist notions of the church, and a consequent impulse to separatism. That we are saved by grace alone rather than by works, is a principle that might have been applied with more charity to the body of believers called the church that, like every one of us Christians, stumbles somewhat erratically forward in its efforts to be faithful to its Lord. In charting the history of separatism and schism in the evangelical movement, Alister McGrath comments, "Evangelicalism can be very good at self-righteousness, when it ought to be concerned with Christian love."[9] The assumption of a perfectionist ecclesiology that seeks a church without spot or stain might be one contributing cause of this record of fragmentation. What we need instead is an ecclesiology that, like a properly balanced theological anthropology, can tell the truth about the imperfections of the church while at the same time proclaiming the sufficiency of God's forgiveness and grace.

---

[9] Alister E. McGrath, *Evangelicalism and the Future of Christianity* (London: Hodder & Stoughton, 1988), 24.

In this brief survey of possible causes of the relative neglect of ecclesiology in evangelical theology we may also mention the ecumenicity of evangelicalism. To its credit, evangelicalism characteristically transcends denominational boundaries and properly exposes them as without real relevance to the establishment of genuine bonds of fellowship with other Christians. Early evangelical leaders like Wesley, Newton, and Whitefield tried to affirm a new kind of ecumenism on the basis that true Christians were to be found across all branches of the church.[10] Seeking to safeguard the benefits of this trans-denominational character, evangelicalism has generally avoided making claims about ideal ecclesiastical form and the like. It has sought Christian unity and fellowship across denominational boundaries and has counted authentic Christian faith and commitment as more important than one's ecclesiastical affiliation. A corollary of this, I suggest, is that ecclesiology has not presented itself as a pressing issue for evangelical theology in the same way that it has for theologians more occupied with the defence and critique of their own denominational identity.

Towards an evangelical ecclesiology

I turn now to the more constructive task of identifying what ought to be key features, I shall argue, of an evangelical ecclesiology. We shall be seeking an ecclesiology that is clearly founded on the biblical witness, that upholds the importance of personal faith and conversion without individualism, that recognises the soteriological importance of the new community in Christ, and that replaces human and ecclesial perfectionism with trust in the God who calls into his service sinful men and women who have no merit to offer on their own account.

---

[10] I take the point from Bruce D. Hindmarsh, "'Let Us See Thy Great Salvation': What Did It Mean to Be Saved for the Early Evangelicals?" in *What Does it Mean to be Saved? Broadening Evangelical Horizons of Salvation* (ed. John G. Stackhouse; Grand Rapids: Baker Academic, 2002), 61.

Biblical starting points.

One of the most disputed of ecclesiological texts in the New Testament is Matthew 16:18-19: "And I tell you [Jesus says], you are Peter, and on this rock I will build my church... I will give you the keys of the kingdom of heaven, and whatever you loose on earth will be loosed in heaven." Whatever may be the matters open to dispute in the interpretation of this verse, and those following, it is at least clear that it was Jesus' intention to establish a church and that Peter, furthermore, who is shortly to be rebuked for protesting against the necessity of Jesus' death and who will later deny Jesus three times, was to be given a critical role in that church, whether as the rock upon which the church was to be built, or, more clearly, as one who will be entrusted with the keys of the kingdom. Either way, this is an awkward text for evangelicalism to deal with for it introduces into the drama of salvation an institution, ordained by Christ himself, to be sure, but constituting just the same, a path of access to the kingdom that is tended, watched over, and closed off, even, by human rather than divine hands. Christ entrusts into human stewardship, apparently, the means of access to his kingdom. The evangelical tradition, by contrast drawing sustenance from its Protestant roots, has long emphasised the open access to God provided by Jesus Christ and has denied the need for any human mediation. What does Jesus mean here, then, by suggesting that the way of salvation, the way to the kingdom, passes through the church? That is a first question that we shall seek to address as we proceed.

A second, and related, question is prompted by the account of Pentecost given in Acts 2, another key ecclesiological datum of the New Testament. Following the preaching of the Gospel and the descent of the Spirit, those who were being saved were drawn into the fellowship, the *koinonia*, of a new community. Salvation for them, it seems, involved reconciliation not only with God but also with the many who were being added to their number. What insight does this give us for a theology of the Christian community? Does it mean that Christian identity is necessarily ecclesial identity and that the tendency, all too prevalent in evangelicalism, to conceive salvation in terms of some sort of spiritual individualism is profoundly mistaken?[11]

Two further questions will give us more than enough to deal with in what remains of this paper. They arise this time from Paul's declaration to the Corinthians no less – this disputatious and divisive people – that they are the body of Christ (1 Cor 12:27). The image is used again in the letter to the Ephesians and in Colossians. The first question is straight-forward and arises especially from Paul's correspondence with the Corinthians. Although Paul urges them toward a transformation of their life together, he doesn't hesitate, despite their all-too-evident failings, to address them as saints and to call them the body of Christ. What might we learn from this starting point about the nature of the church as a community of forgiven sinners? Like the first of our texts considered above, the image of the church as the body of Christ has occasioned much debate. Should this language of the body be understood in merely metaphorical terms so that the church is simply an association of members forming a body corporate, or does Paul intend an ontological understanding of the image? Is there some sense in which the church really is Christ's body, the mode of Christ's availability in space and time? This has been a point of difference between the Lutheran and Reformed traditions, the former giving ontological weight to the language of the body of Christ, and the latter preferring a "merely" metaphorical reading. The Lutheran reading entails that being "in Christ" means being a member of the church, and supports the ancient Cyprianic contention that outside the church there is no salvation, while the latter view dissolves the connection between life "in Christ" and membership of the church. One can be a Christian, on this reading, without belonging to the church.

---

[11] I owe the phrase to John G. Stackhouse who writes with reference to his experience of teaching at Regent College in Vancouver, "Over and over, students have betrayed an understanding of salvation that amounted to a sort of spiritual individualism that is little better than Gnosticism." John G. Stackhouse, Jr., "Preface," in *What Does it Mean to be Saved?* 9.

The humanity of the church.

The text of Matthew 16:18, concerning the establishment of Christ's church on the rock Peter and the handing over of the keys of the kingdom to Peter, raised the question of the human and ecclesial mediation of the relationship that every Christian is called to enjoy with God. Does the way to the kingdom of God necessarily pass through the fallible and erring institution of the church? I think, on the basis of the New Testament evidence, that we need to answer, yes. It is made clear again and again, and consistently across all four gospels, that Jesus entrusts the continuing work of the kingdom and the mediation of salvation to the hands of his disciples. He hands over the keys of the kingdom to Peter (Matt 16:19); he commissions his followers to make disciples and to baptise in the name of the Father, the Son and the Spirit (Matt 28:19); he appoints the apostles to declare his message and invests them with power and authority to cast out demons (Mark 3:14-15; Luke 9:1); and while praying for the twelve, he says to the Father, just as you have sent me, so I send them into the world (John 17:18). Finally, in preparation for this service, the disciples are promised the gift of the Spirit, who will guide them into all truth (John 16:13). The disciples are then told by Jesus that on account of the Spirit's empowering of them if they forgive anyone's sins, they will be forgiven, and if they retain the sins of any, they are retained (John 20:23). This commissioning and anointing and investing of the disciples with power and authority is to be understood as the working out of Christ's own promise to build his church. It is clear here that the church exists to serve. It is not an enclave for the pious who wish to avoid the imperative to go into all the world.

Evangelical theology has generally done well in recognising that the being of the church is missionary being. I suggest that we might learn also from this appointment of the disciples that the mediatorial role of the church, established by Christ himself, is not to be understood as denying direct access to God for every believer, but rather as the means that Christ himself establishes to open up that access. Christ builds his church to be his witness precisely so that the world will learn that its sins are forgiven, its disobedience pardoned, and its alienation from God overcome through his life and death and resurrection. The church when it is faithfully engaged in the task to which it has been appointed does not get in the way of our access to God, therefore, but declares the way open by proclaiming the good news of Jesus Christ. Every one of us has cause to be grateful that the church, by divine appointment and grace, has preserved and passed on the news of salvation. The church, for all its fallenness, beginning with the weaknesses and inadequacies of Peter himself, is God's gift to us, his means of calling us to himself.

The community of forgiven sinners

The gospel writers make it plain that Jesus does not appoint people to apostleship on the basis of their own natural capacities, nor even on the basis of their moral worth. As the example of Peter makes clear, conformity to the perfection of Christ is the endpoint not the pre-requisite of service in the church of our Lord. Those who constitute the church are forgiven sinners. No other kind of human being is available for incorporation into the community of God's people. Followers of Christ yet understand only in part, and are still being formed into the likeness of Christ. They are *simul iustus et peccator*, at once justified and sinners. In making this point I am siding with Calvin's conception of the church as a community of forgiven sinners who are still on the way to complete sanctification, and in need, therefore, of the church's nurture and guidance,[12] and I am opposing the conception of the Puritan William Ames who insisted that the church is a community of saints from which sinners must be excluded.[13]

For all that Christian life involves moral striving, evangelical theology has generally understood very well that we have no worthiness of our own to offer in God's service, and that we are

---

[12] See Calvin's *Institutes of the Christian Religion*, IV.I.5.

[13] I take this point about Ames from McGrath, *Evangelicalism and the Future of Christianity*, 74.

adopted as children of God solely in virtue of God's grace. It is essential, therefore, that evangelical ecclesiology corresponds to this evangelical anthropology. What I am suggesting is that the impulse towards separatism that has been a fairly consistent, though not universally endorsed, feature of evangelicalism, must be critically reappraised.[14]

There is no church that has yet attained the fullness of salvation. Nor will we find any such church this side of the eschaton. We must recognise with more grace, therefore, that God has entrusted his purposes to a motley lot of sinners, among whom we ourselves are privileged to belong. The sometime failure to look graciously upon the failings of the church accounts in part for a marked preference in evangelical ecclesiology for the invisible over the visible church. This preference can have the effect of absolving Christians from commitment to any particular Christian community, and, as C. Norman Kraus has pointed out, leaves evangelicalism bereft of an ecclesiology that can undergird any actual gathering of disciples.[15]

It has been remarked that the church is a place where we get plenty of practice in forgiving others as Christ has forgiven us. Christ's strategy in the face of the continued weaknesses and failings of those he gathered to be his disciples was to forgive them and pray for them, and entrust to them again and again the task and privilege of sharing in his mission. The same must be true of our dealings with one another in the church. This is not to say that there will never be any cause for such separation as took place, for instance, at the Reformation. We would do well to learn from Luther, however, that separation was not desired. It was the sad outcome of his efforts to reform from within. The holiness of the church, grounded as it is in the holiness of Christ, is undoubtedly a goal for which we must

---

[14] For an historical account of this separatist impulse, see McGrath, *Evangelicalism and the Future of Christianity*, Chapter 1.

[15] C. Norman Kraus, "Anabaptism and Evangelicalism," in *Evangelicalism and Anabaptism* (ed. C. Norman Kraus; Scottdale: Herald, 1979), 177–78. Cited in Grenz, *Revisioning Evangelical Theology*, 174.

strive, but so too are the unity and the catholicity of the church. Fragmentation can be justified, if at all, only as a temporary expedient on the way to that day when all will be made one in Christ.

Soteriology

We have noted already a tendency in evangelicalism toward individualistic construals of salvation. Concern about this occasioned a conference at Regent College in Vancouver in 2001 dedicated to the task of broadening evangelical horizons of salvation.[16] A properly biblical understanding of salvation, the contributors to that conference argued, involves far more than getting individual souls to heaven. In particular it involves incorporation into a new community, the community of the risen Christ.[17] "Reconciliation" is one of a cluster of biblical terms used to bear witness to the transformation wrought through Christ's life, death, and resurrection. It is a transformation, what is more, that pertains to the whole of creation. The biblical vision of the heavenly city, of the new creation, characteristically refers to a reconciliation of all things with God, but, just as emphatically, it refers also to the reconciliation of God's creatures with one another.

> The wolf shall live with the lamb,
> the leopard shall lie down with the kid,
> the calf and the lion and the fatling together,
> and a little child shall lead them. (Isa 11:6)

This is one such biblical expression of the harmonious co-existence among God's creatures that will be established by the

---

[16] The proceedings have been published under the editorship of John G. Stackhouse as *What Does it Mean to be Saved? Broadening Evangelical Horizons of Salvation*.

[17] The point is supported by John Stott who writes, "The very purpose of [Christ's] self-giving on the cross was not just to save isolated individuals, and thus to perpetuate their loneliness, but to create a new community whose members would belong to him, love one another and eagerly serve the world." John Stott, *The Cross of Christ* (Leicester: IVP, 1986), 255.

Lord's anointed one. "In Christ," Colossians 1:20 asserts, "God was pleased to reconcile all things, whether on earth or in heaven, by making peace through the blood of his cross." Cherith Fee-Nordling expresses the matter well when she writes,

> God finds us in our sin, one by one, and brings us home. But that's just it. He doesn't then set up individual, relational dyads with us. He doesn't go off and have a "one-on-one" with the lost sheep. The sheep is rejoined with the flock, where it finds its life, safety, and identity under the care of the shepherd *with* the other sheep. The coin is put back with the rest of what perhaps is the woman's dowry. The "disgraced" son is restored with honor and love to his position in the household, much to his "faithful" brother's chagrin. Our heavenly Father brings us home, gives us new birth by his Spirit, and in Jesus restores us to the relational reality that defines us (John 3:1-8; Romans 8). He brings us back into relationship, first with the divine communion of Father, Son and Holy Spirit and then into human community formed ontologically *by* and *in* that divine communion.[18]

The ontological emphasis is key here. Church membership is not an optional extra for Christians. The church is not simply a gathering of the like-minded for mutual support and encouragement. Membership of the church, through baptism, is constitutive of one's new identity in Christ. To be "in Christ" is to be in his body, the church, a part of the new community that is both witness to and foretaste of the coming kingdom of God. Ecclesiology belongs, therefore, to the doctrine of salvation. To regard incorporation into the *koinonia* of the new community in Christ as secondary or incidental to the promise of salvation is to depart from the biblical conception of what salvation entails. As Stanley Grenz points out, "We are rescued from sin in order that we may participate in the fellowship of the redeemed humanity..."[19]

---

[18] Cherith Fee-Nordling, "Being Saved as a New Creation: Co-Humanity in the True Imago Dei," in *What Does it Mean to be Saved?* 117-18.

[19] Stanley Grenz, *Theology for the Community of God* (Nashville: Broadman & Holman, 1994), 572.

This relational ontology has its basis, of course, in the triune life of God himself. Stanley Grenz, drawing upon the recovery of Trinitarian doctrine in wider Protestant and Roman Catholic Theology, as also upon the Trinitarian theology of the Orthodox tradition, has done much to recover for evangelical theology too, a proper appreciation of the irreducibly relational character of new life in Christ.[20] True personhood, we learn from the life of God, consists in the perichoretic relationality of love between the three persons of the Trinity. The three persons each owe their identity, their very being, to the communion of love in which they *exist*. It is ecstatic being, a being directed outward to the other, and having its ground in the mutuality of relations between the three persons. That ecstatic, personal being is also the ground of creation, for the love of God flows creatively outward and brings into being that which is not God, the world and all its creatures. Just as the dynamic communion of God's love is the basis of creation, so also is it creation's goal. The reconciliation and consummation of all things in the kingdom of God is nothing other than the full and perfect enjoyment of his love. The church, in the meantime, especially so when it gathers at the Lord's table with no division between male and female, Jew and Gentile, slave and free, is both witness to and foretaste of the heavenly communion that is the basis and the purpose of creation itself. A truly evangelical ecclesiology, therefore, is an ecclesiology that testifies to this good news.

The body of Christ

Paul's image of the church as the body of Christ is commonly utilised in service of the quest for Christian unity and as an expression of the dependence of Christians upon one another. Paul himself uses the image in this way.[21] That is where evangelical

---

[20] See for example, Stanley Grenz, *Revisioning Evangelical Theology*, 186-89, and more extensively, *Theology for the Community of God*.

[21] See especially, 1 Cor 12.

readings of the Pauline texts have tended to begin and end.[22] But there is more to the image of the body of Christ. For Paul it also carries ontological weight. We are told in 1 Corinthians and in Colossians that through baptism we die with Christ and are raised to new life in his body (1 Cor 12:12–14; Col 2:9–14). The church as Christ's body is described in Ephesians 1:23 as "the fullness of him who fills all in all," while again in 1 Corinthians 6:12–20, we are reminded that our bodies are members of Christ, not this time to indicate the corporate nature of Christian life, but rather to emphasise the holiness of our bodies that comes through their being united to Christ. Paul means the image to carry ontological weight and does so by aligning the ecclesial image of Christ's body with the eucharistic one: "the bread that we break, is it not a communion in the body of Christ? Because there is one bread, we who are many are one body, for we all partake of the one bread" (1 Cor 10: 6–17). The church somehow *is* the body of Christ on account of its receiving the one eucharistic bread. This claim appears to plunge us back into the sphere of Reformation disputes about the body of Christ in the eucharist and may therefore be resisted by some.

Allegiance to hard-won positions of Reformed theology, however, may blind those of us belonging to that tradition to an important feature of Paul's thought. We must be prepared to recognise too that ecclesiastical polemics often encourages the drawing of excessively bold lines of demarcation. I suggest, therefore, that there might be something important to learn from these Pauline texts that a Lutheran reading of them may help us to recover. The *Systematic Theology* of Robert Jenson is a helpful means of access to the Lutheran line of thought. That the church is the body of Christ, Jenson explains, means that the church is "the object

---

[22] Wayne Grudem, for example, recognises that the "metaphor" extends beyond Paul's plea for Christians to recognise their dependence upon one another, but he does not discuss the point at any length. See Wayne Grudem, *Systematic Theology: An Introduction to Biblical Doctrine* (Leicester: IVP, 1994), 859.

in the world as which the risen Christ is an object for the world."[23] The church is, in other words, Christ's availability to the world, perhaps not exclusively, but nonetheless *really*. Consistent with Christ's appointment and commissioning of the apostles to be his witnesses throughout the world, Jenson's point is that Christ makes himself available precisely through the community thus appointed and commissioned. He does not leave them without his presence, but enlivens them with his Spirit and thus ensures that through their life and witness the hearers of their testimony will be brought to encounter Christ himself. The church is Christ's availability to the world, and just so it is his body.

Resistance to this claim may be traced, not only to Reformation polemics, perhaps, but also to a dualistic and docetic Christology. It is however the Word become flesh who is Lord of the church, the one, that is, who is made known not apart from but in and through material means. Incarnational theology does not legitimate the divinisation of the material world itself, as some have supposed, but it does entail that where God ordains that it should be so, he will be truly present for us, in bread and wine, and in the community of his body. We don't need a mystical account of transubstantiation to undergird this affirmation. All that is needed, as Jenson himself remarks, is that the risen Christ's personal self-understanding determine what is real.[24] We need have no more difficulty affirming the church as the body of Christ in this way than we do in accepting Christ's promise that wherever two or three are gathered in his name he will be in the midst of them.

The benefits to evangelical theology of this line of thought are several. First, it enhances, I think, our understanding of scriptural references to the body of Christ. Second, it defeats any pretension of the church to stand in the way of access to Christ and recovers a proper appreciation of the way in which the church under the headship of Christ is the means by which Christ himself determines

---

[23] Robert W. Jenson, *Systematic Theology: Volume 2, The Works of God* (New York: Oxford University Press, 1989), 213.

[24] Jenson, *Systematic Theology: Volume 2*, 214.

to be available to the world. Again we must emphasise that Christ remains free to make himself available by other means, but the Lutheran reading of Paul's image of the body suggests that the church, the two or three or more gathered in the name of Christ, is the normative mode of the risen Christ's availability in space and time. A truly personal relation with Christ is possible, therefore, in and because of the church. It is in the church, above all, that we may say "it is no longer I who live, but it is Christ who lives in me" (Gal 2:20). A third benefit to evangelical theology is the direction this thinking leads us in with respect to the institutional form of the church. If the church as Christ's body is interpreted in merely metaphorical terms, the temptation will be to interpret Christ's headship in the same way, and thus to seek a "real" head elsewhere. There has been no shortage of pretenders to that role across most branches of the church. Recognition of the real headship of Christ, however, will require in many cases a reformed church practice, and renewed submission to his Lordship of the body and not that of any one else.[25]

Conclusion

It will be obvious that the themes discussed briefly in this essay are not the only features of a comprehensive ecclesiology, and even those touched on have been treated all too briefly. What I have attempted here is merely the identification of some themes that evangelical theology has tended to neglect. Such neglect has led, I suggest, to an impoverished ecclesiology. I have attempted to argue also that failings in ecclesiology may be caused by and may produce in turn weaknesses in the treatment of other essentials of evangelical theology. Christology, soteriology, and the doctrine of God are particular cases in point.

---

[25] A similar point about the headship of Christ is made by Donald Bloesch in *The Church*, 85, although Bloesch has no extended discussion of the church as the body of Christ.

Chapter Nine
Evangelical ecclesiology? Witness, faithfulness, and "success" in the gospel

Andrew Burgess

Ecclesiology is not generally regarded as a strong area of evangelical theology. Perhaps this is due to a suspicion that an over-developed interest in ecclesiology is itself not very evangelical, and is rather more the preserve of Catholic and Anglo-catholic theologies and of liberal theology more generally. Ecclesiology looks likely to involve (what many evangelicals would consider to be) an inappropriate elevation of the role of the church in God's economy in general, and salvation in particular. This suspicion is grounded in genuine insight. There is often a tendency to immanentise God's reconciling work in the human agency of the church, variously in forms such as: *koinonia* derived more or less directly from the communion of the Trinity; ecclesial polity formed in practices and habits derived from Christian renditions of virtue ethics; a community formed in sacramental action; and combinations of these among other offerings. The danger is that emphasis on the immanence of God's reconciling action displaces or compromises the sovereign and majestic freedom in which God saves and in saving continually sanctifies a community as God's own. The church's ministry of reconciliation is a genuine and free human work exactly as it takes place *within* the magisterial reconciling work of the active and present Lord. Evangelical church leaders inhabit a tradition with a long history of distrust of anything that looks likely to elevate the human and impinge on the sovereignty of God.

Theology matters
However to note all this is not to claim that evangelicals have no ecclesiology, or in fact that evangelicals have a particularly "low" view of the church itself. Many evangelicals would be quite comfortable with some very strong claims about the importance of

the church within God's economy; for example, Bill Hybel's much quoted claim that "the local church is God's plan for the salvation of the world" seems to have struck a chord with many New Zealand evangelical leaders. At the very least an incipient ecclesiology is at work which certainly holds that the church serves within God's ministry of reconciliation – as Paul has it, that God has through Christ "given us a ministry of reconciliation... entrusting the message of reconciliation to us" (2 Cor 5:18-19).[1]

In keeping with this sort of comment, evangelicals tend to be very clear that the task of the church is mission, or evangelism, and to be strongly committed to working out relevant ways to engage in evangelism. There can be no complaint with this. However, evangelicals often need to go deeper in thinking about the church, and add greater insight to this fundamental commitment. Without deeper reflection on the being and work of the church – that is, without fundamentally *theological* reflection – a superficial ecclesiology can end up *solely* driven by pragmatic concerns, and New Zealanders are often given to a particular pragmatism. If pragmatic considerations overrule such that theological perspective is lost, the ability to measure *faithfulness* to God in serving God's mission must also be lost. If God's people have a concern and a willingness to work for as many people as possible to hear and to respond positively to the good news of Jesus then that is very well indeed. But a question remains: are responses to any particular form of proclamation proof of the faithfulness of that message? Indeed, are new members choosing to join a fellowship proof of faithfulness in "being God's people"? We might ask that another way: is numerical growth decisive in our discerning churchly obedience to the Spirit of Christ? These are questions evangelical church leaders need to be particularly concerned with.

---

[1] For a very helpful reflection upon 2 Corinthians 5 and a theology of the church's ministry of reconciliation see John Webster, "Christ, Church and Reconciliation," in *Word and Church: Essays in Christian Dogmatics* (Edinburgh: T. & T. Clark, 2001), 211-30.

We noted above the genuine evangelical concern that "overblown" ecclesiologies maximise the role of the human institution of the church and of human agency. It is absolutely crucial to note that pragmatism yields precisely the same result: the human pole eclipsing the control that genuine Christian doctrine should exercise. Pragmatism lacks an explicit theology, but in supplanting and thus assuming the role theology should have, an implicit ecclesiology is at work. The problem is that it does so without reference to the essential controls, encouragements, challenges, and insights that derive from the doctrine of God, Christology, soteriology, eschatology, and so on. Assumptions need to be brought to light and engaged within a theological frame. So for example, it may well be appropriate to think about the being of the church primarily in terms of "being-in-action," and thus to recognise that there is no church which is not active in the proclamation of the gospel, and so in pursuing justice, seeking communion with God in the Spirit, and with one another in the same Spirit. Yet within this recognition this churchly action must be accounted for within the field encompassed by the being-in-action of the Triune God. Further, even to begin to orient the mission of God's people within the frame of the *missio Dei* requires considerable attention to doctrinal expositions of the being of God (the Trinity) and of God's works *ad extra* as God's seamless self-determined mission in the perfection of God's own being.

In fact, pragmatic emphasis on technique can be even more dangerous than church-aggrandising ecclesiologies, precisely because this emphasis is non-theological and there is no necessity to attend to much (or any) "God-talk" in discussing the relative strengths of techniques and methods. Ecclesiologies that evangelicals quite rightly view askance at least have the advantage that they are theologies of the church's ministry and life and therefore cannot but be engaged with questions of the nature of salvation and of the being, identity, holiness, and love of the Saviour – at least to some degree.

Complaints as to the danger of a hegemony of method nonetheless cannot direct us toward a sterile and wholly theoretical approach. (As if true theology can ever be truly sterile!) God *is* at work, the ministry of reconciliation *is* real, God *is* making God's own appeal. In bearing witness in the real world – and there is no witness to be borne except in the real world, where God is actually at work – pragmatic insights do count, but they do not count above all. Worship of God counts above all, and worship of God is more than success in our endeavours.

In pointing toward the dangers of a non-theological ecclesiology allow me to become autobiographical for a moment: I will never forget a particular instance of being "taught" by two leaders of very large – "successful" – Christian fellowships. The context was a training session for church leaders, and one key piece of wisdom offered several times through the session was this: if a church leader wants people to be interested in joining his or her church fellowship, then that leader must make sure that they drive an expensive car, and have a nice home, and dress in a way that indicates some affluence. The concomitant claim was also made: a church leader who does not appear to be affluent, by virtue of the quality of their possessions, will attract no one to their fellowship.

What is wrong with such "wisdom"? An answer to that question can only come from theology. Pragmatically these statements may well be proven to be true. Real estate agents, and other sales-people, know that the appearance of success is a useful and important component in persuading people to listen to "the pitch" and to take the sales-person seriously. A church leader who embraces this "wisdom" may well find that it "works" and that their fellowship grows numerically. But theologically there are enormous issues: What sort of community is God's church to be? What sorts of motivators are appropriate – that is, express faithfulness to the gospel – in the way that the church goes about proclaiming Jesus? For the gospel is God's message and is not a possession of the church, or a matter of our revision and adaptation. Theology matters, for only ever deeper penetration into worship and ever deeper comprehension of the height, breadth, length, and depth of God's amazing grace will do!

So, this essay represents an attempt to reflect on the sort of ecclesiology found in a New Testament source, the Revelation of John, and then draw that into some *theological* reflection on the present age as a particular *theological* phenomenon, in such a way as to recommend that our ecclesiology draw far more heavily on the concepts of "witness" and "faithfulness."

Jesus as the "true witness," and the witness of the church

It involves no new insight to note that various Christological titles are applied to Jesus throughout the New Testament, but one that is particularly important in the book of Revelation is Jesus as "the faithful and true witness." What is involved in this title, and what does it have to do with ecclesiology?

First and foremost a sense of the context for the title within Revelation is essential. Several key titles and metaphors for understanding Jesus appear through the book. Jesus is the victor in God's war with Satan and the kingdoms of this world, represented as they are by the dragon and beasts. Jesus is also the Passover lamb slain for the world; indeed it is as the slain "lamb" that Jesus is victor.[2] However, the identification of Jesus as the true witness has a particular import in that Revelation also echoes throughout with the call for the *church* to bear witness, indeed to maintain Jesus' own witness. Jesus is the true witness whose life and death, in particular, are the ultimate human expression of faithfulness and obedience to the Father. Jesus' obedience is the perfect witness to the sovereignty of the Father in the face of all violent coercion, and ungodly pressure from "the powers." Jesus obeys his God – obedience

---

[2] In Revelation 5 we are told that the "Lion of the tribe of Judah, the Root of David, has conquered" and by virtue of this victory can open the scroll with seven seals. When John looks for this "victorious lion" what he sees is the "slain lamb." There is a marvelous interplay of hearing and seeing and the juxtaposition of the audible metaphor and visual image involved; the mighty lion who conquers does so in the (seemingly) powerless suffering and death of God's lamb (Rev 5:5-6).

characterizes his entire life and his death also – and it is in this fashion that he bears witness before the world.

In fact the three key Christological titles – victor, slain lamb, and witness – are clearly linked, each with the other two, but also with the reality of the church. Christians are pictured as those who, like Jesus, conquer Satan and the various satanic powers – Christians share Jesus' victory – but they do so "by the blood of the lamb and by the word of their testimony" (Rev 12:11a). In fact, the witness of Christians, like that of Jesus, is exemplified in faithfulness to God and God's truth even unto death, a fact made commonplace by the subsequent adoption of the word "martyr" (Greek *martos/martyr* = witness) to indicate one who *dies* for the faith. The importance of the connection between the call to "overcome" or "conquer" – expressed to each of the seven churches as the condition upon which will come Jesus' reward – and faithful witness must not be underplayed. The unity of chapters 1-3 and the rest of Revelation is perhaps less recognised, but the whole letter is introduced as the message of the One who walks among the lampstands – the message of the Lord to his church. Each local fellowship of Christ's church receives its particular words, but as each receives the same call to "overcome" the rest of the message provides a vision of what such overcoming involves; God grants a vision of what the church's victory looks like. We will see below that this overcoming may well be weak, and even a failure when viewed with eyes that do not share the vision that comes from God. The interlinking of Jesus as *the* "faithful witness" who overcomes in radical and costly obedience and the church as God's people of witness, who are likewise called to overcome, is of extraordinary significance.

All this contributes to a broad message running through the whole of Revelation, that the church is called to bear witness among the nations that Jesus is Lord, in opposition to the lordship of the demonic powers manifest in the godless empires of the world. However, this witness is to *hidden* reality, and even the form of witness itself is somewhat counter-intuitive, because every appearance indicates that it is the world that conquers the church (just as every appearance would lead to the conclusion that Jesus was at best a failed messiah who died in defeat and ignominy). The saints conquer Satan by Jesus' blood and the word of their testimony; but this is achieved in that they do "not cling to life even in the face of death" (Rev 12:11b). *Even in the face of death!* We might just as well say "even in the face of utter and total defeat." The imposition of a death sentence is the way the lordless powers declare total victory over and the absolute degradation of those who stand against them. Those who are put to death in such a way are declared non-persons and insignificant except as objects of rejection and wrath. It cannot be elided: on this account the saints appear defeated in every way that matters; they are pursued and harassed even to death and it is the powers who win. *But God speaks a different word* and precisely in their defeat lies their victory as they bear ultimate witness to the truth of God that opposes all the self-aggrandisement both of the dragon and of fallen humanity. Jesus' people turn out to look rather like him.

Perhaps no other book of the New Testament so broadly describes the situation of the church as she awaits Jesus' return and the end of the age.[3] If Richard Bauckham is right to reject interpretation of Revelation as a predictive list of (then) future events, and instead to describe the book as a prophetic description of the *nature* of the time leading up to Jesus' return,[4] then we must look less for accurate and detailed predictions of particular events, and more for depictions of the metanarrative of our age, an age in which Christians confront the powers and bear prophetic witness through faithful living, even unto death. Once again, within this the church is held up before us as a community of witness, and that witness is anchored in the agency of the Spirit, who mediates the

---

[3] We need to note the contrast that is often drawn between Acts and Revelation in presenting what are claimed to be rather different pictures of the church's situation. However this contrast is perhaps overplayed, and might be argued to fail to take seriously Acts' own depiction of struggle and suffering, even seeming defeat, in the life and mission of the church.
[4] Richard Bauckham, *The Theology of the Book of Revelation* (Cambridge: Cambridge University Press, 1993), 150.

presence and power of the risen Christ, and who is the power of the church's faithful life.

Thus Bauckham can say: "The essential form of Christian witness, which cannot be replaced by any other, is consistent loyalty to God's kingdom. In this powerless witness the power of the truth to defeat lies comes into its own."[5] What does such witness mean? Essentially witness is no more or less than faithfulness: Christians, the church, living in utter faithfulness to the call of God over and against all other lordships and dominions. By this we mean *obedience*. The characteristic form of Christian ethics is obedience to God. And in this space the church occupies the place of those who live within the life-giving judgement of the God who says "Your *sins* are forgiven you."[6]

But witness is such faithfulness in its *public* dimension, as an historical datum. This is not to say that such witness, such public faithfulness, is unambiguous in its reality and that anyone viewing even the most faithful Christian community in operation will be forced to "convert." That witness is public faithfulness does not remove the uncertainty that attends all faithfulness to God within a world ruled by the powers; it simply identifies the mundane nature of the socio-historical realm within which it is acted out.

To this degree Bauckham's comment also requires that we guard a definition of witness as public faithfulness by disregarding any notion of a distinction between public and private versions of faithfulness. There are not two types of faithfulness but only one, so that in reality no firm distinction may be drawn between public and private faithfulness, and to that degree we must acknowledge that all faithfulness is in fact witness in that it occurs in the public realm

---

[5] Bauckham, *Theology of the Book of Revelation*, 163.

[6] It should not need to be so, but perhaps some explanation is required. The forgiveness of sins is judgement, not avoidance or refusal of judgement, for to forgive sins is to name them for what they are and to *destroy* them in such a fashion as to give life in doing so. God's forgiveness is no wink at evil; it is the manner in which God puts evil to death.

of words and actions.[7] This means that "this powerless witness"[8] cannot involve any falsification for the purpose of presenting a better public face for the gospel. In other words, the church cannot elect to show an "attractive" and "successful" public face when such success flies in the face of the gospel. There can be no private set of values which recognise the antithesis between Jesus' lordship and the lordship of mammon, or any of "the powers", and a public display of wealth or any other false "overcoming." Revelation holds out to Christians a command to be that people in whom the faithfulness of Jesus is *re*presented even at the cost of lives, and whose faithful living may well appear as failure *within* the realms dominated by the powers, but whose witness will be revealed to be a victory empowered by the very Spirit of God, *on the last day*. The church cannot and must not betray such witness for any other, no matter how attractive to the world around, nor how much more "successful."

All this, of course, indicates an ecclesiology with a focus on witness expressed in an age that is entirely eschatological in focus. What sort of theology of the present age might be in view here?

The present age: ascension and the church

Karl Barth described the current age as "the time-between," meaning, specifically, the time between ascension and *eschaton* (or Jesus' final *parousia*).[9] In doing so Barth was doing something that we should take very seriously; he was applying a *theological* description to the present age, so that a Christian might understand the present time not merely as the wheel of mundane history rolling on in its rut, nor simply as late modernity or early post-modernity, or the age of globalisation, and not even geologically or climatically as the age of global warming, but rather as the age defined by its

---

[7] Clearly this also assumes no legitimate bifurcation between private devotion and public action.

[8] Bauckham, *Theology of the Book of Revelation*, 150.

[9] For more on this, and what follows, see Andrew Burgess, *The Ascension in Karl Barth* (Aldershot: Ashgate, 2004).

start and finish within the history of Jesus of Nazareth. In typical fashion Barth acknowledges Jesus as the measure of all creaturely reality, and defines history by reference to him.

This being so, what understanding of the nature of this age follows? As the time inaugurated by Jesus' ascension, this is the age of Jesus' *physical* absence and of his agency in the Spirit and the church.[10] Jesus withdraws into the hidden "place" of God – to the Father's "side" – and his return will signal the end of the age. We may at this point be reminded of the old chestnut "the delay of the *parousia*." The question certainly becomes "for what purpose does this 'time-between' exist; why is there *any* age between ascension and *eschaton*?" Such a theological question receives a theological answer. We will be unsurprised to hear that the present age is in fact the "time of the church," and specifically the age of mission, of witness.

> The community is and has the answer which has to be given to the question of the good and gracious purpose of God in the puzzling distance between the first *parousia* of Jesus Christ and the second, the question of the time between, in which the world is held, as it were suspended between the provisional and transitory and particular revelation of its reconciliation with God in Jesus Christ and the perfect and definitive and universal revelation of it in His final coming.[11]

Thus mission and witness function within the very being of the church as a creature of the "time-between." As Barth puts it, the church's "mission is not additional to its being. It is, as it is sent and active in its mission."[12] As Jesus lives as the "true witness" to the Father, so the church exists as his body in this age, and is made by

---

[10] This reference to physicality in regard to ascension causes many some pause. However, the ascension is certainly to be understood as introducing a *lack* of physical availability of Jesus and equally the pictures we have of his *parousia* in the *eschaton* are of his physical return and presence.

[11] Karl Barth, *Church Dogmatics* [hereafter *CD*] (4 vols; Edinburgh: T. & T. Clark, 1936-69), IV/1, 733-34.

[12] *CD*, IV/1, 725.

him to be a community through which his witness is made present within the world.[13]

In parallel to the emphasis in the Book of Revelation, Barth enters into considerable discussion of Jesus as "the true witness."[14] The church as his earthly "body" is therefore very much the community of witness "between the times," living out the reality of God's victory and reign within an age dominated by the old world, the old creation, which is passing away. The witness of the church in such an age is a provisional and sometimes ambiguous matter, but its power is anchored in the power of God, and as such it remains true and genuine witness.

The suffering and rejected witness of Jesus himself once again provides the model. The church is that community whose faithfulness to the walk and work of the suffering Saviour is at one and the same moment its witness to him. Thus Barth encourages us to see the present age as that age given specifically for this work of witness and mission. Why does the world roll on, seemingly unchanged by the victory of God? So that there may be witness *within* this world that is perishing, and the church is that community tasked with, and created for, this work of witness. But as in Revelation, it is not insignificant that the world does appear to overcome. It is fundamental to the character of the "time-between" and Jesus' relationship to it. The current age is the age which *precedes* the eschaton – the age of the "not-yet" – and this time is precisely that time in which Jesus and his victory are *not* immediate. Indeed this reality is concealed under the sign of the broken – even sinful and defeated – witness of those who overcome by the blood of the lamb and the word of their testimony.

---

[13] Barth describes Jesus' risen and ascended body as his "heavenly-historical" reality, and the church as his "earthly-historical" reality. See e.g., *CD*, IV/1, 661.

[14] The whole of *CD*, IV/3 (parts i and ii) is given over to the theme of Jesus, risen and ascended as "The True Witness," as Barth gathers up the traditional *munus triplex* themes of Jesus as King and Priest in the third office of Prophet.

The link between Jesus' walk, witness, and victory on the tortuous route from Bethlehem to Golgotha and the work of God in the church has already been made, but let us note further here the way in which the victory of God, manifest in Jesus' resurrection and ascension, remains hidden at the Father's side as long as Jesus remains there. The age of faith and hope is the age of witness to things unseen, to victory concealed in the absence of the victor. Yet such witness redounds with the power of the one whose victory is accomplished in, through, and beyond a cross and a grave. Ambiguity is not an obstacle to God's self-witness, but is intolerable to us if we think it is in any way our job to save, or that witness has in some way been devolved to the church. No, "we are ambassadors of God" it is true, "*since God is making his appeal through us.*" Let no fear of failure or sense of ultimate responsibility lead God's people away from this fraught walk of victorious failure and powerful weakness. Let no angst at the uncertainty of our appeal to the world send Christ's body in search of a better word. Jesus' blood speaks the better word, but it was spilt by the powers, and they still understand it not.

Witness and the powers
Ecclesiology is therefore best shaped by attention to witness and faithfulness, not to diminish attention to such themes as worship and holiness, or to such practices as Holy Communion, confession, and prayer, but to recognise all faithfulness and obedience as essentially the church bearing witness. This age is without doubt the age of witness, and the church is not *God's* church if it is not a community of witness, plain and simple.

Yet the church, and evangelicals as much as any churchly group, can falsify this faithful witness, and especially in accommodating to the "spirit of the age," even and although resistance to the *Zeitgeist* is often assumed to be somewhat of a evangelical speciality. The greatest danger is surely the way in which this happens subtly and insidiously, and especially when the church is tempted to mistake the values and/or methods of the powers for faithfulness itself. As earlier, evangelicalism may be particularly vulnerable to this in what is often held to be the greatest strength of the movement: evangelism and church-growth. The danger manifests particularly in adoption of consumerist approaches to church practices *when they lead to a falsification of the gospel and the reality of Jesus' relation to this world*. As above, this is by no means a blanket rejection of all technique or of a radical commitment to the communication of the gospel, but attention to the nature of witness as described by the Book of Revelation, and a theologian such as Barth, should help us to recognise the danger inherent in too much attention to "success" in growing a particular fellowship, or in a particular evangelistic technique.

At its most fundamental the radical witness of the church must be the willingness to forsake all else for the Name of Jesus Christ, and to worship him in a world dominated by idolatrous worship of the powers. There can be no escaping the fact that this may well look like failure to the world around, and that in our greatest weakness we may well be serving God best. This flies in the face of that current wisdom with which we began: "If you don't drive a good car, and have a nice house, who's going to want to come to your church?" Such adoption of the standards of the powers is an extraordinary falsification of the gospel, and betrayal of the Saviour reviled upon the cross, the man with no place to lay his head, despised and rejected by all.

We might hope that few evangelical leaders would readily accept this line. But the other more subtle temptations are still there. Take for example the assumption that a church leader whose congregation is growing is a "success". If we are satisfied with such assumptions we fail to ask the deeper questions that might allow us genuinely to measure Christian "success," that is, we fail to look for signs of faithful witness. We cannot assume that numerical growth *automatically* equates to faithfulness. Equally, and perhaps even more strongly, we cannot assume that numerical decline in a fellowship must indicate a lack of faithful witness. What if, like Jesus our Lord, our faithful witness actually sends people running from the difficulty of the message? "This teaching is difficult; who can accept it?" (John 6:60) say Jesus' followers, and many cease to follow.

The call to witness provides a deeper framework than simply looking for numerical growth, even as the call to witness will itself lead to considerable celebration of genuine growth in numbers of people living as disciples. Witness opens up an ecclesiology that is active and "mission focussed," but an ecclesiology with resources to counter the attraction of unfaithful methods and manners of mission. It does not exclude the wealth of attitudes and actions that make for the practice of "doing church," but rather gathers them up within a rich framework of obedience and worship. God's church is a faithful, hopeful community which bears witness in radical eschatological hope which is itself the ground of equally radical engagement in the here and now. Eschatological vision is the gift of the Spirit of Christ who thrusts God's people into all sorts of powerless victory and unmasking of the powers as the defeated beasts they are.

Such theological vision cannot but have a profound bearing on what we regard as "successful" mission, on what outreach activities we will consider faithful, on what words, songs, and actions form the liturgy of our worship, and so on and so on. Let us pray that we might be witnesses and members of a community of witness that is conformed to *the* faithful witness. Amen.

Chapter Ten
Beyond Henry's nominalism and evangelical foundationalism: Thomas Torrance's theological realism.

Myk Habets

The careers of Carl Henry and Thomas Torrance share many similarities in their general outlines, and yet they could not have chartered more different courses in theology had they tried. Both men were born in 1913 and lived into their 90s. Both were professors of theology: Henry at Fuller Theological Seminary, which he helped to establish; Torrance at the University of Edinburgh. Both were prolific authors: Henry's *magnum opus* being the six-volume *God, Revelation and Authority*;[1] Torrance's *magnum opus* being *The Christian Doctrine of God* (and *The Trinitarian Faith*).[2] Both were also editors of significant theological journals: Henry of the popular *Christianity Today*,[3] and Torrance of the *Scottish Journal of Theology*. Both were international speakers and first order systematic theologians. Finally, both were guardians of what they considered orthodoxy: Henry of the evangelical heritage which developed out of fundamentalism,[4] and Torrance of an orthodoxy developed in line with the Great Tradition.

---

[1] Carl F.H. Henry, *God, Revelation and Authority* (6 Vols; Waco: Word, 1976–1983).

[2] Thomas F. Torrance, *The Christian Doctrine of God: One Being Three Persons* (Edinburgh: T. & T. Clark, 1996); *The Trinitarian Faith: The Evangelical Theology of the Ancient Catholic Church* (2nd ed; Edinburgh: T. & T. Clark, 1995).

[3] While *Christianity Today* has become a popular, lay-driven magazine, it started out as a theological magazine–journal in opposition to *The Christian Century*.

[4] Even though, in Grenz's estimation, Henry remained a fundamentalist in many respects. Stanley J. Grenz, *Renewing the Centre: Evangelical Theology in a Post-Theological Era* (Grand Rapids: Baker, 2000), 87.

While clearly of the same mind regarding a range of theological beliefs, Henry and Torrance did not share the same epistemic commitments and thus their theological methods were drastically different and this resulted in what can only be considered radically differing theologies. Having met on several occasions they disagreed considerably and this spilt over into their respective *oeuvres*. What follows is a focused reflection on what may be considered the heart of their theological disagreement: the nominalism of Henry versus the realism of Torrance.

Carl Henry vs. Thomas F. Torrance

In *God, Revelation and Authority* Henry sought to establish the foundations of an apologetic theology, an evangelical response to modernity on modernity's terms, with the aim of establishing the intellectual coherence and academic credibility of a Christian "world-life view," as Henry termed it. In volume one, *God Who Speaks and Shows*, he sets forth the nature of theology, and in volumes two, three, and four he comments at length upon fifteen foundational theses on divine revelation. Volumes five and six, *God Who Stands and Stays*, develop a classically orthodox approach to the doctrine of God. The ordering of the work is important; Henry privileges treating method before theology proper, for Scripture is epistemologically prior to God in his theology. To be clear, it was Henry's express conviction that the foundation for correct theology can only be found in the divine revelation of God as deposited in the Holy Scriptures.

Henry defined revelation as

> that activity of the supernatural God whereby he communicates information essential for man's present and future destiny. In revelation God, whose thoughts are not our thoughts, shares his mind; he communicates not only the truth about himself and his intentions, but also that concerning man's present plight and future prospects.[5]

---

[5] Henry, *God, Revelation and Authority*, 3:457.

Revelation is thus objective and available to unaided human reason. So insistent was Henry on this point that he rejected all attempts by the so-called neo-orthodox of his day (read here Barth, Bultmann, and Brunner especially), to establish a relational and participatory theology whereby only those united to Christ and enlivened by the Spirit could know God. Henry wrote, "If a person must first be a Christian believer in order to grasp the truth of revelation, then meaning is subjective and incommunicable"; and further, "the new birth is not prerequisite to a knowledge of the truth of God."[6]

According to Henry, the Bible is almost entirely propositional in content, thus God communicates in order to convey truths in the form of propositional sentences.[7] The purpose of theology is to take such sentences and form doctrines or propositions from them. In this regard we might note the affinities of Wayne Grudem's approach to systematic theology with that of Henry when Grudem defines theology as "any study that answers the question: 'What does the whole Bible teach us today?' about any given topic?"[8] John Franke calls this the "concordance conception of theology" which has characterized evangelical theology in general, to the extent that it has assumed the methodology of post-Reformation Protestant scholasticism.[9] In a programmatic passage Henry sets forth his "basic epistemological axiom" as follows:

> Divine revelation is the source of all truth, the truth of Christianity included; reason is the instrument for recognizing it; Scripture is its verifying principle; logical consistency is a negative test for truth and coherence a subordinate test. The task

---

[6] Henry, *God, Revelation and Authority*, 1:229.
[7] Henry, *God, Revelation and Authority*, 1:181–409.
[8] Wayne Grudem, *Systematic Theology: An Introduction to Biblical Doctrine* (Grand Rapids: Zondervan, 1994), 21. Grudem's definition is insufficient and deficient in that it ignores the interplay in all knowing between tradition, reason, and experience.
[9] See John R. Franke, *The Character of Theology: An Introduction to its Nature, Task, and Purpose* (Grand Rapids: Baker, 2005), especially 88-89.

of Christian theology is to exhibit the content of biblical revelation as an orderly whole.[10]

One may enquire about the relationship between Scripture and general revelation, given the epistemological axiom above. Henry states that:

> The scriptural revelation takes epistemological priority over general revelation, not because general revelation is obscure or because man as sinner cannot know it, but because Scripture as an inspired literary document republishes the content of general revelation objectively, over against man's sinful reductive dilutions and misconstructions of it.[11]

It was Henry's conviction that general revelation was sufficient for the independent use of reason for a knowledge of God. He thus believed that special revelation was an objective given. In a 1964 work, *Frontiers in Modern Theology*, Henry, in Grenz's words, "charted an agenda that proved to be an apt summary of his entire theological program":[12] "If Christianity is to win intellectual respectability in the modern world, the reality of the transcendent God must indeed be proclaimed by the theologians – and proclaimed on the basis of man's rational competence to know the transempirical realm."[13]

This is not to say that Henry was an advocate of natural theology; he wasn't. Henry was a biblicist who rigorously upheld the inerrancy and infallibility of Scripture.[14] Thus, right thinking about

---

[10] Henry, *God, Revelation and Authority*, 1:215 (in italics in the original). This is not to deny that the triune God is Christianity's basic ontological axiom. Henry, *God, Revelation and Authority*, 1:219.

[11] Henry, *God, Revelation and Authority*, 1:223.

[12] Grenz, *Renewing the Centre*, 92.

[13] Carl F.H. Henry, *Frontiers in Modern Theology A Critique of Current Theological Trends* (Chicago: Moody, 1964), 154–55, cited in Grenz, *Renewing the Centre*, 92.

[14] For his defence of inerrancy, infallibility, and inspiration see Henry, *God, Revelation and Authority*, 4:103–219. Henry did not, as many other fundamentalist-evangelicals have done, including the ETS, make inerrancy a

God can only be found through Scripture, for here alone one finds the authoritative word of God in objective form. While Henry does allow that revelation is personal, simply because God and humans are personal, his theology amounts to a rejection of personal revelation in favour of an absolute propositional revelation. This is asserted in his Thesis Ten: "God's revelation is rational communication conveyed in intelligible ideas and meaningful words, that is, in conceptual-verbal form."[15] Henry clarifies that he is opposed to all definitions of revelation which are expressed as God's "*self*-revelation, or to *cosmic* revelation, or to *historical* revelation, in express contrast to a divine disclosure of truths and information..."[16] Henry cites Karl Barth and Thomas Torrance as two such champions of the sort of dialectical and existential (read, non-evangelical) theology he is opposed to.

Focusing specifically upon Torrance's doctrine of the knowledge of God drawn largely from his 1969 work *Theological Science*,[17] Henry devotes an entire chapter of *God, Revelation and Authority* to rebutting Torrance's position.[18] In Henry's estimation, Torrance's formulation of what he terms "theologic" is evangelically inadequate and an example of the "unstable neo-Protestant formulation of man's knowledge of God."[19] What exactly Henry takes exception to is Torrance's attempt to relate human logic to the logic of God in a non-formal way.

Acknowledging that Torrance rises above the neo-orthodox (a pejorative and inaccurate term in itself) antithesis of propositional and personal revelation by locating revelation in Jesus Christ,

---

badge of evangelical orthodoxy. See Carl F.H. Henry, "Reaction and Realignment," *Christianity Today* 20 (2 July 1976): 30.

[15] Henry, *God, Revelation and Authority*, 3:248.

[16] Henry, *God, Revelation and Authority*, 3:248.

[17] Thomas F. Torrance, *Theological Science* (London: Oxford University Press, 1969).

[18] Chapter 14, 'The Logos and Human Logic," in Henry, *God, Revelation and Authority*, 3:216-29.

[19] Henry, *God, Revelation and Authority*, 3:216.

himself the Truth and the one who manifests the truth, Henry then accuses Torrance of "unjustifiably converting the fact that God objectifies himself for us and meets us in Jesus Christ into an eclipse of general revelation, a devaluation of the prophetic revelation, and a cognitive deflation of all Logos-revelation."[20] What Henry takes umbrage to is the idea that outside of Jesus there is no knowledge of God.[21] Henry appeals to the Old Testament in the first instance (then after to nature, history, and the conscience), as evidence that God has spoken in propositional form through prophets, kings, priests, and directly in divine manifestations. Henry considers these to be defeating arguments against Torrance's insistence that outside of Christ there is no knowledge of God. But this is to misunderstand Torrance's position that Jesus Christ is epistemologically determinative and thus there is no knowledge of God outside of Jesus Christ, given that Christian theology as a science is posterior to an actual encounter with an actual event.

Henry agrees with Torrance that humanity after the fall is estranged from God and thus cannot think rightly – about God, truth, or reality. However, that does not mean, argues Henry, that we must attribute this to an "epistemic deficiency" in humanity whereby only through regeneration and repentance may one actually know God.[22] Henry then levels his charge against Torrance:

> Torrance here overstates the deformity of human reason in relation to divine revelation; he disregards the general revelation that penetrates man's reason and conscience with the knowledge of God which confronts him consciously with light and truth and knowledge and in relation to which he is culpable. The change in logical structure which a revelation is held to require, it develops, is nothing less than a rejection of the law of

---

[20] Henry, *God, Revelation and Authority*, 3:217.

[21] This is the fourth of Torrance's five points as to what characterises theological science, Torrance, *Theological Science*, 137; and Torrance, *Christian Doctrine of God*, 1.

[22] Henry, *God, Revelation and Authority*, 3:218. See Torrance, *Theological Science*, 147.

contradiction and if that be the case – so we shall argue, against Torrance – nonsense can be regarded as divine truth.[23]

Henry was not one to lack rhetorical flourish or force a point!

Interpreting Torrance accurately, I think, Henry shows that according to Torrance, only Jesus, who is the Logos, can know the truth through human concepts and statements, because Christ is the God-man. For all other people our statements point away from ourselves to some objective truth, but for Christ he is the Truth incarnate thus his statements do not point away from himself but to himself. Torrance can thus say: "Theological knowledge and theological statements participate sacramentally in the mystery of Christ as the Truth."[24] As such revelation is, for Torrance, *uniquely* personal and *uniquely* propositional to Christ, and mediated to others to the extent that they participate in Christ.[25] It is thus faith (revelation) in Christ and not philosophy which forms the conceptual bridge between God and humanity.

What Henry is pushing back against is Torrance's dialogical/dialectical theological method. According to Henry, truth and statements of the truth correspond so that the truth is objectively known despite the condition – fallen or otherwise, Christian or not – of the subject. Henry's correspondence theory of the truth (similar to Wittgenstein's "picture language")[26] comes up squarely against Torrance's realistic theory of the truth. In Henry's

---

[23] Henry, *God, Revelation and Authority*, 3:218.
[24] Torrance, *Theological Science*, 150, cited by Henry, *God, Revelation and Authority*, 3:219.
[25] Torrance, *Theological Science*, 42, 148, cited by Henry, *God, Revelation and Authority*, 3:219.
[26] See David Munchin, *Is Theology a Science? The Nature of the Scientific Enterprise in the Scientific Theology of Thomas Forsyth Torrance and the Anarchic Epistemology of Paul Feyerabend* (Leiden: Brill, 2011), 205–209, for a description of various correspondence theories of truth, including that of Torrance.

estimation, all such dialectical/dialogical reasoning must end up "either saying nothing or of stating gibberish."[27]

Henry also appears to misunderstand Torrance's claim that only those united to Christ genuinely know Christ. Torrance, it seems to me, does not insist that there is no general revelation, simply that general revelation does not provide enough information for the unredeemed person to come to a saving knowledge of God. This is the "new natural theology" which McGrath and Molnar, to name but two, have canvassed.[28] Henry also appears to adopt something of a Thomistic theology of conversion whereby reason acts as a genuine and natural *preambula fidei*, the means by which one is led to faith. Any other view, Henry avers, amounts to fideism – the blind leap of faith, with Kierkegaard mistakenly being the poster child of such a theology. In short, what Henry would seem to take exception to in this part of his argument is Torrance's Reformed doctrine of election whereby faith itself is a gift imparted to the believer. In relation to the work and role of human reason, Henry is a semi-Pelagian as opposed to Torrance's Reformational *sola gratia* and *sola fidei* commitments. In Henry's best estimation, "the insistence on a logical gulf between human conceptions and God as the object of religious knowledge is erosive of knowledge and cannot escape a reduction to scepticism."[29] And finally, "We are therefore back to the emphasis that the laws of logic belong to the *imago Dei*, and have ontological import."[30]

Henry is particularly critical of what he sees as the illogical presuppositions of Torrance's intuitive theology. Torrance rejects the form of propositional revelation espoused by Henry in favour of a "personal knowing." Reality is to be known in faith through an existential encounter with the ultimate Reality – Jesus Christ the

---

[27] Henry, *God, Revelation and Authority*, 3:221.
[28] See Alister E. McGrath, *The Open Secret: A New Vision for Natural Theology* (Oxford: Blackwell, 2008); and Paul D. Molnar, *Thomas F. Torrance: Theologian of the Trinity* (Farnham: Ashgate, 2009), 93–99.
[29] Henry, *God, Revelation and Authority*, 3:229.
[30] Henry, *God, Revelation and Authority*, 3:229.

incarnate Word (Logos). Henry believes this amounts to mysticism, something he is not favourably disposed to.[31]

Henry sees the critical mistake of Torrance's epistemology, derived in part from Kierkegaard but more from Polanyi, to lie in his seeming rejection of any objective revelational knowledge. From Kierkegaard, Torrance is committed to the idea that the truth of God is communicated through personal relations, not, as Henry would have it, "objectively" and even dispassionately.[32] However, Torrance holds that theology which accepts the absolute primacy of its proper object of inquiry can be considered rational and scientific – hence objective. Torrance understands Kierkegaard's "truth as Subjectivity" as in fact theological objectivity and realism, the subject's proper relation to the Object.

Henry appears to misread Torrance (and Polanyi) also at this point and interprets the notion of "personal knowledge," which acknowledges the necessity for "responsible commitment" – Polanyi's term for personal knowledge – in terms of subjectiv*ism*. This is especially so when "personal knowledge" is applied to religious knowing and is virtually equated with biblical "faith."

Utilizing as he does Polanyi's epistemology, Torrance would no doubt react to this criticism that Henry, and other critics, are perhaps looking to an impersonal procedure which operates along detached and mechanical lines and ultimately appeals to the concept of autonomous reason. This autonomous reason is then directed at an external authority, in this religious case the Holy Scriptures, and

---

[31] On mysticism see Myk Habets, "T.F. Torrance: Mystical Theologian *Sui Generis*," *Princeton Theological Review* 14 (2008): 91–104. Also see the brief discussion in Titus Chung, *Thomas Torrance's Mediations and Revelation* (Farnham: Ashgate, 2011), 127–29.

[32] For an interesting insight into how Torrance articulated some of these convictions in response to a liberal Christian methodology see the account of his job interview for Princeton University in I. John Hesselink, "A Pilgrimage in the School of Christ – An Interview with T.F. Torrance," in *Reformed Review* 38 (1984): 54–55; and Alister E. McGrath, *T.F. Torrance: An Intellectual Biography* (Edinburgh: T. & T. Clark, 1999), 57-58.

a system of propositional truth is worked out in a purely impersonal but logical way. It is this program that Torrance is particularly concerned to eradicate.

This use of Polanyi further explains Torrance's form of realism in his theological method. It is this commitment to *critical* realism that constitutes one of Torrance's main reasons for drawing on the work of Polanyi. In Polanyi, Torrance finds a philosophical ally and one who has illustrated Torrance's own point in the natural sciences as Torrance is seeking to do in Christian theology.

Not only is Polanyi appealed to, but also the theological method of Athanasius, Anselm of Canterbury, John Calvin, and not least, Karl Barth. Throughout his reading of the tradition Torrance develops what he calls a *kata physic* form of theological methodology which is as applicable to the sciences as it is to the humanities, and here specifically to systematic theology. An overview of Torrance's theology illustrates his methodology and an examination of his use of Scripture in particular highlights the fundamental differences between the fundamentalist orientation of Henry's – and popular evangelicalism's – theological methodology and biblical hermeneutics.

As can be gleaned from this brief survey of Henry's critique of Torrance's theological method, Henry's theology may be characterised as rationalist, foundationalist, and nominalist, at least to some extent. As Grenz observed, Gordon H. Clark, Henry's professor of philosophy when he was a young student at Wheaton College, was perhaps the single most important intellectual influence on Henry's thought, giving it its rationalist-oriented worldview.[33] Not all would agree with this assessment though. "Put simply, if the term 'foundationalist' is to be applied to Henry's

---

[33] Grenz, *Renewing the Centre*, 90.

theological outlook, his sounds more like that of a soft than a hard foundationalist,"³⁴ writes Mavis Leung. Chad Brand agrees:

> Is Henry a foundationalist? If one means by 'foundationalist,' the search for Cartesian certainty through the discovery of indubitable and noninferential truth claims arrived at through reason or reflection, then the answer is a resounding, 'no'... It might be correct, on the other hand, to call Henry a scriptural foundationalist...³⁵

And further,

> In regards to Scripture, Henry is certainly a firm, biblical foundationalist; in regards to the outworking of the theological implications of biblical asseverations, it appears that Henry is a soft foundationalist, one who is willing to admit that all our claims to understanding are subject to... God's judgment.³⁶

Wider critique of T.F. Torrance

Henry is not alone in his critique of Torrance and others who adopt a similar theological method. One example will be useful, that of an appreciative critic of Torrance's, Colin Gunton. Gunton tells us that he first met Torrance at a student conference in 1963 when Gunton was a student and Torrance was a keynote speaker. Since then the two men were known to each other and respected each other's work, despite disagreeing on many points. Gunton later organised a day conference in Torrance's honour at the King's College's Research Institute in Systematic Theology, and he contributed to a volume of essays interacting with Torrance's theology edited by Elmer Colyer

---

³⁴ Mavis M. Leung, "With What is Evangelicalism to Penetrate the World? A Study of Carl Henry's Envisioned Evangelicalism," *Trinity Journal* 27NS (2006): 240.
³⁵ Chad O. Brand, "Is Carl Henry a Modernist? Rationalism and Foundationalism in Post-War Evangelical Theology," *Trinity Journal* 20NS (1999): 18.
³⁶ Brand, "Is Carl Henry a Modernist?" 19.

in 2001. Torrance's doctrine of God was the subject of Gunton's appreciative critique,[37] and of a short response by Torrance.[38]

Gunton's critique of Torrance's method is best explored through his published lectures *Revelation and Reason*, where Torrance's idea of "theological science" is critiqued in chapter 2, §2.[39] The focus of Gunton's lectures is on the relationship between revelation and reason. In the wake of Enlightenment philosophy revelation was consigned to the periphery of human knowledge, if not rejected outright, and in its place reason assumed the centre. Whereas the Patristic thinkers simply assumed divine revelation, post-Enlightenment theology felt it had to establish a basis from which revelation could be accepted and then utilised by human reason. Thus it was that foundationalism found its way into theology. Gunton refers to this as "faith seeking foundations," a phrase coined by Ronald Thiemann, and an obvious play on Anselm's "faith seeking understanding." Gunton is using a definition of foundationalism as the proposition that every coherent belief system rests upon certain convictions. These convictions are assumed to be true, or even self-evident, and thus provide stability for the framework of belief. The coherence of many other beliefs depends upon the acceptance of these beliefs as true.[40] In his use of

---

[37] Colin Gunton, "Being and Person: T.F. Torrance's Doctrine of God," in *The Promise of Trinitarian Theology: Theologians in Dialogue with T.F. Torrance* (ed. Elmer M. Colyer; Lanham: Rowman & Littlefield, 2001), 115-37. Paul Molnar has provided a thorough critique of Gunton's essay in *Divine Freedom and the Doctrine of the Immanent Trinity: in Dialogue with Karl Barth and Contemporary Theology* (London: T. & T. Clark, 2002), 317-30.

[38] Thomas F. Torrance, "Thomas Torrance Responds," in *The Promise of Trinitarian Theology*, 303-40.

[39] Colin Gunton, *Revelation and Reason: Prolegomena to Systematic Theology* (trans. and ed. Paul. H. Brazier; London: T. & T. Clark, 2008), 49–51; also see pp. 33–36. The work is based on tape recordings of a seminar programme for MA students given by Gunton at King's College, London, 1999–2000.

[40] Gunton is using the definition provided by Ronald F. Thiemann, *Revelation and Theology: The Gospel as Narrated Promise* (Notre Dame: University of Notre Dame Press, 1985), 13–15. Thiemann's work is critical of Torrance's

Thiemann, Gunton believes Torrance is a foundationalist of a sort in that he grounds revelation in the ability to explain causally revelation as coming from God; thus belief in God is the foundation. According to Gunton, "By intuition Torrance does mean, well, integrity, a kind of integration of data rather than leaping into another world [revelation]. There is a very rationalistic side to Tom Torrance; he would use a foundationalist argument if he could."[41] It is unclear in the context what Gunton means exactly by this last phrase, "if he could." He goes on to say that Locke and Schleiermacher are certainly foundationalist, thus we may aver that he thinks Torrance is a qualified foundationalist of some sort.

When Gunton turns his attention to Torrance directly he examines his use of "science" to describe his theological method. Science in this context is the activity in which we observe objects and reduce the description of their workings into a coherent explanation. Thus Torrance allows God the Object to impose himself on us rather than appealing to philosophical foundations or some such. By means of a Polanyian integration, the scientist then integrates all the evidence into a logical coherence. Thus Torrance reads from the Object (God) to the subject (the enquiring mind).

Later in the work, under a discussion of Vatican II, Gunton provides a chart in which Torrance's view of revelation as an act and an event is pictured. In it Gunton explains that when revelation means Jesus Christ it is different from revelation as a series of propositions.[42] And so, when we come to ask if revelation is personal or propositional, as Henry does, unless Torrance's twofold view of revelation is acknowledged, there is going to be confusion.

"epistemological foundationalism" and in its place a coherentist account of epistemology is offered. For a critical interaction see Tom McCall, "Ronald Thiemann, Thomas Torrance and Epistemological Doctrines of Revelation," *International Journal of Systematic Theology* 6 (2004): 148–68.

[41] Gunton, *Revelation and Reason*, 35.

[42] Gunton, *Revelation and Reason*, 98. This distinction approximates Torrance's distinction between "coherence-statements" and "existence-statements" in Torrance, *Theological Science*, 164–72.

It will appear that Torrance does not believe in propositional revelation, leaving many evangelicals to assume that Torrance is merely a more sophisticated mystical theologian for whom doctrine is either Gnosticism on the one hand, known only to the initiated (something we have seen Henry accuse Torrance of in other words); or one is a liberal or postmodern theologian for whom there is no truth but only personal experience. Torrance is neither.[43]

Gunton contrasts Torrance's view with that of Roman Catholicism, even post-Vatican II. According to the latter view God's personal act presupposes all our traditions and our writings such that church tradition must be considered as authoritative as Scripture, given both affirm the same content of propositional truth. If we were to apply this to Henry and some other evangelicals then we would have to conclude that a commitment to a strong propositional revelation that is not nuanced in the twofold way that it is by Torrance necessarily ends up in a form of narrow foundationalism so that classic Roman Catholicism and fundamentalist-evangelicalism are actually operating out of the same theological methodology and epistemology.

So much for the evaluation and critique of Torrance by Henry and others. It will pay us to consider Torrance's theological methodology directly before forming some critical conclusions.

T.F. Torrance vs. Carl Henry

In 1981 Torrance presented the Payton Lectures at Fuller Theological Seminary (subsequently published as *Reality and Evangelical Theology*), wherein he was "concerned to establish a realist basis in evangelical theology in contrast with the nominalism

---

[43] Interestingly, in Torrance's opinion the fundamentalist and the liberal are not that far removed from each other when it comes to their epistemic commitments in that they both share "a fatal deistic disjunction between God and the World" in that they both cut short the ontological reference of biblical and theological statements to God. See Thomas F. Torrance, *Space, Time and Resurrection* (Edinburgh: T. & T. Clark, 1998), 2–3.

that prevails so widely among so-called 'evangelicals'!"[44] While at Fuller Theological Seminary, Torrance singled out evangelical doyen, Carl Henry, as one such evangelical. In answer to a student's question on the extent of the atonement Torrance replied:

> You see there is nowhere in the Christian faith, there is no such thing as partial representation, as partial substitution. It's a total act and therefore the total being comes under the death and resurrection of Christ and therefore under the judgement of the cross. So that you, whether you are good or evil – Christ died for you. Now for you with your good as well as your evil comes under the judgment of the cross. Now that applies to the whole of creation. That applies to this creation that God made to be good but which has become estranged from him. So there you have to take seriously, dead seriously, the fact that the Creator became creature made atonement for the whole creation, consecrated the whole creation for God, not part of it. Now this is very important, you see.
>
> Carl Henry, for example, in a discussion with me on this very issue, would not agree that Christ died for all of him. There is still an integrity in his reason that doesn't come under the judgement of the cross, you see. So I said to him, Carl Henry do you believe in a partial substitution, and therefore there is something in your reason Carl Henry, that hasn't really come under the judgement of the cross of Christ. And that's why you are a rationalist.
>
> So you see that is the point; and this is where the Gospel comes at its hardest. It's a good man, a righteous man, a man who is rich in goodness, it's as impossible for him to be saved as it is a camel to go through the eye of a needle. And yet that's possible for God, you see. And so the more we cling to our rationality,

---

[44] Torrance, "A Pilgrimage in the School of Christ – An Interview with T.F. Torrance," 60.

the more we cling to our goodness, the more difficult it is for us to have salvation.[45]

Torrance, it appears to me, is accurate in his assessment of Henry. According to Henry, the fall affects the will and not the mind: "Man wills," writes Henry, "not to know God in truth, and makes religious reflection serviceable to moral revolt. But he is still capable of intellectually analyzing rational evidence for the truth-value of assertions about God."[46]

Echoing the same critique, Donald Bloesch rightly observed that Carl Henry and other fundamentalist-evangelicals provided a "transcendence in ontology but not in epistemology, for they are confident that human reason can lay hold of the truth of divine revelation apart from special grace."[47] He then outlines a four-stage taxonomy of ways in which contemporary Christianity has sought to respond to the challenges of modernity. Carl Henry is allocated to stage one, a theology of restoration which Bloesch characterises as a return to the rationalistic idealism of the early Enlightenment: "In this approach we arrive at truth by beginning with universal principles and then proceeding to deduce particular conclusions."[48]

Like Torrance and Bloesch, John Webster makes a trenchant and enlightened case for the need for reason itself to be sanctified and converted if it is to be of use in thinking theologically. "Christian theology is an aspect of reason's sanctification… good Christian theology can only happen if it is rooted in the

---

[45] Thomas F. Torrance, "The Ground and Grammar of Theology," lectures given at Fuller Theological Seminary, 1981: Lecture 6, Q & A, 20.54-22.42. Transcribed from the audio available at Online: http://www.gci.org/audio/torrance [cited 13 November 2011].

[46] Henry, *God, Revelation and Authority*, 1:226–27. Henry locates the *imago Dei* in the cognitive capacity of humanity and does not see this as inoperative after the Fall. See Henry, *God, Revelation and Authority*, 1:394, 405; 2:136.

[47] Donald G. Bloesch, *A Theology of Word and Spirit: Authority and Method in Theology* (Downers Grove: IVP, 1992), 252.

[48] Bloesch, *A Theology of Word and Spirit*, 253. Bloesch identifies the influence of Gordon Clark on Henry, along with the influence of Descartes and Leibniz.

reconciliation of reason by the sanctifying presence of God."[49] This is a central point which Henry misses, even rejects. According to Henry, reason is a natural faculty seemingly unaffected by the Fall, and as such, reason is not involved in the drama of God's saving work. As Webster notes of this approach, "Consequently, 'natural' reason has been regarded as 'transcendent' reason."[50] "Holy reason is eschatological reason,"[51] argues Webster. Torrance accepts the basic orientation of Webster's claims with his dialectical/dialogical method in theology.

Gunton too, follows this basic epistemological stance in discussing Christian claims to knowledge. Gunton glosses 1 Cor 1:22: "For Jews demand signs and Greeks desire wisdom, but we proclaim Christ crucified, a stumbling-block to Jews and foolishness to Gentiles, but to those who are the called, both Jews and Greeks, Christ the power of God and the wisdom of God," as: 'Modernists seek certainty; postmodernists deny it? What do we claim and proclaim?"[52] We proclaim Christ, of course. But knowledge which comes by faith is of a different sort, or at least requires a different epistemic orientation – that which comes by faith.

Torrance directly accuses Henry of being a nominalist in his insistence that revelation is propositional and not also personal. Then follows an example: "This paper is white" is not the truth, according to Torrance, but is a statement about the truth; however, according to Henry, "This paper is white" is truth itself. Torrance is thus a metaphysical realist against Henry's nominalism, presumably in the sense that Torrance thinks Henry rejects universals. Torrance then draws a comparison with law when he says, "I thought lawyers would have seen through this much clearly and more early." Juridical law is based upon actual law and is utterly consistent. A clue is thus found in juridical law – law testifies to actual Law which imposes itself upon us. Thus it may be that Torrance's little book on

---

[49] John Webster, *Holiness* (Grand Rapids: Eerdmans, 2003), 10.
[50] Webster, *Holiness*, 10.
[51] Webster, *Holiness*, 12.
[52] Gunton, *Revelation and Reason*, 17.

juridical law may say more about his hermeneutics and method than has previously been thought.[53]

In Tom McCall's estimation Torrance is a modest foundationalist.[54] While this, in McCall's opinion, is better than Thiemann's coherentism, it is not without its problems. He writes:

> Torrance's epistemological foundationalism will likely continue to draw criticism from his detractors… but the general position seems to be a stable one. If there is a problem with his theology of revelation it will appear when he relates his doctrine of revelation to scripture."[55]

McCall was on the money, as they say, and Henry was one such detractor to make this point. It is thus to Torrance's doctrines of knowledge, revelation, and Scripture that we turn.

Critical realism

For Torrance the truth can be known and apprehended by the human person and this knowledge represents a genuine disclosure of that which is real. Christian theology and natural science operate with an understanding of knowledge which has its "ontological foundations in objective reality." Torrance develops his critical realism in two directions, first, from natural science, especially in the work of John Philoponos, Clerk Maxwell, Albert Einstein, and Michael Polanyi, and second, from theology, especially in the work of Athanasius, Anselm, and Barth. Torrance argues that theology and the sciences share a common commitment to a realist epistemology (given an ordered universe), with each responding

---

[53] Thomas F. Torrance, *Juridical Law and Physical Law: Toward a Realist Foundation for Human Law* (Eugene: Wipf and Stock, 1997). In this work it is legal positivism Torrance is reacting to with his realist epistemology.

[54] McCall, "Ronald Thiemann, Thomas Torrance and Epistemological Doctrines of Revelation," 164–165.

[55] McCall, "Ronald Thiemann, Thomas Torrance and Epistemological Doctrines of Revelation," 165.

appropriately to their respective objects of study (*kata physin*).[56] Each of these disciplines recognises

> the impossibility of separating out the way in which knowledge arises from the actual knowledge that it attains. Thus in theology the canons of inquiry that are discerned in the process of knowing are not separable from the body of actual knowledge out of which they arise. In the nature of the case a true and adequate account of theological epistemology cannot be gained apart from substantial exposition of the content of the knowledge of God, and of the knowledge of man and the world as creatures of God… this means that all through theological inquiry we must operate with an *open* epistemology in which we allow the way of our knowing to be clarified and modified *pari passu* with advance in deeper and fuller knowledge of the object, and that we will be unable to set forth an account of that way of knowing in advance but only by looking back from what has been established as knowledge.[57]

Torrance has a particularly high regard for the work of Einstein and often returns to his scientific insights as illustrations of a realist epistemology in practice. From Einstein's "scientific realism" Torrance sees great application for theology through the means of a "critical realism." Accepting the legitimate status of epistemic realism, what is the nature of correspondence between Reality and our understanding of it? The question of correspondence theories of truth is of great importance to our discussion.[58]

---

[56] Alister McGrath characterises Torrance's method as "scientific realism," in *Reality* (*A Scientific Theology*, vol. 2; London: T. & T. Clark, 2002), 130. The alternative to scientific realism would be constructive empiricism, whereby theories are empirically adequate but may not necessarily correspond to reality.

[57] Torrance, *Theological Science*, 10.

[58] See the discussion of Torrance's christocentric analogy in regards to a "created correspondence" in Roland Spjuth, *Creation, Contingency and Divine Presence: In the Theologies of Thomas F. Torrance and Eberhard Jüngel* (Lund: Lund University Press, 1995), 47–57.

Torrance does not advocate a scientific positivism which argues for a direct correspondence between concepts and experience. He made this clear when he wrote:

> The fundamental difficulty with abstractive and positivist science... is that it operates with a logical bridge between concepts and experience, both at the start and the finish, that is, in the derivation of concepts from the universe as we experience it and in the verificatory procedures relating concepts back to experience... This is not only a difficulty, but an impossibility, for this is not and cannot be any logical bridge between ideas and existence. There is indeed a deep and wonderful correlation between concepts and experience, and science operates with that correlation everywhere, but since there is no logical bridge the scientist does not work with rules for inductive procedures, and cannot finally verify his claims to have discovered the structures of reality by logical means.[59]

Torrance also rejects a "naïve realism" in which there is a direct correspondence between knowledge and reality.[60] What Torrance does advocate is a "critical realism."[61] Perhaps one of the better known advocates of critical realism in biblical theology today is that of N.T. Wright. In his 1992 work he defines critical realism as:

> A way of describing the process of "knowing" that acknowledges the *reality of the thing known, as something other than the knower* (hence "realism"), while also fully acknowledging that the only

---

[59] Thomas F. Torrance, *Reality and Scientific Theology* (Edinburgh: Scottish Academic Press, 1985), 76.

[60] See Spjuth, *Creation, Contingency and Divine Presence*, 94–101. With a phrase borrowed from Nancy Murphy, Spjuth characterizes Torrance's critical realism as "chastened modern" (98).

[61] See Paul M. Achtemeier, "The Truth of Tradition: Critical Realism in the Thought of Alasdair MacIntyre and T.F. Torrance," *Scottish Journal of Theology* 47 (1996): 355–74; John D. Morrison, "Heidegger, Correspondence Truth and the Realist Theology of Thomas Forsyth Torrance," *Evangelical Quarterly* 69 (1997): 139–55; John D. Morrison, *Knowledge of the Self-Revealing God in the Thought of Thomas Forsyth Torrance* (Bern: Peter Lang, 1997).

access we have to this reality lies along the spiralling path of *appropriate dialogue or conversation between the knower and the thing known* (hence "critical"). This path leads to critical reflection on the products of our enquiry into "reality", so that our assertions about "reality" acknowledge their own provisionality. Knowledge, in other words, although in principle concerning reality is independent of the knower, is never itself independent of the knower.[62]

Unless Torrance is misunderstood, we must understand that realism involves at least three elements, identified by Andrew Moore as: ontological (realism vs. idealism); epistemological (realism vs. empiricism); and semantic (realism vs. linguistic idealism).[63] These three elements are distinct and confusion often results in insufficiently distinguishing between them. David Munchin observes, "The debate concerning realism becomes therefore a matter of epistemic degrees…"[64] So Torrance asserts:

> Belief is not something that is freely chosen or arbitrary, that is, without evidential grounds, for that would be highly subjective, a mere fancy. Nor is it something hypothetical or conditional, for then it would not be genuine, since we would entertain it, as it were, with our fingers crossed. Rather does belief arise in us, as we have seen, because it is thrust upon us by the nature of the reality with which we are in experiential contact. It arises as we allow our minds to fall under the compelling power of an intelligible structure or order inherent in the nature of things which we cannot rationally or in good conscience resist.[65]

---

[62] Nicholas T. Wright, *The New Testament and the People of God* (London: SPCK, 1992), 35.

[63] Andrew Moore, *Realism and Christian Faith: God, Grammar and Meaning* (Cambridge: Cambridge University Press, 2003), 1.

[64] Munchin, *Is Theology a Science?* 190.

[65] Thomas F. Torrance, *Belief in Science and in Christian Life: The Relevance of Michael Polanyi's Thought for Christian Faith and Life* (Edinburgh: Handsel, 1980), 13.

This leads us to ask about the relationship between Scripture and theology within Torrance's scientific theology.

Scripture and dogmatics

There is an inseparable relation between Scripture and dogmatics for Torrance, which may be explained around three interrelated movements. First, dogmatics explains Scripture and Scripture explains Christ. Second, Christ explains Scripture. Third, dogmatics is only rightly conducted when Christ is rightly known.[66] As a consequence, Scripture stands in a middle relation between Christ and dogmatics, as the mediator of Christ, but it needs illumination itself from both ends, from Christ and from dogmatics. The result is that Christ the Word is known both through and in the Word written, which means the written Word has a unique and normative authority in our knowledge of him.

There is a *theological* reason for Torrance's method. For Torrance revelation is always divine self-disclosure in which God communicates *himself* to his creatures. This self-revelation was made decisively through the Incarnation. Scripture thus plays a secondary (but indispensable) role to the self-revelation of God through Christ. In Torrance's theology revelation determines both Scripture and the *depositum fide*. The *depositum fide* is a gracious work of God in which knowledge of God through Christ is made possible in a personal and participatory way in the knower.

While Scripture is an imperfect and inadequate text, when it is appropriated by God's full, final and Holy Word, Jesus Christ, it is made to serve his reconciling revelation and infallible communication of his truth. Thus, explicating the relationship between the Word incarnate and the Word written becomes one of Torrance's central tasks. In a sermon on Matthew 18:1-22, "Christ in the Midst of His Church," Torrance narrates the relationship

---

[66] These relations are articulated in Robert T. Walker, "Editor's Foreword," in Thomas F. Torrance, *Incarnation: The Person and Life of Christ* (ed. Robert T. Walker; Milton Keynes: Paternoster, 2008), xxvi.

between Christ and Scripture by means of a meditation on the fact of "Christ in us." Christ lodges permanently within us by means of his Word, but they are more than merely human words, they are "creative words," "personal words," "life-giving words" which create personal communion and presence, they "germinate in the human heart and create room for Christ there."[67] Christ and Holy Scripture are in such an intimate union that Torrance can say:

> It is as we allow the Word of the Gospel to saturate our minds and imaginations, to penetrate into our memories, and to master all our thinking, that Christ is born within us, that all that He is and has done becomes, as it were, imprinted upon us within, and becomes so truly and permanently the very centre of our being that we are transformed into His image and likeness, and even partake of His nature.[68]

Here the goal of Scripture is clearly stated,[69] related as it is to the Word incarnate. We also begin to see how Torrance clarifies how the Christological analogy and the Chalcedonian formula are integral to his understanding of the relation between the Word written and the Living Word.[70]

Between realism and idealism

Torrance's use of Scripture avoids a fundamentalist and Roman Catholic foundationalism on the one hand, and on the other hand, a liberal and neo-Protestant idealism; both approaches Torrance considers to be mistaken.[71] In relation to fundamentalist-

---

[67] Thomas F. Torrance, "Christ in the Midst of His Church," in *When Christ Comes and Comes Again* (London: Hodder and Stoughton, 1957), 110.

[68] Torrance, "Christ in the Midst of His Church," 110.

[69] For more on the ultimate goal of salvation see Myk Habets, *Theosis in the Theology of Thomas Torrance* (Surrey: Ashgate, 2009).

[70] For his articulation of this point see Thomas F. Torrance, *Atonement: The Person and Work of Christ* (ed. Robert T. Walker; Downers Grove: IVP, 2009), 333–40.

[71] Torrance deals with both fundamentalism and liberalism on many occasions. See for instance Thomas F. Torrance, *God and Rationality* (London: Oxford

evangelicalism, Christian dogmas or doctrines are not to be read directly off the pages of Scripture in a propositionalist kind of way:

> The assumption that the Scriptures are impregnated with universal, changeless divine truths which can be read off the sentential sequences of the inspired text, provided that it is properly or authoritatively interpreted, is admittedly the view that was long held, and often still is held, by Roman Catholic and Protestant fundamentalism alike.[72]

Fundamentalisms of this sort result in a position in which faith is placed *in* Scripture directly rather than in that to which Scripture bears witness – God's being and act. To mistake the text of Scripture for the truths they seek to reveal is to adopt some form of nominalism or extreme realism.[73] According to Torrance:

> in a scientific theology, on the contrary, we are concerned not with thinking thoughts, far less with thinking statements themselves, but with thinking realities through thoughts and statements, and with developing an understanding of God from his self-revelation mediated to us by the Holy Scriptures in the Church, in which the connections we think are objectively and

---

University Press, 1971), 36; *Space, Time and Resurrection*, 1-26; and *Reality and Evangelical Theology* (Downers Grove: IVP, 1999), 52-83. Barth avoided both positions as well but in Hunsinger's words he labelled the two extremes "literalism" and "expressivism." See George Hunsinger, "Beyond Literalism and Expressivism: Karl Barth's Hermeneutical Realism," in *Disruptive Grace: Studies in the Theology of Karl Barth* (Grand Rapids: Eerdmans, 2000), 210-25. In his own work John Webster labels both poles as objectification and spiritualisation respectively, and argues that both are pneumatologically deficient. See Webster, *Holy Scripture*, 33-36.

[72] Torrance, *Space, Time and Resurrection*, 7-8. Similar ideas are expressed in Torrance, *Reality and Evangelical Theology*, see especially 17.

[73] As background to Torrance's discussion on truthfulness and the Truth see Thomas F. Torrance, "Truth and Authority: Theses on Truth," *Irish Theological Quarterly* 39 (1972): 215-42, especially thesis 5. Torrance's commitment to critical realism is also at play here.

ontologically controlled by the intrinsic connections of God's *self*-communication as Father, Son and Holy Spirit.[74]

The second position Torrance distances himself from is that of liberalism or neo-Protestantism in which Christian dogmas or doctrines are reached by simple empirical observations of uninterpreted facts, that is, simply existentially.[75] This form of neo-Protestantism is considered the by-product of the scientific world of Newton. This was a radically dualist conception of science that carried over into theology, exemplified, as Torrance notes, by Hermann's distinction between *Geschichte* and *Historie*.[76]

Depth exegesis

In distancing himself from these two positions Torrance argues that what the theologian is really seeking to do is to penetrate the depths of meaning that Scripture is witness to. Thus a genuinely theological reading of Scripture is attempted. The theologian "operates with the whole apostolic tradition in its stratified depth in order to allow himself to be directed from all sides to the objective realities under the creative impact of which all the apostolic tradition incorporated in the New Testament took its rise and shape in the primitive church."[77] Throughout this process the theologian is under the influence of the self-revelation of God in Jesus Christ

---

[74] Torrance, *Space, Time and Resurrection*, 8.

[75] Torrance believes contemporary existentialists to have distorted the referring function of language so that people are thrown back upon themselves to supply meaning, something already seen in the late medieval times. Torrance concludes that modern exegesis has much in common with the allegorical exegesis of the Augustinian tradition and that "as we look back upon allegorical exegesis with a little pathetic ridicule, so they in the days ahead will look back upon modern existentialist exegesis with the same sort of pathetic ridicule because it was oblique and rejected the *intentio recta*." Torrance, "Truth and Authority," 221, cf. 219.

[76] Torrance, *Space, Time and Resurrection*, 8-9; and *Preaching Christ Today* (Grand Rapids: Eerdmans, 1994), 42-43.

[77] Torrance, *Space, Time and Resurrection*, 10.

and the Holy Spirit, through Scripture and beyond. This process involves a form of spiralling upwards from one level to another as successive layers of meaning and order are uncovered. This is the essence of Torrance's depth exegesis, realist hermeneutics, and theological interpretation of Scripture.[78]

Torrance is highly indebted to Barth's doctrine of Scripture, especially his 1930 work on Anselm, *Fides Quaerens Intellectum*, which Torrance considers to be the turning point in Barth's theological method.[79] Scripture contains a word of God in rational form. This word is not an end in itself but is accompanied by the living Word of God in the *event* of revelation.[80] Due to this event true knowledge of the Object of our study is also true knowledge of the Subject – God himself. This involves penetrating into its inner

---

[78] See Richardson, "Revelation, Scripture, and Mystical Apprehension of Divine Knowledge," 185-203; and Colyer, *The Nature of Doctrine in T.F. Torrance's Theology*. I am aware that the metaphors suggest an incompatible spiralling "upwards" and a burrowing "downwards," but these are simply analogies and thus spatial imagery is just that, imagery.

[79] Thomas F. Torrance, *Karl Barth: An Introduction to His Early Theology, 1910-1931* (1962 repr.; Edinburgh: T. & T. Clark, 2000), 183.

[80] See the articulation of this in Karl Barth, *Church Dogmatics* [hereafter *CD*] (4 vols; Edinburgh: T. & T. Clark, 1956-1975), I/1, 113. According to a Barthian exposition of revelation as event which Torrance subscribes to, "the term revelation refers *not to the objective self-manifestation alone, but equally to the act of faith in which it is heard and received and obeyed.*" Trevor Hart, *Regarding Karl Barth: Toward a Reading of his Theology* (Downers Grove: IVP, 1999), 30 (italics in original). See Christina Baxter, "The Nature and Place of Scripture in the Church Dogmatics," in *Theology Beyond Christendom: Essays on the Centenary of the Birth of Karl Barth* (ed. John Thompson; Allison Park: Pickwick, 1986), 35. In a sermon Torrance explains this event when he says, "That is how God always speaks to us, not directly out of the blue, as it were, nor simply through the witness of others. It is when both these come together, the vertical Word of God from above, and the horizontal witness of others, that we know God and hear His Word personally and directly for ourselves." Torrance, "The Lamb of God," in *When Christ Comes and Comes Again*, 56.

rationality: the practice of depth exegesis.[81] Elsewhere Torrance refers to depth exegesis as a "cross-level movement of thought" in which we understand the text and the *realities* to which it bears witness.[82] It is also a "bi-polarity" (dialectic) between the words and the Word, the worldly form of revelation and its divine content that renders Scripture a *witness* to the self-revelation of God.[83] Torrance traces his method of depth exegesis back to the Athanasian difference between *lalia* and *Logos*, according to which the *lalia* or human words are to be interpreted in terms of the *Logos*.[84] On other occasions Torrance refers to this method as a "stereoscopic" reading of Scripture in which the *scope* of the Bible means its sacramental frame of reference, so that we must look not only at the text of Scripture but through it to the reality it signifies. When theologically interpreted, Jesus Christ becomes the *skopos* of the Bible.[85] Torrance is explicit at this point:

> Strictly speaking Christ himself is the scope of the Scriptures, so that it is only through focusing constantly upon him, dwelling in his Word and assimilating his Mind, that the interpreter can discern the real meaning of the Scriptures. What is required then is a theological interpretation of the Scriptures under the

---

[81] The term "depth exegesis" is taken from William Manson. See Torrance, *God and Rationality*, 110; and Thomas F. Torrance, "Introduction," in William Manson, *Jesus and the Christian* (London: James Clarke & Co, 1967), 9-14. The idea, however, is directly attributed by Torrance to the Greek Fathers. See Thomas F. Torrance, "Introduction: Biblical Hermeneutics and General Hermeneutics," in *Divine Meaning: Studies in Patristic Hermeneutics* (Edinburgh: T. & T. Clark, 1995), 5.

[82] Thomas F. Torrance, *Reality and Evangelical Theology* (Downers Grove: IVP, 1999), 99.

[83] T.F. Torrance, *Karl Barth: Biblical and Evangelical Theologian* (Edinburgh: T. & T. Clark, 1990), 111-12.

[84] See Torrance, *Space, Time and Resurrection*, 5, 167.

[85] This is articulated in Torrance, *Reality and Evangelical Theology*, 100-107; *Space, Time and Resurrection*, 166-169; and *Theology in Reconstruction* (Grand Rapids: Eerdmans, 1965), 88-89.

direction of their ostensive reference to God's self-revelation in Jesus Christ and within the general perspective of faith.[86]

Accordingly, the function of theological understanding or *intelligere* is the act of reading (*legere*) the text embedded within (*intus*) the object. Torrance remarks:

> God reveals himself to us by his Word in the Holy Scriptures, but our task in reading the outward text is to get at its inner meaning and basis, to read it at the deeper level of the solid truth on which the text rests. By a special act of the understanding that goes beyond mere reading, we penetrate into the objective *ratio* of the Word which enlightens and informs us.[87]

Ratio carries within it a three-fold sense: first, it refers to the means we employ (noetic *ratio*); and, second, the end of our quest (ontic *ratio*); but ultimately, third, to the transcendent rationality of God behind all this (*ratio veritatis* or *ratio* of God). "*Ratio* is used then in a dimension of depth," writes Torrance, "of the ultimate Truth, the *ratio* of God himself; of the words and acts of God in Revelation, the *ratio* proper to the object of faith; and of man's knowledge of the object, the knowing *ratio* which corresponds to the *ratio* of the object."[88]

This final *ratio veritatis* is identical with God's being; it is the Divine Word consubstantial with the Father. Theological activity is derived from and is determined by the activity of God himself in his Word, for it is that Word (Christ) communicated through Holy Scripture which is the real object of our knowledge. When our statements are simply and formally identical with statements of the text of Scripture in which Christ speaks his Word to us, they are directly authoritative. Any other theological statements have a derived and thus lesser authority status and are constantly open to revision in light of the Word of God. Recall the distinction of

---

[86] Torrance, *Reality and Evangelical Theology*, 107.
[87] Torrance, *Karl Barth: An Introduction to His Early Theology*, 186.
[88] Torrance, *Karl Barth: An Introduction to His Early Theology*, 187.

Vanhoozer's between the magisterial authority of Holy Scripture and the ministerial authority of churchly interpretations.[89] But theology is not content merely to recite or repeat biblical texts but rather seeks to make statements about the truth revealed in the inner text, and so must seek a conformity to the truth at a deeper level beyond formal conformity to the external text. "Hence, scientific theological activity begins where straightforward biblical quotations end, precisely because it is the task of theology to penetrate to the solid truth upon which biblical statements rest."[90] Torrance's method of depth exegesis or realist hermeneutics thus involves taking the biblical text and seeking to discern the inner, deeper structures of reality or truth inherent in it. It never leaves behind the text for another for this is *Holy* Scripture.[91] But it never rests content on the mere *ipssisma vox*.

Torrance is insistent on the fact that the "voice" of God must be heard through Scripture alone – *sola scriptura*, but not *nuda scriptura*. In a sermon on Christ the redeemer Torrance asserts that "We cannot see Jesus just by piecing together picturesque historical detail about Him,"[92] clearly a rejection of the historical-critical method as an end in itself in biblical exegesis. Rather, "Jesus must be transfigured before our very eyes."[93] This is accomplished through his cross and resurrection, by means of which he now stands at the door of the church and knocks, and whose voice is heard inside the

---

[89] Kevin Vanhoozer, "Interpreting Scripture Between the Rock of Biblical Studies and the Hard Place of Systematic Theology: The State of the Evangelical (Dis)union," delivered at *Renewing the Evangelical Mission* Conference held at Gordon-Conwell Theological Seminary from October 13-15, 2009.
[90] Torrance, *Karl Barth: An Introduction to His Early Theology*, 188.
[91] For a recent account of what it means to call Scripture "holy" see Webster, *Holy Scripture*.
[92] Torrance, "When Christ Comes to the Church," 26.
[93] Torrance, "When Christ Comes to the Church," 26.

church "speaking to us out of the pages of the Bible."[94] Torrance speaks of this as a miracle:

> We cannot see Jesus, for He has withdrawn Himself from our sight; and we will not see Him face to face until He comes again – but we *can hear* His *voice* speaking to us in the midst of the Church on earth. That is the perpetual miracle of the Bible, for it is the inspired instrument through which the voice of Christ is still to be heard... The Church is, in fact, the Community of the Voice of God...[95]

Theology is an inherently rational discipline for the precise reason that faith itself is inherently rational. In revelation God himself is being communicated so that in the Word we are confronted with an Object which is Subject, that is, with one who is both person and message. "Hence, Christian Theology cannot tolerate the idea that faith is not rational in its own right and that it is the task of theology to give it rational interpretation through employing conceptual forms drawn from elsewhere."[96] From this premise Torrance concludes that the real issue is one of *ratio*, in both senses of the word, *rationality* and *method*, and this is what defines a scientific theology or dogmatics. Scientific theology or dogmatics is thus different from biblical theology which remains content with the linguistic and phenomenological exegesis of the Scriptures. Theology must press on to inquire into the relation between biblical thought and speech and their source in the truth and being of God. It is the specific task of theology to inquire into what we ourselves have to say on the basis of the biblical revelation, and to articulate its relation to the object in such a way that our knowledge may be established as true. Torrance goes even further in suggesting that unless this happens "we have not engaged upon genuine exegesis, for then we are setting aside the all-important relation between the external text and the inner meaning and

---

[94] Torrance, "When Christ Comes to the Church," 27.
[95] Torrance, "When Christ Comes to the Church," 27.
[96] Torrance, *Karl Barth: An Introduction to His Early Theology*, 182.

objective basis upon which it rests."⁹⁷ We may conclude from this that Torrance would only consider *theological* interpretation of Scripture as ultimately worthy of the epithet "Christian exegesis."

Torrance is trying to clarify how an exegesis of Scripture by a believer is different from that of the unbeliever. One could rephrase this somewhat to show that Torrance was pointing out the necessary ecclesial commitments and contexts for a correct reading of Scripture. According to Torrance "the decisive point in interpretation is not reached until there is inquiry into the reality signified. True interpretation arises where perception of the meaning of the letter of Holy Scripture and understanding of the reality it indicates are one."⁹⁸ This form of argument is another application of one of Torrance's fundamental commitments in theological science: the *kata physic* nature of scientific inquiry in which the method of inquiry is dictated by the object under study.⁹⁹ "It belongs to the rationality of theology that the reason should operate only with objects of faith, for faith is the specific mode of rationality which is demanded of the reason when it is directed to the knowledge of God."¹⁰⁰

A depth exegesis of Scripture can be illustrated by employing an analogy that Polanyi used in communicating what he meant by "tacit knowledge" and "indwelling," that of a blind man's walking stick. Gunton summaries it in the following way:

> When a blind man uses a stick… he learns about the world by their instrumentality, *from* them *to* the object of

---

⁹⁷ Torrance, *Karl Barth: An Introduction to His Early Theology*, 189. This is followed by a clarification: "No exegesis that is content only with noetic rationality can be regarded as properly scientific, for scientific activity must penetrate through noetic rationality into the ontic rationality of its basis and so lay bare its inner necessity."

⁹⁸ Torrance, *Karl Barth: An Introduction to His Early Theology*.

⁹⁹ Or alternatively: the nature of the object prescribes the mode of rationality proper to its investigation. See a potted summary of this position in Torrance, "Truth and Authority," 223-24.

¹⁰⁰ Torrance, *Karl Barth: An Introduction to His Early Theology*, 192.

the knowledge. Employing these tools tacitly, we *indwell* them, "this indwelling being logically similar to the way we live in our body... [Indwelling] applies here in a logical sense as affirming that the parts of the external world, when interiorised, function in the same way as our body functions when we attend from it to things outside". It is the fact that there is a real relation, in which there is a rational linkage between mind and matter, that makes the generalisation from body to tool to sophisticated theory a possibility... The way in which our bodies and by extension our tools, both physical and theoretical, make a real indwelling in the world possible is fundamental to Polanyi's case. Without it, there would be no knowledge of the world at all. Thus the theory of indwelling is the obverse of the theory of tacit knowing.[101]

When applied directly to a realist hermeneutics, Scripture is the walking cane, the medium through which reality can be conceived, and yet it is not the reality itself but points to it.[102] According to Polanyi, things are only understood by indwelling them, not merely by observing them.[103] Hence, when Torrance applies this philosophy of science, or epistemology, to theological method, he concludes that we only know the truth through indwelling the Word, both written and incarnate.[104] In this light evangelical

---

[101] Colin E. Gunton, "The Truth of Christology," in *Belief in Science and in Christian Life: The Relevance of Michael Polanyi's Thought for Christian Faith and Life* (ed. T.F. Torrance; Edinburgh: Handsel, 1980), 98.

[102] It is Webster's contention that "the referential or signifying function of Scripture is... a primary element in Torrance's understanding of biblical interpretation." John Webster, "T.F. Torrance on Scripture," Keynote address at the annual meeting of the T.F. Torrance Theological Fellowship, Montreal (6 November 2009), 12.

[103] Michael Polanyi, "Science and Man's Place in the Universe," in *Science as a Cultural Force* (ed. H. Woolf; Baltimore: Johns Hopkins, 1964), 54-76; and Michael Polanyi, *The Tacit Dimension* (London: Routledge & Kegan Paul, 1967), 21.

[104] Webster, *Holy Scripture*, 68-106, presents a similar view.

exegesis should not be the mere study of a text but a way of life in which God, through Christ, and by the Holy Spirit, leads us into a deeper communion with himself through the Word written.[105] The ends of exegesis are thus kept squarely at the forefront of Torrance's theological interpretation of Scripture.

Inspiration and revelation

Torrance's revised Barthian doctrine of Scripture regards revelation as dynamic because it is initiated by Christ and enabled by the Holy Spirit. This means Scripture is not, strictly speaking, revelation but a vehicle for revelation or a medium through which God's revelation in Christ and by the Spirit can be given. Donald Bloesch is one of a number of contemporary evangelicals who follow this line of reasoning carefully. Bloesch maintains that "The Bible in and of itself is not the Word of God – divine revelation – but it is translucent to this revelation by virtue of the Spirit of God working within it and within the mind of the reader and hearer."[106] Scripture is a human medium of the divine Word and as such cannot be, according to Torrance, simply mistaken for God's living eternal Word who is Jesus Christ. All human speech must have a reservation about it until all is revealed by God. Torrance brings out

---

[105] Though not identical, see the sort of participatory exegesis recommended by Matthew Levering, *Participatory Biblical Exegesis: A Theology of Biblical Interpretation* (Notre Dame: University of Notre Dame Press, 2008).

[106] Donald G. Bloesch, *Holy Scripture: Revelation, Inspiration, and Interpretation* (Downers Grove: IVP, 1994), 27. Bloesch's use of "translucent" is reminiscent of Torrance's language of Scripture as a "transparent medium" through which "the divine Light shines from the face of Jesus Christ into our hearts." Torrance, *Space, Time and Resurrection*, 12, and *Theology in Reconstruction*, 257. In addition to Bloesch see other contemporary evangelical theologians who share the same basic convictions, especially: Grenz, *Renewing the Center*; and Alister E. McGrath, *A Passion for Truth: The Intellectual Coherence of Evangelicalism* (Leicester: Apollos, 1996), 53-118; and *The Genesis of Doctrine: A Study in the Foundation of Doctrinal Criticism* (Grand Rapids: Eerdmans, 1990).

this eschatological character of revelation in his early work *Theological Science*:

> While God has made His Word audible and apprehensible with our human speech and thought, refusing to be limited by their inadequacy in making Himself known to us, He nevertheless refuses to be understood merely from within the conceptual framework of our natural thought and language but demands of that framework a logical reconstruction in accordance with His Word. Hence a theology faithful to what God has revealed and done in Jesus Christ must involve a powerful element of apocalyptic, that is epistemologically speaking, an eschatological suspension of logical form in order to keep our thought ever open to what is radically new.[107]

The relation between God's self-revelation and Scripture is fundamentally asymmetrical.[108] Indeed, Torrance is even willing to describe the Bible as a product of human authorship and thus "faulty and errant."[109] However, due to the dual-authorship of Scripture, Torrance regards its human imperfections as the very means through which God lays hold of our sinful, fallen human condition and redeems it. This is yet another reason he sees for not regarding the text of Scripture as the truth or as the Word of God in any absolute or final sense. Scripture points to, and is the divinely chosen medium for, the revelation of God's eternal Word. I at least would want to affirm that it would thus be closer to the truth to say Holy Scripture *is* revelation, but must not be misunderstood as the *end* of revelation or as authoritative as Christ the Word.

Torrance develops this realist hermeneutic more fully in a discussion on the referring relation of language. If statements are absolutely adequate to the object, asks Torrance, then how can we distinguish the object from statements about it? If language and statements are to perform their denotative function adequately,

---

[107] Torrance, *Theological Science*, 279-80.
[108] Torrance, *Reality and Evangelical Theology*, 96.
[109] Torrance, *Divine Meaning: Studies in Patristic Hermeneutics*, 10.

directing us to reality/truth beyond themselves in such a way that there takes place a disclosure of reality/truth, then, Torrance concludes, they must have a measure of inadequacy in order to be differentiated from that to which they refer.[110] "The Scriptures of the Old and New Testaments rightly evoke from us profound respect and veneration not because of what they are in themselves but because of the divine revelation mediated in and through them. This is why we speak of them as 'Holy' Scriptures."[111] Barth's formulation of the dynamic between God's revelation in Christ and in Scripture was to propose his famous three-fold distinction of the Word: the living Word, the written Word, and the proclaimed Word. Barth understands that only when the written or proclaimed Word is united with the revealed Word does it become revelation proper. Torrance, in line with Barth, considers the Word written to point to God's revelation, yet for Torrance, revelation cannot be detached from the Bible for in space-time this is how God has "uniquely and sovereignly coordinated the biblical word with his eternal Word, and adapted the written form and contents of the Bible to his Word, in such a way that the living Voice of God is made to resound through the Bible to all who have ears to hear."[112]

Critical conclusions by way of a summary

As I conclude, it is clear that I am favourably disposed to the theological methodology of Torrance, as opposed to that of Henry. Henry's theological method does fall foul of what Kevin Vanhoozer has dramatically termed "epic classicism," Lindbeck's "cognitive-propositional" approach.[113] It is also clear where I disagree with

---

[110] See the discussion in Torrance, "Truth and Authority," 229-31, especially 231.
[111] Torrance, *Reality and Evangelical Theology*, 95. In a footnote Torrance then directs the reader to Barth's *CD*, I/2, Ch. III on "Holy Scripture," 457–537.
[112] Torrance, *Karl Barth: Biblical and Evangelical Theologian*, 88.
[113] Kevin J. Vanhoozer, *The Drama of Doctrine: A Canonical Linguistic Approach to Christian Theology* (Louisville" Westminster John Knox Press, 2005), 83.

Henry and where I might want to push back on his fundamentalist-leaning ideas.

However, before Carl Henry is dismissed as some fundamentalist fossil of an embarrassing history, I do think there are aspects of his critique and his perspective which are important to note and which most evangelicals will appreciate.

It can appear that Torrance sees Scripture as less than revelation and that it only *becomes* revelation through personal communion with Christ by the Spirit. Indeed, if that is the case then evangelicals would want to push back, with Henry, and say that our response to revelation does not make it revelation but rather makes it *revelatory* and personally affective. We must say, then, that Scripture *is* divine revelation regardless of whether or not one is in union with Christ. In the words of McCall:

> Perhaps what Torrance needs is a strong dose of his own epistemological medicine. The trajectory of his thought might well result in belief in scripture as the written revelation standing in a direct but subordinate relation to the self-revelation of God in Jesus Christ.[114]

If this were the case then Torrance would be able to affirm, with Carl Henry, that Scripture *is* revelation, without this being a denial that ultimate or final Revelation is found in Jesus Christ alone. Scripture is revelation as far as it is a divinely given witness to the God revealed in Jesus Christ by the Spirit.

I conclude with the words Marguerite Shuster used to finish her short article on Torrance's theological method: "What is truth? The True Man said, 'I am the truth.' True men, responding in the faith of God's grace, can start nowhere else than to proclaim, 'Indeed, *he* is the truth.'"[115]

---

[114] McCall, "Ronald Thiemann, Thomas Torrance and Epistemological Doctrines of Revelation," 167.

[115] Marguerite Shuster, "'What is Truth?' An Exploration of Thomas F. Torrance's Epistemology," *Studio Biblica Et Theologia* 3 (1973): 56.

Chapter Eleven
Stanley Grenz' theological method: revisioning evangelical theology or business as usual?

Brian Harris

Stanley Grenz' theological method has occasioned much comment amongst evangelicals. There are those who believe that he speaks for younger evangelicals and articulates a method capable of reflecting their convictions.[1] Pentecostal theologians have been largely approving of his work, finding that his pneumatological emphasis helps rectify some of the shortcomings they have perceived in traditional evangelical theology.[2] In *Revisioning Evangelical Theology* Grenz identifies seven areas in need of revisioning if evangelicalism is to successfully transition from modernity to postmodernity, namely evangelical identity, evangelical spirituality, the theological task, sources for theology, biblical authority, theology's integrative motif, and the church.[3] This 1993 publication served as his programmatic work,[4] and

---

[1] Webber suggests that Grenz is the representative theologian for the emerging church. Robert E. Webber, *The Younger Evangelicals: Facing the Challenges of the New World* (Grand Rapids: Baker, 2002), 92.

[2] See e.g., Cross' tribute to Grenz in the opening footnote of his article. Terry L. Cross, "Proposal to Break the Ice: What Can Pentecostal Theology Offer Evangelical Theology," *Journal of Pentecostal Theology* 10 (2002): 44–73. Offsetting Cross, see Smith's plea that Pentecostal theology distance itself from evangelical theology. However, Smith's concerns are largely addressed by Grenz' method. James K.A. Smith, "The Closing of the Book: Pentecostals, Evangelicals, and the Sacred Writings," *Journal of Pentecostal Theology* 11(1997): 49–71.

[3] After a general introduction, the book is structured to allocate a chapter per area in need of revisioning. Stanley J. Grenz, *Revisioning Evangelical Theology: A Fresh Agenda for the Twenty First Century* (Downers Grove: IVP, 1993).

[4] Grenz was later to speak of it in these terms. See Grenz, *Renewing the Center: Evangelical Theology in a Post-Theological Era* (Grand Rapids: Baker, 2000), 8.

helped direct his subsequent theological research and emphasis. Grenz' theological project was brought to an abrupt end by his sudden death on 12 March 2005. While many have expressed enthusiasm for his work, others have been more guarded, and yet others have been hostile. The range of response necessitates asking if Grenz has genuinely revisioned evangelical theology. In this paper I suggest that while Grenz' method is capable of leading evangelical theology along new and fresh paths, Grenz' selective and cautious application of his method leaves a gap between the promise of his theology and its product. I argue this on the basis of an examination of the application of his method in the sphere of theological ethics[5] in *Welcoming but Not Affirming*.[6]

---

[5] The appropriateness of testing a *theological* method with a case study in *ethics* can be queried. The debate as to whether theology and ethics should be seen as integrally related or as two distinct specialities is valid. While recognising the concerns of those who prefer to work with the disciplines separately, in this paper I have chosen to treat them seamlessly. I think this is justified for two reasons: 1) Most importantly, Grenz treats the disciplines seamlessly. His expressed conviction is that whenever theology fails to flow over into ethics, it falls short of its calling. His publications move back and forth between those that can be classified as theology and those that can be classified as ethics, but often the lines are blurred. His ethical construction is clearly shaped by his theological method. And 2) Devising a post-foundationalist theology for a postmodern context presupposes an interdisciplinary approach. Neatly dividing the theological enterprise into clear compartments reflects the systematising mindset of the modern era. Any theological method that does not allow for the free flowing interchange between theological disciplines is unlikely to be successful in revisioning theological method for a postmodern era. The greater the interchange, the less clear the borders between disciplines. In light of this, my decision to choose *Welcoming but Not Affirming* as the test case for Grenz' theological method is understandable. The selection meets Grenz' own standard of requiring a revisioned theological method genuinely to inform and guide the life and practice of the community of God. Grenz, *Revisioning Evangelical Theology*, 84.

[6] Stanley J. Grenz, *Welcoming but Not Affirming: An Evangelical Response to Homosexuality* (Louisville: Westminster John Knox, 1998).

Grenz has proposed a model for evangelical theological construction that utilizes Scripture, tradition, and culture as the sources for theology; and the Trinity, community, and eschatology as its focal motifs. He supplements these with the belief that the Spirit guides the church as it communally attempts to discern truth in changing contexts. Grenz believes that his method moves beyond foundationalism as it appeals to a trio of interacting, conversing sources that are guided by three related motifs, rather than to the single source of Scripture. I will unpack each of these components in what follows.

Three theological sources

Suggesting Scripture as a source for theological construction is something of a non-negotiable for any theological method that wishes to be considered evangelical.[7] For evangelical method, the debate is more over seeing Scripture as *a* source or *the* source for theological conclusions, with the latter serving as the default drive. There is therefore nothing inherently novel in Grenz' suggestion that Scripture serve as theology's norming norm.[8] Of greater interest are the shifts in emphasis proposed by Grenz.

Grenz argues that post-fundamentalist evangelical theology has continued to adopt a propositionalist approach, with the theological task being conceived as the discovery and articulation of the one doctrinal system embedded in the Bible.[9] We should not accept Grenz' analysis uncritically, as he is a little one-sided in his

---

[7] Bebbington can be seen as representative when he suggests that biblicism is one of the defining characteristics of evangelicalism. David Bebbington, *Evangelicalism in Modern Britain: A History from the 1730s to the 1980s* (Grand Rapids: Baker, 1989), 12–14.

[8] Grenz unpacks his understanding of this in Stanley J. Grenz and John Franke, *Beyond Foundationalism: Shaping Theology in a Postmodern Context* (Louisville: Westminster John Knox, 2001), 57–92.

[9] Grenz and Franke, *Beyond Foundationalism*, 60–63.

presentation of propositionalist approaches.[10] Rather than follow a propositional programme, Grenz suggests that theology should be conceived as the "reflection on the faith commitment of the believing community."[11] He suggests that its authority derives from it being "...the source for the symbols, stories, teachings and doctrines that form the cognitive framework for the worldview of the believing community."[12]

Second, he believes that many evangelicals "...take loyalty to the Bible to heights not intended by the Reformers and not in keeping with the broader trajectory of the evangelical movement."[13] He argues that such loyalty is misguided and unnecessary. The Bible's status as the foundational text of the faith community guarantees its place of importance in the theological enterprise. Grenz' approach at this point is essentially pragmatic and functional. If theology is the reflection on the faith commitment of the believing community, it is a reflection that cannot begin without an understanding of the "book of the community."[14]

---

[10] See e.g. Helseth's critique of Grenz' historical reconstruction in Paul Kjoss Helseth, "Are Postconservative Evangelicals Fundamentalists? Postconservative Evangelicalism, Old Princeton and the Rise of Neo-Fundamentalism," in *Reclaiming the Center: Confronting Evangelical Accomodation in Postmodern Times* (eds Millard J. Erickson, Paul Kjoss Helseth, and Justin Taylor; Wheaton: Crossway, 2004), 223–50.

[11] Grenz, *Revisioning Evangelical Theology*, 87. The adequacy of this definition must be questioned. It implies a descriptive, rather than prescriptive, role for the theologian. Perhaps a church historian might be willing to be limited to a descriptive role, but it is improbable that many systematic theologians would be willing to accept such an abbreviated description of their task. Indeed, Grenz himself does not, for in spite of this definition, he carves out a far more ambitious role in his own theological work. Perhaps it should be enlarged to be a "reflection on the *adequacy* of the faith commitment of the believing community *in the light of...*" with relevant theological criteria inserted (e.g., Scripture, the tradition of the church, certain ethical criteria, etc.).

[12] Grenz, *Revisioning Evangelical Theology*, 88.

[13] Grenz, *Revisioning Evangelical Theology*, 93.

[14] Grenz, *Revisioning Evangelical Theology*, 94.

From a traditional evangelical perspective, this is provocative. Evangelicals assign a place of prominence to the Bible out of a conviction that its message is the truth, and its revelation the sole surety for statements made about the nature and character of God.[15] The constituting role of the Bible in the life of the church is seen as of secondary importance to the claim that it is an accurate and authoritative revelation of the character, will, and actions of God. Grenz' stance seems a short step from relegating the Bible to a text of historical (but not authoritative) importance. His argument that the Bible's role as the repository of the original *kerygma* of the faith community guarantees it a role of ongoing importance is not self evidently true. Belief systems can change and evolve, and most would not consider a stance definitive simply because it was the one originally adopted.

A third aspect of Grenz' proposal on Scripture, and one which reflects something of the heartbeat of his concern, is expressed in his approving discussion of the Pietists. He notes, "For the Pietists, talk about the truth claims of the Bible was less important than the fact that 'truth claims' – that the Scriptures lay hold of the life of the reader and call that life into divine service."[16] This, however, is a false dichotomy. Brand accuses Grenz of driving an artificial wedge between those who focus on the Bible as a source of correct doctrine and those whose focus is on the Bible as a source of spiritual sustenance. Dismissing this typology as overly simplistic, Brand argues that balance between the two has usually characterized evangelicalism.[17]

---

[15] A correspondence theory of truth is what is envisaged here.

[16] Grenz, *Revisioning Evangelical Theology*, 112. While hard to dispute, this does seem to beg the question. Is it not the task of the theologian to articulate why this happens and how to evaluate the validity of such an "encounter"? In addition, this presentation of the Pietists is one sided according to Travis. See William G. Travis, "Pietism and the History of American Evangelicalism," in *Reclaiming the Center*, 251–79.

[17] Chad O. Brand, "Defining Evangelicalism," in *Reclaiming the Center*, 298. Smith, in his work on the relationship between Pentecostalism and

Grenz then moves to an important stage in his thinking, namely, that the meaning and impact of Scripture is pneumatologically mediated. He laments that the theological method of most Protestant theologians separates bibliology and pneumatology.[18] In practical terms, Grenz calls evangelicals to pay as much attention to the doctrine of illumination as they do to inspiration. By placing the emphasis on the inspiration of Scripture, a static view of Scripture can dominate. Arguments revolve around the once for all divinely given message of Scripture, rather than around the need to listen to the ongoing voice of the Spirit speaking through Scripture (illumination).

This focus on illumination shifts the subject-object locus. So long as we have an inspired text to study, the theologian can approach Scripture as an objective text whose message can be interpreted and explained. If, however, the focus shifts to Scripture as a Spirit illuminated text dynamically interacting with the life of the community, the static 'given' of the text is replaced by uncertainty, ambiguity, and the subjectivity of a required response. The approach has Barthian overtones where the Word of God shifts from being authoritatively inspired Word to divinely

---

evangelicalism, is more nuanced when he distinguishes between evangelical theology and grass-roots evangelical experience. He writes: "This issue (the relationship between Pentecostalism and evangelicalism) situates us in the midst of an ongoing historiographic debate between Donald Dayton and George Marsden... Dayton has been insisting on a 'pentecostal paradigm' for understanding evangelicalism over against what he calls Marsden's 'presbyterian paradigm.' I think both of them are right, but on different levels. I think Marsden is correct in asserting the dominant influence of the Princeton tradition on mainstream evangelical *theology*; but in agreement with Dayton, I think evangelicalism at a grass-roots level has been significantly influenced by a more Wesleyan-holiness piety as found, for instance, in Finney." Smith, "The Closing of the Book: Pentecostals, Evangelicals, and the Sacred Writings," 61.

[18] Grenz follows up on his own suggestion in Stanley J. Grenz, *Theology for the Community of God* (Nashville: Broadman and Holman, 1994), 494–527. His discussion of Scripture in the middle of the book within the section on the work of the Spirit makes for a refreshing point of difference.

illuminated Word. In this limited sense, the Scripture *becomes* the Word of God in interaction with a particular person or community.[19]

Grenz' pneumatologically mediated approach to Scripture has led to concerns being expressed. A major refrain is that the approach is subjective and undermines the concept of the authority of Scripture by taking the locus of authority from the text and placing it within the contextualized, Spirit guided, community of faith. Consequently some evangelicals have been dismissive of Grenz' proposal, Carson complaining, "I cannot see how Grenz's approach to Scripture can be called 'evangelical' in any useful sense."[20]

Grenz' second source for theology is tradition. In exploring tradition as a theological source which serves as theology's hermeneutical trajectory, Grenz attempts to answer the question of how the insights gained from the Spirit's guidance and leading of the church over the last two thousand years can be utilized in the process of theological reflection.[21] In suggesting that tradition serves as a hermeneutical trajectory, pointing toward the eschatological future of the church on the basis of insights from the past, and in turn being critiqued on the basis of the eschatological vision, he hopes to overcome static views of tradition that have historically led to an impasse between opposing groups, as each try to justify their tradition as the valid one.

---

[19] Grenz is well aware of the reservation evangelicals have of Barth, and especially of the subjectivity implicit within his approach. He writes: "Several recent theologies of Word and Spirit have come close to subjectivism. Thinkers influenced by Karl Barth and neo-orthodox Word of God theologies routinely differentiate between the Bible and the transcendent Word in a manner that seems to reduce biblical authority to our subjective reception of the divine address that confronts us through the human words of the Bible." Grenz and Franke, *Beyond Foundationalism*, 67.

[20] Donald A. Carson, *The Gagging of God: Christianity Confronts Pluralism* (Grand Rapids: Zondervan, 1996), 481.

[21] Grenz and Franke, *Beyond Foundationalism*, 94.

Grenz' revisioned theology is intended to win over two audiences. On the one hand, it is *evangelical* theology that he revisions, and his hope is to draw traditional evangelicals to a broader vision of the movement. On the other hand he writes for the *postmodern* context, and seeks to develop a theology that is true to its evangelical roots, but which is a respected player in the postmodern arena. For neither of these audiences is tradition an obvious choice as a source for theology.

However the roots of evangelicalism are traced, it is never less than a movement supportive of the Reformers' cry of *sola scriptura*. Indeed, the perceived use of tradition at the expense of the Scriptures was a key factor in the Protestant Reformation.[22] In suggesting tradition as a source for theology Grenz therefore has to indicate how to move beyond the hermeneutics of suspicion from which evangelicals usually operate when appeals to tradition are made in theological construction. Neither is the choice of tradition for a postmodern audience a self evident one. Wentzel van Huyssteen accurately summarizes a key postmodern concern about the use of tradition when he writes:

> By seeking to disturb any easy relationship with our past by arguing that our assertion of continuity is itself an invention of our need to control the destiny of our culture and society, a sceptical form of the postmodern critique of continuity thus calls into question the very possibility of tradition.[23]

While aware of these reservations, Grenz provides four persuasive reasons for using tradition as a theological source. First, past doctrinal statements and theological models are instructive for the present theological quest and help to avoid the pitfalls from the past. Secondly, traditions serve as a reference point. Thirdly, some

---

[22] Which is not to suggest that the Reformers made no use of tradition. Attempts to apply *sola scriptura* literally are, inevitably, naïve. While the Reformers held a theoretical commitment to *sola scriptura*, their hermeneutical practice is better described as *suprema scriptura*.

[23] Wentzel van Huyssteen, "Tradition and the Task of Theology," *Theology Today* 55 (1998): 217.

doctrinal formulations have withstood the test of time. Fourthly, as a second order task, theology is undertaken by theologians who are themselves members of a faith community which spans the centuries.[24]

While Grenz' case for appropriating tradition as a conversation partner with Scripture and culture is sensible, he glosses over the problems inherent in the approach. His claim that the believing community will be guided by the Spirit to know which aspects of tradition to embrace flies in the face of the very history of the church that Grenz wishes to uphold. Even a cursory glance through church history establishes the wide range of conflicting answers that have been adopted by different segments of the faith community. Grenz is silent on how this impasse is to be overcome, other than to note the helpfulness of having the interacting voices of Scripture, tradition, and culture rather than a monologue by Scripture alone.

A key issue Grenz leaves unresolved is therefore what criteria can be seen as valid in testing the authoritative status of any particular theological tradition. At the very least, tradition needs to be an interactive player subject to other criteria. Acknowledging the input of both Scripture and culture in reaching a decision is useful, but still leaves wide and vague parameters. Openness to pneumatological mediation may reflect a pious and reverent approach to theology, but its hazy boundaries make it hard to either affirm or refute.

Grenz' third source for theology is culture. This is his most controversial selection. To Grenz' suggestion that culture is a source for theology, evangelicals are likely to respond that while culture provides the location within which a particular theological system is developed, to suggest that culture is a *source* for theology goes beyond the mandate of evangelical theology.

Because Grenz writes in a nuanced way, it is dangerous to assume that one can respond to his broad categories without

---

[24] Grenz, *Revisioning Evangelical Theology*, 95–97.

carefully examining the meaning he attaches to them.[25] When he suggests culture as a source for theology, at times he seems simply to be calling for a "culture-sensitive theology," a plea that is neither original nor divisive.[26] At other times he views culture as a "resource" for theology, another essentially uncontested insight. More often, however, the suggestion is that culture is one of three conversation partners sourcing theology. This last stance has been the cause of debate amongst those who have responded to Grenz' work. Bloesch is representative when he writes, "My problem with Grenz is that he sees mainly promise in cultural achievements and not also deception and self-aggrandizement… In a viable biblical, evangelical theology culture is neither deified nor demonized but relativized."[27]

Grenz' argument is that the Spirit and community mediated interaction between culture and Scripture enriches the understanding of Scripture and unearths aspects of biblical truth that would otherwise be overlooked. It also allows the theologian to speak to areas not directly addressed in Scripture. The whole is therefore greater as a result of the interaction, and culture has thus genuinely sourced theological conclusions.[28]

---

[25] Both Carson and Erickson can be accused of responding superficially. Donald A. Carson, "Domesticating the Gospel: A Review of Grenz's Renewing the Center," in *Reclaiming the Center*, 33–55; Millard J. Erickson, *The Evangelical Left: Encountering Postconservative Evangelical Theology* (Grand Rapids: Baker, 1997); Millard J. Erickson, "On Flying in Theological Fog," in *Reclaiming the Center*, 323–47.

[26] Stanley J. Grenz, "Culture and Spirit: The Role of Cultural Context in Theological Reflection," *Asbury Theological Journal* 55 (2000): 40.

[27] Donald G. Bloesch, "Donald Bloesch Responds: On Grenz," in *Evangelical Theology in Transition: Theologians in Dialogue with Donald Bloesch* (ed. Elmer M. Colyer; Downers Grove: IVP, 1999), 186.

[28] Grenz' comment that "our theological reflection can draw from the so-called 'secular' sciences, because ultimately no truth is in fact secular" and later that "theology seeks to show how the postulate of God illumines all human knowledge," is important. Instead of the common evangelical reactionary default drive to that which is new in society, this approach allows the

Three focal motifs

In addition to utilizing Scripture, tradition, and culture as sources for theology, Grenz argues that a theology suited to the postmodern situation will utilize three focal motifs, namely, the Trinity as a structural motif, community as an integrative motif, and eschatology as an orienting motif.[29] He reasons that while the use of Scripture, tradition, and culture provide a rounded trio of conversation partners, these should be supplemented by the focal motifs of Trinity, community, and eschatology. Placing contemporary theological construction in eschatological perspective, and in this way working backwards from the ultimate *telos* of human existence, helps to address the concerns of the present without being held hostage to them. It ensures that theology retains a prophetically anticipatory character. If the eschaton will see the creation of a community that reflects and interacts with the communion experienced by the triune God, focusing theological construction around Trinity, community, and eschatology provides a seamless trio of motifs.

In moving from a single source for theological construction to a trio of sources filtered through three focal motifs, a fundamental methodological problem appears. Grenz uses the image of the three sources acting as conversation partners, but how does one decide if a conversation partner is speaking too loudly? Put differently, if we say tradition is a source for theological construction, we must ask "which tradition?" Some theologians make their commitments in this regard clear. Thomas Oden, for example, has proposed that theology draw from a pyramid of sources, with Scripture occupying the wide base of the pyramid, and modern theologians the narrow

---

embracing of that which is not directly addressed in Scripture on the basis of the insights which arise from the interaction. Stanley J. Grenz, "What Does Hollywood Have to Do with Wheaton? The Place of (Pop) Culture in Theological Reflection," *Journal of the Evangelical Theological Society* 43 (2000): 310–11.

[29] Grenz and Franke, *Beyond Foundationalism*, 24–25.

apex.³⁰ After Scripture come the patristic interpreters of Scripture. Modern sources are given less prominence because, as recent participants in the historical conversation, they have had little time to influence the overall consensus. To the question, "which tradition should have the dominant voice?" Oden answers that the ancient sources should be given greater weight than recent ones.

While Oden's model does not need to be embraced, he has alerted us to the need for criteria to discern the appropriate "volume" of each conversation partner.³¹ Grenz has made no commitments in this regard, but seems to believe that the natural back and forth of the conversation will help set an appropriate volume for each source. By insisting that Scripture remains the norming norm, the implication is that Scripture has sufficient prominence to mute other sources if they are moving in a direction contrary to Scripture. If this is the case, then Grenz is not methodologically transparent in his proposal that there are three conversation partners. A more nuanced approach would acknowledge that while three sources are conversing, they have significantly different amounts of influence.

It is Grenz' use of the term "source" that is problematic. Claiming that theological construction flows from three sources implies that any of the sources can add to or direct the path taken by the theology constructed. However a careful reading of Grenz reveals that while he treats Scripture as a genuine source for theology, both tradition and culture serve more as what Maquarrie describes as "formative factors."³² By opting to use the term "source"

---

[30] Thomas C. Oden, *The Word of Life* (San Francisco: Harper & Row, 1992), xv–xx.

[31] While accepting the usefulness of seeking areas of consensus in the church's tradition, Harmon points out how fruitful times of dissent have been. Steven R. Harmon, "The Authority of the Community (of All the Saints): Toward a Postmodern Baptist Hermeneutic of Tradition," *Review and Expositor* 100 (2003): 611–12.

[32] Macquarrie prefers to speak of formative factors as this clarifies that each factor is not on the same level or of the same importance. While acknowledging

Grenz has claimed more for tradition and culture than he is willing to give.[33] Those who have reacted against Grenz have usually accepted Grenz' use of the term "source" at face value, without observing the significant limitations he places upon both tradition and culture in theological construction. The criticism is therefore often unfounded, but flows from Grenz' misleading terminology.

If it is valid to assert that in Grenz' method Scripture serves as the source for theology and tradition and culture as formative factors, the question arises as to whether Grenz' method represents a genuinely post-foundationalist contribution to theological construction, or if it is better described as a model utilizing a "chastened" foundationalism. In Grenz' work, ultimately Scripture is the source for theological construction, but other factors are encouraged actively to participate in the construction process. The introduction of additional voices ensures that Grenz has moved beyond a crass foundationalism, but this does not represent anything more than a chastened foundationalism. This becomes apparent in his text on homosexuality, *Welcoming but Not Affirming*.

Homosexuality as test case

In analysing Grenz' treatment of homosexuality we are able more fully to assess the role he allows culture to play as a source for theology, largely because the clamour for evangelicals to change

---

many formative factors, he discusses six: experience, revelation, Scripture, tradition, culture, and reason. John Macquarrie, *Principles of Christian Theology* (rev. ed.; London: SCM, 1977), 4–18.

[33] For example, Grenz very modestly suggests that "the tradition of the Christian church serves as a source or a resource for theology, not as a final arbiter of theological issues or concerns but a hermeneutical context or trajectory for the Christian theological enterprise." Even when speaking of the ecumenical consensus represented by statements such as the Apostles and Nicene Creeds Grenz cautions, "Despite their great stature, such resources do not take the place of canonical scripture as the community's constitutive authority. Moreover, they must always and continually be tested by the norm of canonical scripture." Grenz and Franke, *Beyond Foundationalism*, 120, 124.

their understanding of homosexuality has not come from either church historians or biblical scholars, but from those who are aware of the significant shift in public attitudes to homosexuality in recent years.[34] What was once largely portrayed as a matter of personal morality is now more commonly seen as a human rights issue closely inter-woven with the question of social justice.[35] The context in which evangelicals are trying to understand Scripture and the traditional attitudes of the church to homosexuality has thus undergone considerable change. If culture is genuinely a source for theology, it would seem reasonable to expect that a changed cultural context will result in different theological conclusions.

In *Welcoming but Not Affirming* Grenz draws from his three sources for theological construction to guide his response to homosexuality. In chapter two he investigates the biblical material. He affirms that "homosexual conduct is not a major theme in the Bible" but that Christian ethicists when examining the limited number of relevant biblical passages have "found in these texts a clear rejection of all genital homosexual behaviour." He notes that recently "a growing chorus of exegetes" has voiced disagreement with traditional conclusions and has argued that the text has been misread.[36]

From a methodological perspective, Grenz then makes an important comment when he states: "My intent is not to offer a complete exegesis of any one text, but to determine whether recent

---

[34] This is not to suggest that there is not lively debate amongst evangelicals as to either what constitutes a valid biblical approach to homosexuality or a valid understanding of the church's tradition on the matter. It is simply to note that the more pressing questions seem to surround the role context and culture (or science and psychology) should play in arriving at an ethical response to the issue.

[35] So e.g., Loughlin, who chastises the church for inconsistency in advocating for the rights of homosexuals outside the church while denying them to homosexuals within the church. Gerard Loughlin, "Gathered at the Altar: Homosexuals and Human Rights," *Theology and Sexuality* 10 (2004): 73–82.

[36] Grenz, *Welcoming but Not Affirming*, 35.

scholarship has provided sufficient new insight into these texts to warrant our rejection of the traditional interpretation."[37] Two points should be noted. Though Grenz views tradition as a source for theology, if "recent scholarship" can show traditional interpretations to be flawed, the traditional stance will be ignored. At this point it is hard to see how tradition is a genuine source for theology. If it is a source only if it is deemed accurate in the light of another more definitive source, namely valid biblical interpretation, this assigns tradition little more than a supporting role when and if convenient.

Second, one needs to determine if "recent scholarship has provided sufficient new insights." The obvious question is to ask how this will be determined. While the field of hermeneutics and biblical exegesis is its own speciality, what is noteworthy is what is not suggested. At the heart of Grenz' methodological revisioning of the role of Scripture in sourcing theological insights was the need to reclaim the doctrine of the illumination of Scripture. Grenz' proposal is that this illumination comes to the faithful community of God in their historic and geographic location and that it is pneumatologically mediated and communally received. Rather than this revisioned agenda being implemented when the text is approached, what follows is a standard evangelical exegesis of the text, which is assumed to be inspired and therefore able to be propositionally analysed to yield timeless truths and propositions. None of this is remarkable for evangelical ethics, but what is disappointing is that it falls well short of the revised evangelical theology that Grenz proposes.

At another level, it raises the question of how Grenz' methodological proposals can be implemented. While it is easy to affirm the importance of illumination, in practice it is difficult to concretize. Certainly when Grenz reflects upon a pressing ethical issue facing the evangelical church, he finds a more traditional evangelical method easier to work with. The critique is not necessarily of the concept, but of its implementation. In essence, how can we objectify the more subjective aspects of the faith (what

---

[37] Grenz, *Welcoming but Not Affirming*, 36.

the Spirit is saying to us)?[38] There is an inherent tension in trying to do so, and it is not clear how it can be resolved.[39] While Grenz' method attempts to overcome individual subjectivity by locating illumination within a communal setting, communities, like individuals, are prone to whims and bias. They are also often "stakeholders" in the outcome. Indeed, later in the book Grenz politely but firmly rejects the biblical insights of those who are both welcoming and affirming of those engaged in same-sex sexual unions, indicating that he is not easily convinced by their plea that their biblical insights represent the Spirit mediated biblical illumination of a Christian community.[40] Grenz' propositional unpacking of the relevant texts on homosexuality leads him to the conclusion that same sex genital activity is always forbidden in Scripture.

Chapter three sees Grenz utilize the source of tradition for his exploration of homosexuality. He examines the argument that while there is a widespread assumption of a uniform rejection of homosexuality in the church's history, a more nuanced reading of the church's tradition is possible. He concludes that "explicit moral references to such behaviour in the Christian tradition were

---

[38] This is well illustrated by Gray Temple's book where Temple claims to have heard a direct word from God ("My Trinitarian discernment is sometimes fuzzy, but it felt like the First Person") instructing him that same sex unions are to be sanctioned, and then had that confirmed when another friend (also a theology graduate) claimed a comparable experience. Using Grenz' method, Temple could claim that his experience was communally supported. Gray Temple, *Gay Unions: In the Light of Scripture, Tradition and Reason* (New York: Church Publishing, 2004), 129.

[39] Yoder tackles this question more fully than Grenz. His argument that communal discernment takes place via the interaction of agents of direction (prophets), agents of memory (scribes), agents of linguistic self-consciousness (teachers), and agents of order and due process (elders, bishops, and overseers) helps to flesh out one possible way that communal discernment might take place in practice. See John Howard Yoder, *The Priestly Kingdom: Social Ethics as Gospel* (Notre Dame: University of Notre Dame Press, 1984).

[40] Grenz, *Welcoming but Not Affirming*, 153–55.

consistently negative," and that "In each era, Christian moralists rejected the same-sex practices of their day."[41] Though he acknowledges alternate readings of the church's tradition, Grenz does not find them sufficiently compelling to be taken seriously. The implicit answer to the question which tradition should be used as a theological source is, therefore, the dominant tradition. While not surprising, it is hard to see how genuine revisioning can take place if only dominating themes are allowed to inform the discussion.[42]

In short, Grenz' listening to the voice of Scripture and tradition as relevant to an evangelical understanding of homosexuality leads him to the conclusion that on this topic, it will be business as usual. But what does he make of the voice of culture, which one would anticipate as the voice calling for a revisioned understanding of homosexuality? For example, Philip Culbertson claims:

> In today's counselling world, the American Psychiatric Association of Social Workers, the American Psychological Association, the National Association of Social Workers, and the National Association for Marriage and Family Therapy state that it is unethical for members to treat gayness as an emotional disorder or to discriminate in any way on the basis of sexual orientation.[43]

How does Grenz treat this changed context? An analysis of *Welcoming but Not Affirming* leads to the conclusion that Grenz is

---

[41] Grenz, *Welcoming but Not Affirming*, 80.

[42] This would be particularly true for a question like homosexuality. There is no serious doubt that heterosexuality is a majority preference. By virtue of its minority status, homosexuality is unlikely to receive a substantial or sympathetic focus in the church's tradition. Grenz is willing to acknowledge that negative evaluations of homosexuality are often on the basis of obvious immorality (promiscuous rather than faithfully committed relationships), but does not seriously explore the implication of the church not accepting homosexuality as a permanent sexual orientation for a minority group.

[43] Philip Culbertson, *Caring for God's People: Counseling and Christian Wholeness* (Minneapolis: Fortress, 2000), 191.

highly selective in the cultural voices he heeds. Indeed, while willing to acknowledge other voices, he appropriates those that concur with his understanding of Scripture and tradition. The introductory chapter thus begins with a search for the causes of homosexuality. The search for a cause reflects an ideological bias, as the causes examined presuppose some form of pathology.[44] A similar search for the cause or causes of heterosexuality is not undertaken. If one works from the premise that homosexuality reflects some form of shortfall, its practice is unlikely to be sanctioned. By contrast, if the premise is that homosexuality is a normal, albeit minority, preference, the ethical evaluation is likely to be different.[45] Even as he embarks on the search for causes of homosexuality Grenz acknowledges that "since the mid-twentieth century the belief that homosexuality is a sexual orientation and that it may be the normal condition for some people has gained wide acceptance in professional and academic circles," but the implications of this statement do not impact what follows.[46] Later in the text when Grenz asks if homosexuality can represent a stable and fixed sexual orientation, he precedes it by a discussion of the "naturalistic fallacy" that derives "an 'ought' from an 'is'," thereby making clear his unwillingness to allow any findings in this regard seriously to impact his position.[47] Other criticisms could be added. For example,

---

[44] Grenz is fully aware that he lays himself open to this charge: "I embark on this task conscious, however, that a number of writers look askance at the research into the 'causes' of homosexuality. They worry that these endeavours are intrinsically hostile to homosexual persons..." Grenz, *Welcoming but Not Affirming*, 14.

[45] The tendency to confuse a "minority preference" with an "*abnormal* preference" is one that must be avoided. Indeed, if homosexual people are a minority group, it could be argued that the ethical focus should shift to the safeguarding that the Bible encourages for vulnerable groups. The issue is then not one of preventing certain perverse behaviours, but of protecting a susceptible group as a matter of social justice.

[46] Grenz, *Welcoming but Not Affirming*, 14.

[47] He writes: "Thus, even if homosexuality were indisputably 'natural' for certain people, this would not, in and of itself justify their engaging in same-sex

though well versed in the social sciences, Grenz chooses not to interact seriously with constructionist views of either homosexuality or gender.

Grenz' selective use of culture as a source for theology highlights a problem of his method. Having three sources for theology simply compounds the hermeneutical dilemma – which understanding of Scripture, which tradition, and which view of culture? When focusing on culture, which discipline studying culture should be favoured? Is it sociology, or anthropology, or psychology, and if a choice can be made, which lens within each of these disciplines should be adopted?

Grenz makes some progress toward an answer in his article "Culture and Spirit: The Role of Cultural Context in Theological Reflection." In it he asks and answers,

> How, then, can theology take culture seriously without imperilling the commitment to Scripture as theology's norming norm?... The answer to this question lies in pneumatology, more particularly in the construction of a theological link between culture and Spirit. The connection between culture and Spirit, in turn, lies in an understanding of culture as the Spirit's voice.[48]

One has to ask how the theological link between culture and the Spirit is to be built. The model adopted in *Welcoming but Not Affirming* suggests that it is via classical biblical exegesis, a mainstream understanding of tradition, and the selective use of culture, where only evidence that supports the insights from the first

---

practices." However, as he does not stipulate any conditions under which it would justify same-sex practice, one is left with the impression that he is unwilling to engage the debate in a serious manner. Grenz, *Welcoming but Not Affirming*, 117.

[48] Grenz, "Culture and Spirit: The Role of Cultural Context in Theological Reflection," 45.

two sources is allowed.⁴⁹ Ironically, this seems a most un-pneumatological pneumatology.

Grenz' three focal motifs for theological construction – Trinity, community, and eschatology – are assigned a modest role in *Welcoming but Not Affirming*. Each could be utilized to support either a conservative or a more daring agenda. While in *Welcoming but Not Affirming* Grenz' choices are consistently conservative, there is no obvious reason for them to be so. For example, Elizabeth Stuart utilizes an eschatological orientation to relativise the importance of the debate surrounding homosexuality, writing: "In the end gay is not good, straight is not good, no one is good but God alone. The Church as a community of the redeemed must play out gender and sexuality in such a way as to reveal their lack of eschatological significance."⁵⁰

Indeed, all three of Grenz' focal motifs can be used to support a pro-gay position. However, Grenz chooses to use them to discredit this stance. Adding content to sources and motifs involves hermeneutical decisions. While Grenz' theological model has been constructed to allow a move beyond foundationalism via a trialogue between three theological sources focused around three motifs, the application of his method in *Welcoming but Not Affirming* suggests that he arrives at little more than a chastened foundationalism. He

---

⁴⁹ This is a strong accusation, but is seen in Grenz' insistence e.g., that scientific research has not established that homosexual attraction "is either innate or an ineradicable trait that for this reason can be said to be normal for some persons." Grenz, *Welcoming but Not Affirming*, 32. We earlier noted Culbertson's claim that such a position flies in the face of the findings of, amongst others, the American Psychiatric Association of Social Workers, the American Psychological Association, the National Association of Social Workers, and the National Association for Marriage and Family Therapy. If the views of mainstream representative bodies from the social sciences are disallowed, one is led to the conclusion that the insights of the social sciences are being used selectively. Culbertson, *Caring for God's People: Counseling and Christian Wholeness*, 191.

⁵⁰ Elizabeth Stuart, *Gay and Lesbian Theologies: Repetitions with Critical Difference* (Aldershot: Ashgate, 2003), 114.

utilizes the insights of tradition, culture, Trinity, community, and eschatology when, and only when, they support the foundational pillar of Scripture. Pneumatological mediation is not seriously entertained. Grenz' conclusions are consequently pedestrian and little more than a charitable restatement of what evangelicals have always stated. Instead of a genuinely revisioned evangelical theology, he settles for business as usual.

Post-foundational and evangelical?

Is a genuinely post-foundational, yet evangelical, outcome possible utilizing Grenz' basic building blocks? While it is clear that Grenz desires to move beyond a crass foundationalism (where only what the Bible says is of any relevance), he has not given sufficient attention to the manner in which the conversation between Scripture, tradition, and culture should be undertaken. A more nuanced approach would provide guidelines on the appropriate "volume" for each conversation partner. Volume might well be related to the topic under investigation.

If Grenz' method is to move beyond the soft (or chastened) foundationalism he embraces, clarification of the rules for the conversation between the sources of theology is needed. Nicholas Wolterstorff's concept of "control beliefs" is useful at this point.[51] Wolterstorff notes that certain beliefs, be they religious, philosophical, biblical, or other, exercise "control" over what can and will be believed. He writes, "Everyone who weighs a theory has certain beliefs as to what constitutes an acceptable *sort* of theory on the matter under consideration. We all have these *control* beliefs."[52] Control beliefs lead us to reject certain sorts of theories, while they are also instrumental in the theories we devise. He notes, "We want

---

[51] See Nicholas Wolterstorff, *Reason within the Bounds of Religion* (Grand Rapids: Eerdmans, 1976). The title of Wolterstorff's work is intentionally contra Kant. Immanuel Kant, *Religion within the Limits of Reason Alone* (trans. Theodore M. Greene and Hoyt H. Hudson; New York: Harper and Row, 1960).

[52] Wolterstorff, *Reason within the Bounds of Religion*, 63.

theories that are consistent with our control beliefs."[53] Rather than attempt to eliminate control beliefs, Wolterstorff argues that they should be acknowledged and embraced. Thus he suggests that in theology "the belief-content of the theologian's authentic commitment ought all the while to be functioning also as control over his theory-devising and theory-weighing."[54]

Using Wolterstorff, we can ask what control belief should be adopted to help adjudicate between the differing sources available for theological construction. Examination of Grenz' method reveals that his control belief is that all theories need to be evaluated in the light of Scripture. To move this beyond foundationalism, he suggests that it is Scripture in interactive conversation with tradition and culture, but this soon leads to a circular argument.[55]

More helpful would be the adoption of a control belief that is allowed to act as a lens through which the contribution of all sources of theological construction is filtered. Attempting to adopt Scripture as both a control belief and a source does not work, as a control belief cannot operate on the same level as a source unless only a single source is allowed. Grenz' attempt to adopt Scripture as one of three sources while at the same time assigning it the role of the control belief is consequently flawed.[56]

The logical question therefore becomes, "Is there a control belief that can be adopted that is consistent with evangelicalism, which can effectively adjudicate between the differing sources for theological construction?" My proposal is that evangelicalism taps into that which it believes most deeply, namely that the gospel, the *evangel*, is, as the word literally means, good news. This can be expressed in different ways. Some slogans come to mind: "It isn't

---

[53] Wolterstorff, *Reason within the Bounds of Religion*, 64.

[54] Wolterstorff, *Reason within the Bounds of Religion*, 82.

[55] For example, which reading of Scripture? That which is appropriate for the embedded cultural context. But which cultural context? That which is consistent with Scripture…

[56] Grenz' expression is "the norming norm." Grenz and Franke, *Beyond Foundationalism*, 57–92.

the gospel if it isn't good news." Or Grenz' own contribution: "participating in what frees."⁵⁷ A suitable synthesis is *the gospel liberates*.

An objection needs to be considered at this point. Is the adoption of a control belief another name for foundationalism? While the question cannot be lightly dismissed, in this instance, a control belief cannot be said to equate with foundationalism. A highly specific and restrictive control belief could be seen as an alternate name for an indisputable foundation, but the control belief adopted is that *the gospel liberates*. While this could be interpreted as a propositional statement (the truth of which needs to be defended), it is better to view it as a statement encapsulating an ethos and projecting a vision. The filtering is on the basis of this expansive ideal. Its edges are soft, and allow for the incorporation of new insights. Rather than a foundation from which all other insights flow, the control belief *the gospel liberates* is enriched by its interaction with sources for theological construction such as Scripture, tradition, and culture.

The adoption of *the gospel liberates* as the control belief needs further explanation. At the finest moments in their history, evangelicals have been at the forefront of meaningful social change. Evangelicals attribute the abolition of slavery to the evangelical convictions of William Wilberforce and the evangelical Clapham sect. Likewise they attribute measures to protect children, the promotion of religious liberty, and the establishment of multiple humanitarian and educational programmes to those who were motivated by a vision of Christian faith forged within the evangelical camp.⁵⁸ An undergirding belief was that *the gospel*

---

[57] He uses the expression in an article with the same title and which suggests that the truth of the gospel is ultimately that which frees and liberates. Stanley J. Grenz, "Participating in What Frees: The Concept of Truth in the Postmodern Context," *Review and Expositor* 100 (2003): 687–93.

[58] For a partisan account not limited to the role played by evangelicals, but providing a useful overview of the way evangelicals understand their own

liberates those who respond to it, and that this liberation finds expression both in the present moment and throughout eternity.

There is also a shadow side. Sectors of evangelicalism have been supportive of a right wing agenda, which on occasion has revealed itself in racism, sexism, homophobia, militarism, ecological and economic exploitation, cultural insensitivity, and more beside.[59]

Evangelicalism's inconsistent track record in the social arena is reflective of an underdeveloped theological method. Whilst evangelicals usually cite biblical references to justify doctrinal and ethical stances, the lens that drives the selection of the supporting biblical material is rarely acknowledged or examined. Acknowledging and privileging the control belief *the gospel liberates* as the lens through which all assertions are filtered would result in a transparent and consistent method. A critiquing lens calls for accountability for the morality that inevitably flows from all theological construction. While the control belief ultimately critiques what is proposed, the lens adopted shapes construction at all stages.

How would adopting the control belief *the gospel liberates* work in practice?

Each of Grenz' sources for theology are susceptible to the "which" question. Which reading of Scripture will be privileged? Which tradition will be heeded? Which cultural voices will be heard? Acknowledging a bias towards liberation helps answer these valid

---

contribution, see Alvin J. Schmidt, *Under the Influence: How Christianity Transformed Culture* (Grand Rapids: Zondervan, 2001).

[59] Jim Wallis, *The Call to Conversion* (Herts: Lion, 1981), 25, laments, "Evangelicals in this century have a history of going along with the culture on the big issues and taking their stand on the smaller issues. That has been one of the serious problems of evangelical religion. Today, many evangelicals no longer just acquiesce to the culture on the larger economic and political issues, but actively promote the culture's worst values on these matters."

questions, and allows for a methodological transparency that is otherwise missing.[60]

It also helps to answer the question of the "volume" of each conversation partner. Privileging a hermeneutic of liberation allows shifting volumes for each conversation partner, depending on the issue at stake. We are quick to respond (not uncritically) to those voices that point in a liberating direction. Thus e.g., in ethical reflection on homosexuality, the voice of culture, and especially those cultural voices that are seriously engaged in helping to understand sexual identity, should be allowed a strident voice. This is not to attempt to mute the voice of Scripture, but it is to be ready to acknowledge that this is an ethical issue Scripture deals with obliquely and fleetingly. On this issue, the cultural voice alerts us to the subtlety of the debate in a way that Scripture does not. Alerted to the subtle innuendoes unpacked by culture, the conversation is able to deepen as broader biblical themes interact with the insights of the social sciences. The conclusions should not be anticipated in advance, nor should they be fossilised. New insights might lead to the conversation reaching a yet deeper level. Authentic conversation thus takes place within a framework that is genuinely post-foundationalist.

Perhaps then, with this modification, the potential inherent in Grenz' proposals can be unleashed. Instead of concluding that Grenz' proposal for a revisioned evangelical theology fizzles to business as usual, adopting the control belief that *the gospel liberates* could see evangelical theology enter an era of renewal and relevance.

---

[60] I am using "bias" to help provide a range of descriptors. However, as bias has a pejorative tone, my inclination is to opt for the more positive "privileging" or the more neutral "preference." However described, the goal is to attain methodological transparency.

Chapter Twelve
Hermeneutics and evangelical identity: a literary critical appreciation

Tim Meadowcroft

The first challenge in broaching the subject of "hermeneutics" is to discern what might be expected of the writer in the context of a consideration of "evangelical identity." It was initially unclear to me which of several questions might be posed by the juxtaposition of hermeneutics with evangelical identity. Three possibilities in particular presented themselves. One was to propose what I consider to be the/an evangelical hermeneutical identity. But I myself do not have a sense of developing a hermeneutic that may primarily be labelled as "evangelical," and I am conscious that there are a range of approaches to interpretation on the spectrum of evangelicalism.[1] I feared that to approach the topic from that direction would entail getting bogged down in a survey of the multifarious hermeneutical approaches that potentially link to evangelicalism. A second option was to develop a hermeneutical approach that constructs evangelical identity. I sensed that the diversity within evangelicalism that stymied the first potential approach would have a similar impact on any such attempt. A third possibility was for me, as one who identifies as evangelical, to present one particular hermeneutical vision or range of hermeneutical possibilities.

I have decided on the last named approach. In doing so I am suggesting that it is not the manner in which Scripture is interpreted that is of vital importance to evangelical identity so much as the fact that it is read and interpreted. This is because the

---

[1] I leave the wider volume within which this essay is nested to explore what might be covered by the term "evangelicalism," although for my present purposes I assume within that a broad consensus as to the importance of reading and interpreting Scripture, which is a body of material that is held to be uniquely true and useful in the life of the church and of the believer.

text itself is considered to hold a unique significance and it is thereby essential that it be read as well as possible. Hermeneutics, or a self-conscious appreciation of what one is doing when one interprets, is correspondingly important. But the exact hermeneutical approach, within some limits, is not central to this understanding. There is more than one way to skin evangelically the hermeneutical cat.

Consequently, in this essay I will attempt to convey something of the hermeneutic that informs and guides my own practice as a student and teacher of biblical studies. My sense of identity as an evangelical with respect to Scripture primarily revolves around the question of reading and interpreting Scripture so as to encounter God as ultimately revealed in the person of Jesus, to whom the Scriptures bear a uniquely true, and hence indispensible, witness. This entails seven simple propositions, each of which is far more nuanced than a single essay can adequately express, but the unpacking of which form the body of this essay. Unsurprisingly in light of my comments above, it will become evident that each of them is potentially shared with others who would not identify as evangelical, but who seek with me to read the Bible faithfully and well. If there is a common thread to my approach, it is probably a literary critical focus on the hermeneutical process as participation in an act of communication, hence the subtitle of this essay.

In what follows I assume a particular understanding of the relationship between Scripture and Christ as the word/Word of God. As hinted at in the paragraph above, I assume that the Bible is both the word of God and a signpost to or vehicle of the Word of God in Christ. Neither aspect should be diminished at the expense of the other in the practice of reading and interpretation.[2]

Seven Propositions

In summary, the seven propositions are these:

---

[2] For a fuller statement of this, see T.J. Meadowcroft, *The Message of the Word of God: The Glory of God Made Known* (Leicester: IVP, 2011), 30.

- First, I expect Scripture to be the primary vehicle of divine discourse with me and the rest of humanity.
- Secondly, to this end I strive to submit myself to Scripture. I aspire to sit under it rather than stand over it. In more technical terms, I seek primarily to be a reader rather than primarily a critic of Scripture.
- Thirdly, because of this I see a central obligation on the reader to follow the paths opened up by the reading and interpretation of Scripture no matter where they may lead.
- Fourthly, to this end I place a high premium on an ethic of respect for the intention, to the extent that it may be discerned, of the authors of Scripture.
- At the same time, fifthly, as a reader I place a similarly high premium on the responsibility to read from within my own context. I assume that the divine discourse of Scripture is context-specific, and that a reader has an obligation to take the risks that this entails.
- And sixthly, my own sense of the challenge of hermeneutics in our times is to understand how each of the above two points may be held together in the quest to hear the voice of God in Scripture. Or, to put it more explicitly, how I may enter fully into the construction of meaning that is part of the responsibility of the reader while equally fully respecting the intentionality of the text?
- As a consequence of that I feel, seventhly, a huge responsibility to develop in myself and to help to form in others the skills for competent reading.

That is my position and my quest.[3] To put it another way, I seek to be a part of the enterprise named by the general editors of the New International Biblical Commentary as "believing criticism."[4]

---

[3] For a fuller expression of this, see T.J. Meadowcroft, "Prolegomena: Reading Haggai as Scripture," in *Haggai* (Sheffield: Sheffield Phoenix, 2006), 1–40.

[4] R.L. Hubbard and R.K. Johnston, in the series foreword in each volume of the NIBC commentary series: "this approach marries probing, reflective

This takes place in the context of a wider intellectual landscape which provides a number of allies in the quest. In the rest of the paper I intend to identify some of those allies as I explore in more detail what I mean by each of those seven propositions.

Scripture as the primary vehicle of divine discourse

First, I expect Scripture to be the primary vehicle of divine discourse with me and the rest of humanity. This is a more defensible position epistemologically than it once was. I have been helped hugely by the work of thinkers such as Michael Polanyi with his concept of tacit knowledge and his exploration of the distinction between the subject and the object,[5] and Bernard Lonergan with his exposition of what he calls "transcendental method."[6] They have given wings to something that many of us have always known instinctively – that knowing is not merely rational – but have been prevented from expressing by the prevailing scientism of modernity. One of the great blessings of postmodernity is a re-appreciation of the subjective. It makes epistemological sense to approach a text from a faith perspective; Cartesian doubt is no longer definitive.

---

interpretation of the text to loyal biblical devotion and warm Christian affection. Our contributors tackle the task of interpretation using the full range of critical methodologies and practices. Yet they do so as people of faith who hold the text in the highest regard."

[5] M. Polanyi, *Personal Knowledge, Towards a Post-Critical Philosophy* (Chicago: University of Chicago Press, 1958), 286, remarks that, "all truth is but the external pole of belief, and to destroy all belief would be to deny all truth." See also M. Polanyi, *The Tacit Dimension* (London: Routledge & Kegan Paul, 1967).

[6] B. Lonergan, *Method in Theology* (London: Barton, Longman & Todd, 1971), esp. 13–25. He comments (p. 24) that "to assign to transcendental method a role in theology adds no new resource to theology but simply draws attention to a resource that has always been used. For transcendental method is the concrete and dynamic unfolding of human attentiveness, intelligence, reasonableness, and responsibility."

In the light of this, a philosopher such as Nicholas Wolterstorff must be taken seriously when he speaks of "divine discourse." I am deeply indebted to his work on *Divine Discourse* in a book of that title, and his concept (as yet somewhat imperfectly expressed) of human entitlement to participate in this discourse through Scripture.[7] The communication mechanics of this is a more complex matter, to which I return below, and Wolterstorff is one of a number of people who are making certain suggestions along those lines also.[8]

Submission to Scripture

Secondly, that I expect to encounter God in Scripture and that I am assuming an epistemology of belief in doing so both direct me towards a particular stance with respect to Scripture.[9] I strive to submit myself to Scripture; I aspire to sit under it rather than stand over it. In more technical terms, I seek primarily to be a reader rather than primarily a critic of Scripture. In that respect I have been helped by the distinction drawn and discussed by Robert

---

[7] N. Wolterstorff, *Divine Discourse: Philosophical Reflections on the Claim that God Speaks* (Cambridge: University Press, 1995), esp. 261–80.

[8] Note N. Wolterstorff, "The Promise of Speech-Act Theory for Biblical Interpretation," in *After Pentecost: Language and Biblical Interpretation* (eds C. Bartholomew, C. Greene, and K. Möller; Grand Rapids: Zondervan, 2001), 73–90.

[9] This is not the same thing as a fatalistic quietism. From within the limitations of my humanity, I am encouraged to question, challenge, rage against, and interpret God, but ultimately I am compelled to trust the intentions of God. That assumption is not universally shared, of course. See for example P.R. Davies, *Whose Bible is it Anyway?* (Sheffield: Sheffield Academic Press, 1995), 113, who concludes from the story of the near sacrifice of Isaac that, "The story says to them: do not trust a deity. He or she or it almost certainly does not trust you, and has no reason to tell the truth." R.W.L. Moberly, *The Bible, Theology, and Faith: A Study of Abraham and Jesus* (Cambridge: University Press, 2000), 170–83, responds to Davies' highly suspicious reading of the story.

Fowler between reader and critic.[10] Fowler himself is feeling his way towards a *via media* of "critical reader," but in doing so notes the antithesis that may arise between the critic who adopts a legislative function towards the text and the reader who enters into rather than objectifies the text.[11] Although neither pole of the reader-critic continuum exists in a pure state, I seek primarily to read well rather than to critique. I am a biblical critic, but not so much in that I assess the message of Scripture as in that I seek to discern within it the discourse of God in my own context.

In that respect the rise of canonical and rhetorical criticism has helped to make possible the type of stance that I am here advocating. Each has built on the older work of so-called "literary criticism," but each in different ways shifts the focus onto the received text of Scripture.[12] Rhetorical criticism, which famously traces its contemporary formulation back to the 1968 Society of Biblical Literature presidential address by James Muilenburg, does so in that it encourages an attitude of listening to what the text seeks to say to the reader, and enhances an assumption of the text as a communicative event in its own right.[13]

Canonical criticism does so in that it argues the position that the task of the church is to read the text that the church has received, albeit in the light of what may be known of the history of that

---

[10] R.M. Fowler, "Who is 'The Reader' in Reader Response Criticism?" *Semeia* 31 (1985): 5–23.

[11] Fowler, "Who is 'The Reader'?" 6.

[12] I prefer to speak of the "received" rather than the "final" form of the text to express the fact that the text as we have it was but one final form among others competing for attention. This is the one that has been received and discerned by the church as in some way definitive. I am grateful to Edgar Conrad, who clarified this point to me in a private conversation.

[13] See P. Trible, *Rhetorical Criticism: Context, Method, and the Book of Jonah* (Minneapolis: Fortress, 1994), 5–90, for a full discussion of the discipline. Trible (p. 25) quotes J. Muilenburg, "Form Criticism and Beyond," *Journal of Biblical Literature* 88 (1969): 4, calling for the biblical critic to "supplement... form-critical analysis with a careful inspection of the literary unit in its precise and unique formulation."

text.¹⁴ This also encourages the reader to take seriously the received form of the text for two reasons. First, because it opens up a whole range of possibilities of appreciation of the text as we have it as what Robert Alter calls "a literary project."¹⁵ While Alter himself does not engage directly with the project of canonical criticism, concepts such as "composite artistry" proposed by him are made more accessible to the biblical critic by the assumptions wrought by canonical criticism.¹⁶ Secondly, it asks the reader to take seriously the historical fact of canonization as a particular reason for reading the text in its received form rather than in any other particular form and for reading other texts in the service of that particular reading.¹⁷

This shift in focus onto the received, or as some would say the "final," form of the text opens up the rich concept of intertextuality. My readerly submission to Scripture also obliges me to take this whole complex field of study seriously, although a discussion of intertextuality is well beyond the scope of this paper. Without getting distracted by the range of non-textual definitions of what a text may be, I agree with Patricia Tull that "there are some things worth saying about individual texts and particular relationships drawn among them."¹⁸ And these relationships are not merely ones of chronological dependence. Once a set of texts has been gathered

---

¹⁴ B.S. Childs, *The New Testament as Canon: An Introduction* (Valley Forge: Trinity Press International, 1994), xviii, summarises the term "canonical" thus: "as a cipher seeking to articulate the special relationship which the Christian church has always confessed to have with its Scriptures."

¹⁵ This is explicated in R. Alter, *The Art of Biblical Narrative* (London: George Allen & Unwin, 1981), 3–22, in a chapter entitled "A Literary Approach to the Bible."

¹⁶ Alter, *The Art of Biblical Narrative*, 131–54, on "composite artistry."

¹⁷ See the discussion of what he calls the "final form" by R. Rendtorff, *Canon and Theology: Overtures to an Old Testament Theology* (trans. and ed. M. Kohl; Minneapolis: Fortress, 1993), 46–65. See also the comment on "received canonical orders" by E.W. Conrad, *Reading the Latter Prophets: Toward a New Canonical Criticism* (Edinburgh: T. & T. Clark, 2004), 59.

¹⁸ P. Tull, "Intertextuality and the Hebrew Scriptures," *Currents in Research: Biblical Studies* 8 (2000): 61.

into a canonical whole, synchronic understandings of their interrelatedness are brought to bear.[19] Questions of allusions and echoes, as well as more linear dependence, come into play.

In my mind this leads on to two other key related hermeneutical discussions: the questions of authority and of history. With respect to authority, this is a subtle question that requires a subtle treatment. The commentator who cannot see it as that is unlikely to come up with an understanding that is expressive of and respectful towards the nature of the received text.

I have been helped most by the metaphor of performance expressed by N.T. Wright and developed in a slightly different direction by Stephen Barton.[20] This approach seems to me to take the best account of the nature of the received text that we have to work with. It expresses that there is interpretive work to do on the part of the reader without losing sight of the intentionality of the author or text. It helps us to live with the fact that the text is inherently incomplete in the form that we have it; it is something that raises many questions that are not answered directly in that it points towards an ultimate authority beyond the text.[21] It is not a kind of divine encyclopaedia. This does not make the discernment of authority an easy matter. In a development of his earlier article Wright argues in his refreshingly short volume, *The Last Word*, that as readers of the Bible become "actors in their own right" the

---

[19] For further on these matters see the above-mentioned article by Tull; R.B. Hays, *Echoes of Scripture in the Letters of Paul* (New Haven: Yale University Press, 1989), 29–32; J.W. Voelz, "Multiple Signs and Double Texts: Elements of Intertextuality," in *Intertextuality in Biblical Writings: Essays in Honour of Bas van Iersel* (ed. S. Draisma; Kampen: Kok, 1989), 27–34.

[20] N.T. Wright, "How Can the Bible be Authoritative?" *Vox Evangelica* 21 (1991): 7–32; S. Barton, "New Testament Interpretation as Performance," *Scottish Journal of Theology* 52 (1999): 179–208.

[21] N.T. Wright, *The Last Word: Beyond the Bible Wars to a New Understanding of the Authority of Scripture* (New York: HarperSanFrancisco, 2005), xi, wonders "how we can speak of the Bible being in some sense 'authoritative' when the Bible itself declares that all authority belongs to the one true God, and that this is now embodied in Jesus himself."

authority of Scripture becomes "a sub-branch of several other theological topics: the mission of the church, the work of the Spirit, the ultimate future hope and the way it is anticipated in the present, and of course the nature of the church."[22]

The second discussion is that of history. There has grown up gradually as a result of the Enlightenment a particular approach to biblical interpretation that has granted what could be called an interpretive hegemony to history. And that hegemony has been exercised under the aegis of a particularly intractable historiography that has always left me unsatisfied. When I was taught in my initial theological training, for example, that claims concerning the resurrection are statements of faith and not the product of historical enquiry I instinctively rebelled. Because that distinction is so deeply rooted in the practice of biblical studies as a discipline, I have learned to accommodate it, but I still rebel. I continue to struggle to put words to that rebellion, and have not achieved a satisfactory resolution in my mind. I do not think that history should be allowed to be the interpretive grid through which all reading of Scripture must be fed in order to be sound. Why should anachronism be the one unforgivable interpretive sin? Understandings of intertextuality suggest that it should not.

Others have also named the problem. Murray Rae speaks of the "great divorce" between theology and history, and proposes in response an ecclesial reading of Scripture.[23] Hans Frei famously tackled the issue in terms of the Enlightenment reversal in hermeneutics that increasingly distanced the meaning of the text from the story itself. This he termed the "eclipse of biblical

---

[22] Wright, *The Last Word*, 30. Wright's concluding comment is that the authority of Scripture is honoured "by a reading of Scripture that is (a) totally contextual, (b) liturgically grounded, (c) privately studied, (d) refreshed by appropriate scholarship, and (e) taught by the church's accredited leaders." (p. 127).

[23] M.A. Rae, *History and Hermeneutics* (London: T. & T. Clark, 2005).

narrative."[24] The fourth volume of the Scripture and Hermeneutics Project, *"Behind" the Text: History and Biblical Interpretation*, tackles the same issue from a variety of angles.[25]

From within the world of Old Testament theology John Goldingay and Walter Brueggemann are recent exegetes to have dealt in different ways with the problem of history in their Old Testament theology volumes.[26] Both of them draw on Leo Perdue's concept of *The Collapse of History* as part of their thinking.[27] By organizing his approach around the category of rhetoric, Brueggemann perpetuates the "eclipse" complained of by Frei by taking shelter in the category of "rhetoric." To my mind Goldingay's is a more satisfactory acknowledgement of Perdue's proposal concerning the "collapse of the historical paradigm as the singular approach for doing Old Testament theology."[28]

However we approach it, a reacquaintance of theology and history with one another is an important component of competent, faithful, and (in the best sense) submissive reading of the biblical text. I note in passing the Scripture Project hosted by the Centre for Theological Inquiry (Princeton) as one example of the ecclesial struggle to wrestle back the text from the clutches of a modernist historical paradigm.[29]

---

[24] H. Frei, *The Eclipse of Biblical Narrative: A Study of Eighteenth and Nineteenth Century Hermeneutics* (New Haven: Yale University Press, 1974). See also the discussion of Frei by Rae, *History and Hermeneutics*, 39–44.

[25] C. Bartholomew, C.S. Evans, M. Healy, and M. Rae (eds), *"Behind" the Text: History and Biblical Interpretation* (Grand Rapids: Zondervan, 2003).

[26] W. Brueggemann, *Theology of the Old Testament: Testimony, Dispute, Advocacy* (Minneapolis: Fortress, 1997); J.E. Goldingay, *Old Testament Theology, Volume One, Israel's Gospel* (Downers Grove: IVP, 2003). See also T.J. Meadowcroft, "Method and Old Testament Theology: Barr, Brueggemann and Goldingay Considered," *Tyndale Bulletin* 57 (2006): 35–56.

[27] L.G. Perdue, *The Collapse of History* (Minneapolis: Fortress, 1994).

[28] Perdue, *Collapse of History*, 11.

[29] See the resulting collection of essays in E.F. Davis and R.B. Hays (eds), *The Art of Reading Scripture* (Grand Rapids: Eerdmans, 2003).

Scripture and truth

But such a competent and faithful reading does not always win friends, because a determined quest for the truth does not always win friends. Thirdly, I see a central obligation on the reader to follow the paths opened up by the reading and interpretation of Scripture no matter where they may lead, and sometimes this entails the slaughter of sacred confessional cows. For those who work in an evangelical context, when the victim of the slaughter is a statement of faith that is assumed by others to be "biblical," this can be particularly difficult. Those who work in a context with different theological assumptions as to Scripture, and who are led to certain convictions about truth in the light of Scripture but which challenge contemporary experience, there is another, equally painful, type of difficulty. Each arises from a commitment to the search for truth.

The proposal concerning Scripture and truth raises the question of the hermeneutical key to Scripture. By what means do we discern the cohesive nature of the divine discourse that I have mentioned? Scriptural texts are diverse in a range of ways: principally in terms of literary genre, historical context, intention, and theological focus. Yet my first two propositions assume that they should nevertheless constitute some kind of coherent whole. One of the key challenges for evangelical hermeneutics is to discover how to express that. I see three key options jostling with each other. Each is attractive, and each brings with it problems.

One is what may be called a Christological hermeneutic, in theory if not always in practice. This says that Scripture is both christocentric and christotelic.[30] This is not a difficult position to

---

[30] The terminology employed by M. Strom, "Walking into One Conversation: Inspiring and Equipping Leaders with an Integrated Vision of Scripture and Life" (unpublished paper, Bible College of New Zealand, 2005). On p. 10 he writes that "Biblical theology is a clear hermeneutical stance: Scripture is read as a coherent unfolding story that has reached its fulfillment in the person and events of Jesus of Nazareth." P. Enns, *Inspiration and Incarnation* (Grand Rapids: Baker, 2005), 154, coined the term "christotelic" to focus on what gives coherence to the biblical story.

promote in an evangelical context; questioning it is a bit like questioning motherhood and apple pie. The danger of such an approach from within an evangelical context, however, is that it can easily lead to a "canon within a canon." It can also lead to a flattening of the diversity of Scripture with the corresponding silencing of some of the uncomfortable voices. It also attracts little attention to the question of how the divine discourse of Scripture actually works. Another danger of this approach, especially when divorced from an appreciation of an ecclesial dimension to the authority of Scripture (of which see more below), is that it becomes highly individualistic and hence ironically unbiblical.

Another option is a Trinitarian approach. Although nobody who advocates a Christological hermeneutic would deny the other persons of the Trinity, there is a difference it seems to me between a Trinitarian and a Christological approach to hermeneutics. The Trinitarian approach brings to bear an appreciation of the activity of the Spirit in the task of interpretation as entering into the narrative, and hence to a fuller understanding of the speech-act of Scripture (of which see more below) and the accompanying appreciation of the inferential nature of the communicative act of reading.

It also allows for an appreciation of the dwelling of God with humanity in the person of Jesus. This in turn leads to a more direct observation of God the creator as revealed in Scripture, which in turn encourages a wider ranging understanding of God at work in the world. This can all be lost in a christocentric reading, which, incidentally, is not at all the same thing as saying it can be lost in a Christ-like reading. It is more likely also to lead to an appreciation of the intrinsic worth of all of Scripture, under whose divine discourse it is important to remain (see my first proposition above).

Another common approach is what I am calling the "rule of faith" approach, although I am not sure that that is the best term. In any case this may embrace a number of traditions or interpretive grids, some more satisfactory than others. What such approaches have in common is that they shift the hermeneutical focus onto the church, however that may be perceived, either in the endowment of interpretative authority to the church or in recognition of the church as the arena within which the hermeneutical endeavour is played out.[31]

This is classically associated with the Roman Catholic position, by which the church not only discerns the canon of Scripture but also moderates its appropriate interpretation.[32] However, it has also been well observed that some Protestant and independent ecclesial traditions give every bit as much interpretive authority to the church, albeit at a local level.[33] Notwithstanding the rhetoric of classical evangelicalism, I suggest that the manner in which we have used our statements of faith, formal and unspoken, sometimes gives authority to an interpretive grid in a manner which is at odds with the *sola scriptura* position that we espouse. And yet, such an approach is a more realistic recognition of the historical facts that the Scriptures have been discerned by the church in the first place.

Beyond that we may also say that the task of reading the witness contained in the text has both a Christological and an ecclesiological dimension, and that we separate them at our peril. This is well expressed in an essay by James Aageson in which he examines Paul's use of Scripture principally by an extended reflection on 1

---

[31] J.B. Green, "Scripture and Theology: Failed Experiments, Fresh Perspectives," *Interpretation* 56 (2002): 19–20, comments: "Reading the Bible as Christian scripture means acknowledging the relation between the words of scripture and the ongoing presence of the crucified Christ, who is the Lord of the church." I acknowledge also a paper by my colleague R.A. Robinson, "Imaginations Yielded to the Theological Vision of Scripture: Four Diagrams and a Puzzle Solved" (unpublished paper presented to Bible College of New Zealand Faculty Colloquium, 2007), 5.

[32] See for example section II of the Catechism of the Catholic Church, "The relationship between Tradition and Sacred Scripture." [cited 23 November 2011]. Online: http://www.vatican.va/archive/ENG0015/__PL.HTM.

[33] See the fascinating argument by J.K.A. Smith, "The Closing of the Book: Pentecostals, Evangelicals, and the Sacred Writings," *Journal of Pentecostal Theology* 11 (1997): 49–71, that this *should* in fact be the case.

Corinthians 10.[34] Aageson negotiates the subtle interaction of both Christology and ecclesiology in the approach of Paul to Scripture. In doing so he rightly protests at the privilege of one over the other. Both dimensions are inescapable, as they should be for all Paul's descendants as readers of the text. Hence, according to Aageson, "Paul's interpretive space is not the text of Scripture alone but also the way Scripture came to be understood and the matrix of symbols that came to surround it over time."[35] Paul read with other readers and so inevitably do Paul's hermeneutical successors. This point is supplementary to the comment by Joel Green noted above that the word of God is expressed both in Jesus and in the ongoing presence of Jesus in the body of Christ.[36]

Whatever the case, some kind of interpretive subjectivity is inescapable in the matter of truth and Scripture. In light of my first proposition above, one might even say that it is an epistemological necessity. Indeed, I will argue shortly that it is the nature of the case. Although I have said that it is not my task to second-guess the discourse of God in my hermeneutics, nevertheless Scripture itself and the church's understanding of the nature of scriptural authority invite the reader to wrestle with and question the text in the search for understanding. The trick is to ensure that the subjectivity inherent in this process, a kind of interpretive privilege, is not untrammelled. To that end, perhaps the best hermeneutic is one that keeps a range of hermeneutical keys in constant conversation with each other as we go about our work.[37]

---

[34] J.W. Aageson, "Written Also for Our Sake: Paul's Use of Scripture in the Four Major Epistles, with a Study of 1 Corinthians 10," in *Hearing the Old Testament in the New Testament* (ed. S.E. Porter; Grand Rapids: Eerdmans, 2006), 152–81.

[35] Aageson, "Written Also for Our Sake," 160.

[36] See also the collection of essays by J. Webster, *Word and Church: Essays in Christian Dogmatics* (Edinburgh: T. & T. Clark, 2001).

[37] In a comprehensive treatment, J.E. Goldingay, *Models for Scripture* (Grand Rapids: Eerdmans, 1994), makes an argument for this approach.

Respect for intention

This leads to my fourth proposition which is an ethic of respect for the intention, to the extent that it may be discerned, of the authors of Scripture. It is that very ethic that ensures that no hermeneutical approach is permitted to attain an authority that outweighs that of the text itself. It is no accident that Kevin Vanhoozer's massive apology for intention should be subtitled as it is: "The Bible, the reader and the *morality* of literary knowledge."[38]

But this is not merely a doctrinaire position taken in the face of the forces of deconstruction.[39] It may also be argued from the psychological perspective that the communicative act is deeply presumptive of intention, a presumption held both by the initiator of communication and by its recipient.[40] Notwithstanding the theory of the "disappearing author" or the practical difficulties of putting an individual or corporate face and name to some texts, especially ancient texts, there is arguably within the consciousness of the one who encounters any text that he/she is encountering the mind behind the text. This is sometimes acknowledged with the categories of implied author and implied reader. This is to some extent a helpful device, but it does seem to me to deny an identity to the creator of the text. Notwithstanding what I say below on the subject of reader response-ability, that the discernment of who the author might be is left entirely up to the judgment of the reader is a contradictory state of affairs. At this point I am somewhat at odds with New Critical theory which has supported a healthy refocusing

---

[38] K.J. Vanhoozer, *Is There a Meaning in this Text? The Bible, the Reader and the Morality of Literary Knowledge* (Grand Rapids: Apollos, 1998), emphasis mine.

[39] Note that Vanhoozer's title is a play on the earlier work by S. Fish, *Is There a Text in this Class? The Authority of Interpretive Communities* (Cambridge: Harvard University Press, 1980).

[40] R. W. Gibbs, *Intentions in the Experience of Meaning* (Cambridge: University Press, 1999), 206: "the multifaceted nature of authorship complicates any simple view of intentionalism. Yet these complications don't eliminate the cognitive unconscious drive toward inferring something about both real and hypothetical authors'/artists' communicative intentions."

onto the text, and to which canonical criticism is arguably in some debt, but whose focus on the text alone does have its drawbacks.[41]

Quite apart from all this theory, at the level of the human experience of relational communication, I as a writer sense a responsibility to represent what I mean as closely as possible in what I write, and correspondingly a responsibility to know and understand as competently as I hope to be known and understood. This is where I am helped by the psychological theory of Gibbs. Yet I recognize the danger of this position being held in a simplistic way. The work of people such as Stanley Fish has demonstrated the limits to a focus on intention.[42] And in the biblical studies field David Clines has argued the limits of a determinate approach to the text.[43] Both push the logic of their arguments to the point of being untenable, but they do rightly alert us to the subjectivity inherent in the process of communication.

Reader response-ability

And so, fifthly, as a reader I place a similarly high premium on the responsibility to read from within my own context, and to incorporate what I read into my own context. In doing so I am assuming that the divine discourse of Scripture, like any textual discourse, is context-specific, and that a reader has an obligation to enter into the risky subjectivity that this entails. And so I affirm in general terms the value of reader response approaches. This affirmation has so far for me two theoretical underpinnings, one epistemological and one theological.[44]

---

[41] See M.G. Brett, *Biblical Criticism in Crisis? The Impact of the Canonical Approach on Old Testament Studies* (Cambridge: Cambridge University Press, 1991), 5; and J. Barton, *Reading the Old Testament* (London: Darton, Longman and Todd, 1984), 208, on the possible relationship of canonical approaches to the New Criticism.

[42] Fish, *Is There a Text in this Class?*

[43] D.J.A. Clines, "Varieties of Indeterminacy," *Semeia* 71 (1995): 17–27.

[44] There are others that I look forward to the opportunity to explore. The pneumatological and the ecclesiological are but two examples.

I have already touched on the epistemological undergirding in my comments on the first proposition. The key point to note is a calling into question of a Cartesian epistemology of doubt that has dominated modern post-Enlightenment reading. In its place may be found an appreciation that believing and knowing have to do with one another. In support of this is an appreciation of the relationship between subject and object, and that what is known has much to do with the knower. The reader of the text and the text itself are intimately related in the matter of meaning.

I have also argued elsewhere that a theological undergirding for this position may be found in the doctrine of the incarnation.[45] Writing early in the last century, Wilhelm Vischer, on the subject of Christ in both the Old and New Testaments, perceived the link between the incarnation and the nature of the Bible, but took the point further than many who have made similar links. His comments bear quoting at some length:

> If the words of the Bible were not really words of men they would not be the true swaddling clothes of the Son of Man. The *scandalon* of the human contingency of the Bible, which historical and literary criticism has brought to our attention, corresponds precisely to the *scandalon* of the incarnation of the eternal Word in the historical appearance of Jesus of Nazareth at a certain point of time.[46]

Vischer's comments ask us to see that the written testimony to Christ that the church has received and formed could be of no other nature if it is to be a true expression of the incarnation, of the fact of Christ Jesus incarnate in the flesh. Accordingly, "In their fleshliness, in their temporal contingency and historical fortuitousness, the

---

[45] T.J. Meadowcroft, "Between Authorial Intent and Indeterminacy: The Incarnation as an Invitation to Human-Divine Discourse," *Scottish Journal of Theology* 58 (2005): 199–218.

[46] W. Vischer, *The Witness of the Old Testament to Christ: Volume I, The Pentateuch* (trans. A.B. Crabtree; London: Lutterworth, 1949), 15. See also the discussion of Vischer's position by Moberly, *The Bible, Theology, and Faith*, 134–38.

writings of the Old and New Testament bear witness to the incarnation."⁴⁷ Correspondingly, not only do we perceive the nature of the Scriptures in the incarnate one to which they bear witness, but we are helped to understand the nature of the incarnation by means of the nature of the Scriptures which bear it witness.⁴⁸ Accordingly, any hermeneutical process that hopes to enter into the divine discourse must itself be able to reflect the incarnational nature of God's self-revelation. This provides a theological basis for a focus on context and particularity. The very particularity of the incarnation and God's engagement with human history invites a respect for context and particularity in the reading of Scripture.

When it comes to an appreciation of the reader's context this induces an honesty and realism about both the limits and potential of one's own particular reading. In the best sense it calls forth a self-critical "hermeneutic of suspicion" as to the reader's own limitations and potential misuse of the text.⁴⁹ It has also induced a renewed sense of the importance of understanding the text of Scripture itself as context specific, and of the reality that the writers of Scripture themselves are context-rich. This is evident, for example, both in the flowering of work on the Greco-Roman context of the New

---

[47] Vischer, *The Witness*, 14.

[48] Although note the caution by Goldingay, *Models for Scripture*, 241, who warns that "there are limits to the analogy between inspiration and incarnation. There is not such an intrinsic link between the nature of Christ and the nature of Scripture that one can argue directly from the one to the other."

[49] In this respect A.C. Thiselton, *New Horizons in Hermeneutics* (Grand Rapids: Zondervan, 1992), 439–40, comments concerning ideological approaches: "Do the systems function as socio-critical ones in the sense that they embody some trans-contextual, metacritical, or transcendental principle of critique, or do they collapse into socio-pragmatic hermeneutics which, on the basis only of narrative-experience within a given context, exclude all interpretative options in advance which would give any other signals than positive ones for the journey already undertaken?"

Testament,[50] and in the growing appreciation of the Jewishness of Jesus and of the New Testament witness to Jesus.[51]

The mediation of intention and response

Such an approach requires that any methodology for reading Scripture be able to discern both the divine intent of and the contingent response to the text, and be able to distinguish the two. And so, sixthly, I believe that to a significant extent the task of evangelical hermeneutics is to understand how both intention and response may be held together in the quest to hear the voice of God in Scripture. Or, to put it more explicitly, how may I enter fully into the construction of meaning that is part of the responsibility of the reader while equally fully respecting the intentionality of the text?

I will not dwell further on the help that the incarnation may be to us in understanding this dynamic. Rather I will comment on how this works in an understanding of the reading and interpretive process. The challenge posed by the need to hold together intention and response for a truly faithful reading will never yield to a neat synthesis. Rather it is a question that must constantly be explored from different angles, each exploration adding to a web of interpretive understanding. I am conscious that there is more yet to be explored, but I have been helped so far in this quest by two particular approaches from the field of pragmatic linguistics.

---

[50] Note for instance The Book of Acts in Its First Century Setting project under the leadership of Bruce Winter. For a list of Winter's own contributions to this field of study see P.J. Williams, A.D. Clarke, P.M. Head, and D. Instone-Brewer (eds), *The New Testament in Its First Century Setting: Essays on Context and Background in Honour of B.W. Winter on His 65th Birthday* (Grand Rapids: Eerdmans, 2004), xiv–xix. See also M. Strom, *Reframing Paul: Conversations in Grace and Community* (Downers Grove: IVP, 2000).

[51] See for instance the influential work by Jewish scholar G. Vermes, *Jesus the Jew: A Historian's Reading of the Gospels* (London: Collins, 1973). And this is a characteristic of the work of N.T. Wright, *Jesus and the Victory of God* (Minneapolis: Fortress, 1996), who, in this and other volumes, consistently pushes his reader back to Jesus' own Jewish context.

The first of these is Speech-Act Theory. I will not go into the history of this developing branch of pragmatics, other than to note the helpful focus on locution. As opposed to the code model of communication, which undergirds most approaches to hermeneutics that focus on authorial intent, this allows for an appreciation that meaning resides not merely in the words used but in the intent with which they are uttered and in the manner in which they are received. Hence the distinction is made between locution, the utterance or text itself, and the illocutionary intent of an utterance or text and its perlocutionary effect. Meaning is more than grammatical and lexical. This goes some way towards helping us to affirm reader response without abandoning intent and determinacy. There are several strands of thought that have alighted on this possibility in their thinking on hermeneutics. It forms the basis of Wolterstorff's philosophical approach to the possibility of divine discourse (on which see above).[52] It is also a key plank in Anthony Thiselton's magisterial Horizons volumes.[53] And Speech-Act Theory provides a key theme in the Scripture and Hermeneutics volume on "language and biblical interpretation."[54] In any case its principal value to my mind is in its conceptualization of the category of locution, for around that concept gather both intention and response as key elements in perceiving meaning.

However, Speech-Act Theory has its limitations. Principally, it does not sufficiently account for the operation of inference that is at the heart of the locutionary distinctions that the theory makes.

---

[52] See especially Wolterstorff, *Divine Discourse*, 19–36, a chapter entitled "Speaking is not Revealing."

[53] Thiselton, *New Horizons*, in various places. See on p. 691 the index entry for 'Speech-acts, speech-act theory" and related topics.

[54] Apart from the essay by Wolterstorff in *After Pentecost*, noted above, see chapters in the same volume by K.J. Vanhoozer, "From Speech Acts to Scripture Acts: The Covenant of Discourse and the Discourse of Covenant" (1–49); D.R. Stiver, "Ricoeur, Speech-Act Theory, and the Gospels as History" (50–72); and N.B. MacDonald, "Illocutionary Stance in Hans Frei's *The Eclipse of Biblical Narrative*: An Exercise in Conceptual Redescription and Normative Analysis" (312–28).

What is the human process whereby illocutionary intent is conveyed and discerned, and perlocutionary effect achieved? Neither illocution nor perlocution may have anything to do with the actual physical utterance. There are a range of non-verbal factors that all add up to inference, and it is inference which determines the relationship between illocution and perlocution. This has been addressed by a branch of pragmatics known as Relevance Theory. It is a theory that seeks to describe the processes by which a piece of communication achieves relevance to a particular audience. It was pioneered by Dan Sperber and Deidre Wilson,[55] and has been picked up by parts of the biblical studies community. In particular, it is proving to be of interest to translators.[56] One of the most comprehensive applications of this approach that I am aware of is that of UBS translation consultant Stephen Pattemore in the context of a study of the Apocalypse in a University of Otago thesis subsequently published by Cambridge University Press.[57]

What I find remarkable about this focus on inference is that it throws into sharp relief two things at once: the importance of intent and the responsibility to respond. First, it demonstrates that meaning is significantly inferred from a knowledge of a range of things about the speaker or writer that may only be implicit. To that extent it enhances the discernment of intention. At the same time, the responsibility for inference is seen to rest significantly with the listener or reader. The meaning that is finally apprehended by any given act of communication depends on the ability of the reader to infer well. In that respect Relevance Theory also highlights the inescapable need to acknowledge reader response in the interpretive

---

[55] D. Sperber and D. Wilson, *Relevance, Communication and Cognition* (2nd ed.; Oxford: Basil Blackwell, 1995).

[56] Note E.-A. Gutt, *Translation and Relevance: Cognition and Context* (Oxford: Basil Blackwell, 1991); and E.R. Wendland, "On the Relevance of 'Relevance Theory' for Bible Translation," *Bible Translator* 47 (1996): 126–37. This continues to work itself out through a group that meets regularly at Society of Biblical Literature meetings.

[57] S.W. Pattemore, *The People of God in the Apocalypse: Discourse, Structure, and Exegesis* (Cambridge: Cambridge University Press, 2004).

process. I have suggested elsewhere that it may be thought of as a "mediating category" in the hermeneutical debate.[58]

Given that the incarnation is the Word made flesh borne witness to in the text of Scripture, it ought not to surprise us that linguistic theory may help to understand how the Word is encountered in the text which bears witness to him.

Competent reading

As a consequence of that I feel, seventhly, a responsibility to develop in myself and help to form in others the skills for competent reading. I will be brief on this point, for it is essentially in support of the previous three that I have made. To my mind there are three aspects of a competent reading. First, it is a reading that understands well the nature of the text that is being read: its language, its genres, its context, its narratology and historiography, the nature of its authority. Secondly, it is a reading that understands well the task of reading: its epistemological undergirding, its purpose, its ecclesiological and Christological framework, its pneumatological significance. Thirdly, it is a reading that understands well the reader: his/her context, his/her distance from the text, his/her responsibilities with respect to the text.

These categories bear some resemblance to the notions of "ideal reader" formed by Fowler and "informed reader" formed by Fish.[59] Of course, the ideal is not attainable and competence is not fully achievable. We see and hear yet "as in a mirror dimly." Nevertheless, they remain goals in the quest to hear the voice of God in the Scriptures, pending the day that "we will see him face to face."[60]

---

[58] T.J. Meadowcroft, "Relevance as a Mediating Category in the Reading of Biblical Texts: Venturing Beyond the Hermeneutical Circle," *Journal of the Evangelical Theology Society* 45 (2002): 611–27.

[59] Fowler, "Who is 'The Reader'?" 15–18; Fish, *Is There a Text in this Class?* 48–49.

[60] 1 Cor 13:12 (NRSV).

Concluding

In the meantime, we read to the end that we might encounter the Word, "the image of the invisible God," "the firstborn of all creation," the one who "is before all things" and in whom "all things hold together," "the head of the church," the one through whom "God was pleased to reconcile to himself all things."[61] This emphasis on the encounter with the word of God, both spoken and revealed fully in Christ, is a mark of evangelical hermeneutics. Similarly, a determination to wrestle meaning from the text by means of faithful and competent reading and interpretation, and to sit in submission to the outcome of that reading, is an undergirding factor in an evangelical approach to Scripture. There are various modes of interpretation that may be employed to express this evangelical approach to the reading of Scripture. What I have offered in this essay is a cluster of attitudes and approaches that I have found to be supportive of the encounter with God in the text of Scripture.

---

[61] Extracted from Col 1:15-20 (NRSV).

Chapter Thirteen
Music as revelation: a comment from over the fence

Judith Brown

Ever since the creation of the world his invisible nature, namely, his eternal power and deity has been clearly perceived in the things that have been made. (Rom 1:20 RSV)

This paper is a response to an essay by Kevin Vanhoozer,[1] in which he asks if music has "something *intrinsic* to do with theology"[2] and more pointedly yet, "Can music ever convey the truths of *special* revelation and so express not only the sentiment of human faith but faith's very substance?"[3] Vanhoozer concludes that music communicates, that what it communicates is true, founded in reality and that at heart some of this truth at least partakes of grace.[4]

Rather than directly engaging with Vanhoozer's thesis I want to offer a supporting argument drawn not from any Christian reflection but from the philosophy of music of the Marxist Ernst Bloch. This is to say, a response not in itself drawn from theology but bearing on complementary terrain. Bloch's Marxism, so messianic and "revolutionary Romantic," is a summons to kingdom living in which the arts and music in particular "foreshadow"[5] what

---

[1] Kevin Vanhoozer, "What Has Vienna to do with Jerusalem? Barth, Brahms, and Bernstein's Unanswered Question." *Westminster Theological Journal* 63 (2001): 123-50.
[2] Vanhoozer, "What Has Vienna to do with Jerusalem?" 131.
[3] Vanhoozer, "What Has Vienna to do with Jerusalem?" 132.
[4] Vanhoozer, "What Has Vienna to do with Jerusalem?" 128.
[5] Michael Andre Bernstein, *Foregone Conclusions: Against Apocalyptic History*, cited in Anson Rabinbach, *In the Shadow of Catastrophe: German Intellectuals between Apocalypse and Enlightenment* (Berkeley: University of California, 1997), 21.

Bloch calls the "changing of the world."[6] And in which there is no end to historical event but an opening out of history.

Statement of themes: the character of music; the form of music

About music let us begin with some entirely representative quotations regarding the character ascribed to it: Josef Pieper speaks of the intimate connection between the music a society makes and listens to and "the inner existential condition of such a society...";[7] "Music is an incursion into the human world of some higher form of reality..." (Nicholas Cook);[8] "Rhythm and harmony find their way into the inward places of the soul, on which they... fasten, imparting grace..." (Plato, *The Republic*);[9] every melody is "an Hieroglyphical and shadowed lesson of the whole World and creatures of God" (Thomas Browne, *Religio Medici*);[10] and "...a blind man, to whom the infinity of the visible is denied, can grasp an infinity of life in the audible" (Goethe, Introduction to *Farbenlehre*).[11]

Such notions as are represented here are saying that music has *truth* status. This is the kind of truth that makes *knowledge* possible.

---

[6] Bloch borrows this phrase from Marx's famous comment about the role of philosophy in his *Theses on Feuerbach*. See David McLellan (ed.), *Karl Marx: Selected Writings* (Oxford: Oxford University Press, 1977, 1987), 156-58. It is the key to what Bloch means when he writes about the orthodox Marxist notion of the revolution.

[7] Josef Pieper, *Only the Lover Sings: Art and Contemplation* (San Francisco: Ignatius, 1990), 48.

[8] Nicholas Cook, speaking of Heinrich Schenker in *Music: A Very Short Introduction* (Oxford: Oxford University Press, 1998), 31.

[9] Plato, *The Republic* (trans. Benjamin Jowett; New York: Modern Books, 1941), 105.

[10] Thomas Browne, *Works: Including His Life and Correspondence* (ed. Thomas Wilkin; Volume II; London: William Pickering, 1835), 106.

[11] Goethe's treatise on colour theory, published in 1810. Quoted in Victor Zuckerkandl, *Sound and Symbol: Music and the External World* (trans. Willard R. Trask; New York: Princeton, 1956), 3.

This truth is that which the human person lives *from*. So music gives concrete presence to the Spirit who makes all truth known. This is a very Christian statement when taken at face value. It is also a comment perfectly acceptable to those who understand things differently, when it is heard as a statement of the capacity of the arts to communicate an *essence*.

To join truth and music in the same sentence is an old practice – for example, an idea similar to this existed in the strand of Renaissance thought which sought to understand the universe through the premise that the Word of God gives unity and harmony, both of which are revelatory.[12] There are many books in which God has hidden the secrets of the universe and they can be read on the basis of this unity and harmony. Music is one of the books of knowledge in which God has hidden the secrets of the universe. It offers more than pleasure or emotion. It offers knowledge of truth beyond that perceived by the senses. John Donne in a 1627 Candlemass sermon said that *all* heaven could be brought before the eyes by the *ear*. Through the ear we learn the harmony that exists in heaven, but also in the universe and our body and soul.[13] Music is concord and proportion: beauty, love, virtue, and peace by another name. William Bryd regarded music as like the miraculous speech of the Apostles at Pentecost, as recounted in Acts 2.[14]

---

[12] See Gretchen Finney "Music: A Book of Knowledge in Renaissance England," in *Studies in the Renaissance* (Volume VI; New York: Renaissance Society of America, 1959), 36-63.

[13] Evelyn M. Simpson and George R. Potter (eds), *The Sermons of John Donne* (Volume VII; Berkeley and Los Angeles: University of Los Angeles, 1954, rev. 1984), 325-48.

[14] The setting of this text was not uncommon. That it was understood as a statement on the nature of music itself is demonstrated in the motets known as *Loquebantur variis linguis*, set by Byrd's contemporaries Peter Philips, Thomas Tallis, and the slightly older John Taverner. Composers outside Tudor England also used this text – including Tomas Luis de Victoria.

Truth *may* be revelation, that knowledge which enables us to gain a perspective beyond the "darkness of the lived moment."[15] Such knowledge is not static and once-and-over-and-done-with but ongoing and contextual. New paradigms and *metanoia* follow. Revelation effects salvation through bringing the new in such a way that there follows substantive transformation. The falling silent of music even symbolizes the end of an entire civilization in Revelation 18:22 (RSV): "And so shall Babylon the great city be thrown down... and the sound of harpers and minstrels, of flute players and trumpeters, shall be heard... no more..."

Further expression of the notion that music has a particular creative quality is found in the myth of Orpheus, one of a number of music-making saviour figures in Greek mythology (other such figures are Linos, Musaios, and Amphion). Orpheus could compel the trees and rivers and wild animals to listen to him and be still. He had authority over creation through his music-making. Orpheus also overcame the Sirens (he travelled with the Argonauts), beings whose music brings death, driving men out of their minds.

While the Siren's song hints at the capacity of music to unravel the material of the human, Orpheus's music speaks of its capacity to remake it. It is in his death, torn apart by the maenads because of his faithful lamentation over Euridyice, on whose account he was worshipped as the only human ever to return from the land of the dead, that Orpheus compels the silence of death to give way to the passion of life.[16] As with his silencing of the Sirens, and his defeat of the Furies in the underworld, this expresses the authority he has from his music to reform and transform both the world and humanity's relation to it. Orpheus stands as the figure who "opens

---

[15] Ernst Bloch, *Spirit of Utopia* (trans. Anthony A. Nassar; Stanford: Stanford University Press, 2000), 200. See also Bloch, *The Principle of Hope* (trans. Neville Plaice, Stephen Plaice, and Paul Knight; Volume 1; Cambridge: MIT, 1995), 287-315.

[16] Bloch, *The Principle of Hope*, 3:1204-5.

the gate" to life by the association of both death and life with the articulation and forming of sound.[17]

We discern the presence of two perspectives: music is revelatory both of what is most authentically human and of what transcends us. It is both a mundane human practice and the breath of the "air of another planet," as Arnold Schoenberg's Second Quartet proclaims.[18]

This material world about us is not without another aspect. And it is this later that lingers after our hearing – the onward travelling element comes *with* the material. It is of course an absurdity to say music falls on our ears from "somewhere else" in the sense of an extra-material origin. Sound is made; it has sources – and in music many of these begin in exertion.[19] Our creative curiosity, our imagination, transforms this given in a manner appropriate to the "otherness" latent in reality. To do this we must pay attention.

The possibility of the self incarnated: musical form

In its symbolic articulation music arises from and speaks to the problem of the "other" and the self. We can discern the

---

[17] The iconographic connection of Orpheus to Christ the Word was clear to the early Christians: see the famous image of Orpheus/Christ from the Peter and Marcellus catacombs in Rome. While it may not have been primarily his music-making that led to the appropriation of such images, nonetheless here we have concrete representation of Christ as musician – something whose implication we may ponder.

[18] In this quartet from 1908 Schoenberg sets the poetry of the German Symbolist Stefan George (1868-1933) in the third and fourth movements. It is in the poem *Entruckung* ("Rapture"), set in the fourth movement, that this phrase appears (the other poem *Litanei* is set in the third movement). See *Stefan George: Poems (In English and German)* (trans. Carol North Valhope and Ernst Morwitz; New York: Schocken, 1967). The poems can be found in many of the booklets accompanying recordings of the work, e.g., that of the Diotima Quartet, recorded on the Naïve label, France, 2010.

[19] Recent changes in technology have made our connection to the physical sources of music less immediate, indeed, even vestigial.

embodiment of this question of our common life in what Bloch calls the "houses of the self" that are built in music.[20]

The classical era sought musical modes of expression analogous to the social interaction of individuals with one another in a way that was inherently progressive, that is, directed toward an ideal resolution. Forms such as the piano concerto were structured as dynamic dialogue in which individual fulfilment was realized through social integration.[21]

In the Romantic era the *individual* ego emerged more forcefully. The essence of romanticism has been described as infinite longing,[22] a sense of awe, and the sublime as terror, suffering, and beauty. In this period the sonata developed a tension between "staticism in [the] emphasis on themes and dynamism in the way they return and are developed and varied."[23]

With post-World War II composers such as Pierre Boulez and the second generation of serialists we find a form of music that attempts a kind of cultural ground clearance. It does this through a formal solution to the shattering of cultural unity that was consequent on the two world wars. An aesthetic was sought in which even the memory of the past, let alone its forms, would be excised. The development of total serialism sought to exclude the repetition of any element and in this way to destroy the traditional

---

[20] On the surface of things this could be orthodox Marxist socio-economic analysis but Bloch's intent differs from this. See his controversial and non-chronological history of music in Bloch, *Spirit of Utopia*, 34-47.

[21] Nicholas Till, *Mozart and the Enlightenment: Truth, Virtue and Beauty in Mozart's Operas* (New York: W. W. Norton & Co, 1994), 177-78. An opera such as Mozart's *Le Nozze de Figaro* may be understood as a consummation of the Enlightenment's dream of a self-regulating society in which social order and ethical truth manifest themselves as aesthetic beauty (pp. 178-86).

[22] Giogio Pestelli, *The Age of Mozart and Beethoven* (Cambridge: Cambridge University Press, 1984), 288.

[23] Pestelli, *The Age of Mozart and Beethoven*, 228. The sonata in this era attains a new degree of complexity and an autonomous language.

function of memory within music.[24] This affected both musical form and the listener's *relation* to what was being heard.

Today, practices such as open improvisation are often cited as examples of music practice in which ideal forms of community are modelled. But the necessity to be "of the present" both constrains and liberates the relational dynamics in this music. While responsive listening structures the individual's participation and gestures, open improvisation can equally be undertaken by those drawn to its possibility for totalizing individual expression. In this form of music "the characteristics... are established only by the sonic-musical identity of the person or persons playing it."[25]

Despite this great diversity in these musics we *hear* the society we live in. Music is inescapably informed by the way those who make it and listen to it are related in society. Yet it has an open-endedness that makes the work available to successive generations to *hear* in *their* way.[26]

Art in general is credited with a reconciling and integrative function. Theon of Smyrna (died c.130 AD) stated that the Pythagoreans, and so Plato, called music the "harmonization of opposites, the unification of disparate things, and the conciliation of

---

[24] Hence repetition served to lay down the themes of the sonata so that they would be recalled and their transformation in the recapitulation recognized. By calling on the listener's memory a composer was also of course enabling the listener to participate in the forward movement of the work.

[25] Derek Bailey, *Improvisation: Its Nature and Practice in Music* (New York: Da Capo, 1992), 83.

[26] Bloch distinguishes a creative product from a "cultural" product. The latter merely reproduces an era's ideology. True art has a cultural surplus that is the objectification of shared human values and possibilities. The surplus in an art work enables us to grasp the conditions and tendencies of when it was made. It critically formulates what was lacking when the work of art was created and which can therefore be grasped by succeeding generations. See "Ideas as Transformed Material in Human Minds, or Problems of an Ideological Superstructure," in Ernst Bloch, *The Utopian Function of Art and Literature: Selected Essays* (trans. Jack Zipes and Frank Mecklenburg; Cambridge: MIT, 1988), 18-71.

warring elements."²⁷ Subject and object, materiality or sensuality, and idea or mind are at the same time distinct and one.²⁸ Music maps the diversely situated geographies of the human self as simultaneously both the individual and the "we".

One of the ways this mapping is done is through time. The very matter of music is formed of duration and rest. It is the "nothingness" of a "rest" that gives articulation to the tone event. Things are continually coming to be and emerging from points that are nothing. This alternation in coming into being and passing out of being into nothingness is seen by Augustine in his *De Musica* (c. 391 AD) as characterizing a universe created *ex nihilo*.²⁹ The nothingness is a necessary part of the true order intrinsic to creation, even if this is a restricted order or beauty.³⁰ The created order is suspended between nothingness and the infinite. This condition necessitates that the order be audible and temporal, not spatial, because as such the passing of time more truthfully acknowledges our condition and can also be a vehicle for the longing for the truly permanent. Hence the "non-closure of time" is the best image of eternity.³¹

Development: Bloch – the summons

Do we know who we are? No. Are we at rest? No. We strive and we yearn. The features of our being are those of restlessness. Our most fundamental drive is that of longing: "From early on we are searching. All we do is crave, cry out. Do not have what we want."³²

---

²⁷ Quoted in Catherine Pickstock, "Music: Soul, City and Cosmos after Augustine," in *Radical Orthodoxy* (eds John Milbank, Catherine Pickstock, and Graham Ward; London: Routledge, 1999), 270.
²⁸ For Bloch coming into our own, completing ourselves, grounds us so that the "other," whether person or world, becomes an encounter with the distinct yet familiar.
²⁹ Pickstock, "Music," 247.
³⁰ Pickstock, "Music," 247.
³¹ Pickstock, "Music," 248.
³² Bloch, *The Principle of Hope*, 1:21.

Music is the darkness already, *as darkness*, pregnant with dawn. It is something we cannot yet name, which is not yet known – but which is waiting to gain "insight into itself."[33]

Music *experientially* transcends conceptual ordering and classification. In the arts we have objects that are of our making, but stand apart from us, and so provide the necessary antithesis that is the beginning of the dialectical movement of development.

There is in us knowledge – but it is of the "not-yet" (*noch nicht*).[34] This incompletion is part of the structure of the world. For Bloch it indicates the directionality of the unfinished world. It arises from hope expressed in the simplest human activity, daydreaming. There are in our daydreams, partially veiled still, expressions of our deepest drives. In the world that we make there are "anticipatory illuminations" (*das Vor-Schein*) of fulfilled humanity and with humanity, the world. These are *Spuren*, literally "spoor" that we can track and study for clues to the form of authentic human being.

Bloch's philosophy takes up Aristotle's doctrine of *entelechy*, the concept of self-moving and self-creating matter. Primarily, Bloch develops the concept of the form-idea that actualizes itself in appearing.[35] The New (*Novum*) is not sheer innovation, but comes from engaging with the actual, with what is mediated in "what exists and is in motion."[36] Our knowledge of the world is difficult *participatory* knowledge (*Mitwissenheit*). This is why the *Now* is the final concern of utopia.[37]

---

[33] Bloch, *The Principle of Hope*, 1:124.

[34] This is a category in Bloch's philosophy that is a signifier. See Wayne Hudson, *The Marxist Philosophy of Ernst Bloch* (New York: St. Martin's, 1982), 19-20.

[35] For Bloch this is a far more fruitful notion than Plato's concept of "recollection," with its idea that we know something only because we are "recollecting" what we formerly knew. If this is so then the fundamentally new is not possible.

[36] Bloch, *The Principle of Hope*, 1:230-31.

[37] For Bloch the utopian does not have a necessary relation to technical advances. Utopia is not latent in the organically evolving constituents of

So *das Vor-Schein* is a sketch for what will be completed at the end of history, when utopia itself passes into its own arrival. Cultural forms that reproduce the status quo reproduce illusions, our false consciousnesses. But *Vor-Schein* is something that carries the utopian consciousness forward. Indeed, it is what turns history from a "temple of memory" into an "arsenal."[38]

Bloch resisted all descriptions of music that are reductive. Among the notions he regarded as such are those known as "music of the spheres" proportionality, which reduces the musician to a mere recorder of the voice of God. Any form of the popular association of music with "number" was anathema to him.[39] For the same reasons Bloch rejected sociological analyses, such as Weber's, as *sufficient* tools of explanation. Such analysis is a form of the many attempts to transform human life through the quantifiable (described by Bloch in any of its guises as "the management of the insignificant").[40]

Bloch's understanding of music has part of what John Cage means when he says the question to ask of art is not whether it is any good but of what use is it to me in living?[41] Does it introduce

---

culture. Nor should utopia be mistaken for a place or even a time. It images a condition transcending individual and societal forms. It is an analogue for the "not-yet" (*noch nicht*). Bloch presents some of his thought on the "content" of Utopia in Bloch, *The Principle of Hope*, 2:178-94.

[38] Bloch, *Utopian Function*, 58.

[39] Bloch explains this common association as a consequence of our inability to rest contently with the dream. We have to tack on "sober fact." Bloch, *Utopian Function*, 184. Such interpretations do not explain the interpretive process of our reception of music. They just quantify vibrations.

[40] Bloch, *Spirit of Utopia*, 159.

[41] John Cage also rejected the idea of music as communication and this situates him in antithesis to Bloch. Music is not a vehicle of "meaning" for Cage. Rather, it is an activity that creates a condition of responsiveness to reality. Cage's thought was indebted to eastern religious thought. His writings on music can be found in a number of publications, notably *Silence: Lectures and Writings* (Hanover: Wesleyan University, 1961). See also *John Cage: An*

us to the world? Though Cage and Bloch are not in fact in any way similar they share a refusal to restrict the evaluation of music to the aesthetic mode – that is, the disinterested contemplation of self-sufficient form.

Our cultural products, supremely music, have in them a surplus that transcends the ideological conditioning of the era in which they arise. Bloch calls this surplus the "cultural heritage." As a process, the cultural heritage sublimates surplus material so minimally that works with this surplus are left open to future appropriation. Such works have not been "thwarted in existence."[42] The cultural heritage is a "tradition of the future."[43] In effect Bloch is saying that "tradition and producing the future" are one and the same.[44]

It is this surplus that is inherited in successive generations and that is in effect an expression of our most basic drive: hope. Music, of all the arts, has this quality of not-yet (*noch nicht*) that is literally a trace or spoor of our human authenticity. Music is a primary player in the project of *Sein* (being) innovation.

Further, revelation privileges a metahistory. And music with its inherent teleological character localizes (materializes), for the period of its sounding, a metahistory. This is not an inevitable or simply linear outcome, but one that requires that we "seize the moment." We are partakers in "participatory knowledge," not reduced *to* a process. Seizing the moment is also known as revolution.

Creativity is no less than a definition of revolution for Bloch. All the arts, but most completely music, express our struggle and movement toward it through *praxis*, or work (*Arbeit*), as more

---

Anthology (ed. Richard Kostelanetz; New York: Da Capo, 1991), for writings by and about Cage.
[42] Bloch, *Utopian Function*, 49.
[43] Bloch, *Utopian Function*, 50.
[44] Bloch, *Utopian Function*, 49-51. Bloch praises Hegel for his insight that what we make in our culture is an heirloom, an *aide memoire* whose material is of the future. The issue here is whether a work of art is a cultural heritage because it is impervious to successive interpretations or whether it survives only because it is, in a purely chronological way, an "embodied particular"?

orthodox Marxism puts it. The revolution is not a manifesto for subjectivism but provides a material intimation of a future state where subject and object are reconciled. Music is a cipher of the utopian project. Indeed, all the arts bring us out *from* ourselves into *the work of art* and in so doing model the encounter with the "other."

The revolution is the "still-travelling vehicle of our authentic selves." The destiny is "home" (*Heimat*), a place no one has yet been.[45] The *creative* work of art shows our true condition or character to ourselves. The arts contain "our secret signature."[46] Bloch paraphrases Heraclitus: God speaks directly in signs. The world is unfinished, its reality *incognito*: "in tendency and latency something is present though not actually existent."[47] Prophecy and hence revelation can only be indirection. As Bloch remarked, "True genesis comes not at the beginning but at the end."[48] Meanwhile, we decipher the signs.[49]

---

[45] Bloch, *The Principle of Hope*, 3:1376. "But the root of history is the working, creating human being who reshapes and overhauls the given facts. Once he has grasped himself and established what is his, without expropriation and alienation, in real democracy, there arises in the world something which shines into the childhood of all and in which no one has yet been: home." *Heimat* is a fundamental concept in Bloch's philosophy. It cannot be dealt with here.

[46] Bloch, *Spirit of Utopia*, 30. Bloch partakes of a critical tradition that finds meaning in what is implicit rather than explicit. The Marxist analysis of ideology is a form of this, as is Freud's interpretation of dreams.

[47] Ernst Bloch, in Michael Landmann, "Talking with Ernst Bloch: Korula, 1968," *Telos* 25 (1975): 175.

[48] Bloch, *The Principle of Hope*, 3:1375.

[49] As Frederic Jameson has remarked, "the world is (for Bloch) an immense storehouse of figures, and the task of the philosopher or critic becomes a hermeneutic one to the degree that [she] is called upon to pierce this 'incognito of every lived instant,' and to decipher the dimly vibrating meaning beneath the fables and the works, the experiences and the objects, which surrounding us seem to solicit our attention in some peculiarly personal fashion." Frederic Jameson, *Marxism and Form: Twentieth Century Dialectical Theories of Literature* (Princeton: Princeton University Press, 1971), 145.

Bloch's resolution of the I/We tension has the orthodox Marxist tinge – the subordination of the individual to the collective[50] – but his ambition is well conveyed by Barth's gospel paraphrase that "whoso means to rescue and preserve the subjective element shall lose it; but whoso gives it up for the sake of the objective shall save it."[51] It is the arts that bring us out *from* ourselves into *the work of art* and in so doing model the encounter with the "Other." Music is the effective counter to philosophies of fragmentation.

The distinct ethical character of music consists in this capacity to show our true condition to ourselves. While the arts as a body contain our "secret signature" – both of our ideological bondage, and the hope of its transformation – music, according to Bloch, is a copy of a different world-principal (*Weltprinzip*) to any of the other arts.[52] The tone travels out and holds us in temporal suspension between the note heard and the one to arrive. Tonal figures are experienced in time as undetermined, open-ended elements. By contrast, and not just literally, colour is fixed.[53] Here Bloch and Augustine are in agreement.

Great art has fissures in it which are opened up by the utopian ground on which the work is built: as, for example, in Beethoven's last quartets, in which "completion itself, driven so deeply into the Absolute, becomes a fragment."[54] This fragmentation is not an

---

[50] Bloch maintains that the true utopian question is that of the Self *(Selbst)* and We *(Wir)*: "I am. We are. That is enough. Now we have to start." Bloch, *Spirit of Utopia*, 187, and see also p. 1. Compare Bloch's understanding with that of Wolfhart Pannenberg: "The individual is humanity as such, the species, and at the same time the individual is not the species, and this conflict is the 'expression for a task' at which human beings have always failed." W. Pannenberg, *Anthropology in Theological Perspective* (trans. Matthew J. O'Connell; Edinburgh: T. & T. Clark, 1985), 57.

[51] Karl Barth, *Dogmatics in Outline* (London: SCM, 1949), 16.

[52] Bloch, *The Principle of Hope*, 3:1056-57.

[53] E. Bloch, *Essays on the Philosophy of Music* (trans. Peter Palmer; Cambridge: Cambridge University Press, 1985), 140.

[54] Bloch, *The Principle of Hope*, 1:220.

endless Derridean displacement of meaning.[55] These fragments are revelatory in their unfinishability; they manifest the eschatological trajectory in whose light all things appear as unfinished "objective fragment."[56] Such fragments are authentic ciphers *through* which the experimental, processing-out world is manifest.

Our not-yet attained authentic self is coterminous with a "music completely arrived."[57] Such music is the "art of the future Kingdom" and will be in nature like "the meaning of a sentence understood and possessed in the same movement."[58]

Music is able to denote the longing that is our most truly human instinct. Music can denote this because "only the musical note, that enigma of sensuousness, is sufficiently unencumbered by the world, yet phenomenal enough at the last to return..."[59] Music is a "viceroy" of the history to come, the Kingdom. Music is a secret *vita* of redemption. Not secret because it is for the few, but because like the Kingdom it is an inner sanctum within capitalism that will change the form of the world. But we must have eyes to read, and ears to hear especially – "the ear is slightly more deeply embedded in the skin than even the eye."[60]

Music models a template that in its open-endedness facilitates the long common highway to liberty. Music situates and locates us – a thing we cannot do because we are too near to ourselves. Indeed, this is Bloch's claim about the arts: they are us but by becoming something external to ourselves they enable self-perspective. In regard to this character Bloch himself says: "There has to be a distance... Proverbs expresses it very simply"; "The weaver knows not what he weaves."[61]

---

[55] Bloch, *Utopian Function*, xl.
[56] Bloch, *The Principle of Hope*, 1:221.
[57] Bloch, *Spirit of Utopia*, 141.
[58] Bloch, *Spirit of Utopia*, 141.
[59] Bloch, *Spirit of Utopia*, 141.
[60] Bloch, *Spirit of Utopia*, 101.
[61] Bloch, in interview, 1974. Quoted in Vincent Geoghegan, *Ernst Bloch* (New York: Routledge, 1996), 36.

Conclusion: recapitulation

God, or at least the traces of his presence that we are graced with, is communicated in the specific and concrete things of this world. And further, in those things that owe their being to the love that must disclose itself – for example our creative and inquisitive nature. Since the Enlightenment we are predisposed to identify knowledge with propositional forms and scientific rationality and so to diminish the diversity of voices communicating God's "invisible nature." That much evangelical thought has fallen in with this Enlightenment agenda need not hinder us; the experience of grace, and therefore the substance of faith, is not constrained by our cultural particulars.

What this wide-ranging material that has been presented offers is a discussion in support of a claim that music is revelatory in nature: a sound-icon of God's communicative being. Sound is the beginning of all things. God spoke, and it was. Hence, though we may not hear God in the form of external auditory sensation his voice falls on our ears in the way that the world is. If this is so, then the world is nothing less than a sounding forth of God. It is the Spirit's speech. And music, in its various shaping of sound, must capture, even incidentally, this presence. Music, I want to say, but not with any specificity, makes articulate and particularizes as substance, grace.

The presence of the One whose kingdom the world is is not necessarily comfortable. We do not always wish to hear Him. Indeed, did not the people on Mt. Sinai cry: "Let not God speak to us lest we die" (Exod 20:19). And God's voice! Always thundering, and the fire and trumpets accompanying it – yet also the still small voice... And long ago even the sound of God in the garden in the still of the day walking and seeking. Yet Adam and Eve hid from the sound of God. For us, God is the personally undue (which is one definition of noise). That the voice of God is "too much" is affirmed by Paul's experience of encountering God. In Acts those accompanying the Apostle were speechless, hearing God. Our being is disturbed. There is no containing this God-aurality. It is both hearable presence and for us unhearable: a kind of erasure – a purity of otherness so indescribable and unencompassable that it can only be spoken of as "a consuming fire" (Heb 12:29 RSV).

Yet Jesus said, "let him who has ears hear…" While the specific reference is to Jesus' parables we may note that these are not the most literal forms of communication. The injunction is made also in the letters to the seven churches in the book of Revelation where it follows statements of commendation and rebuke which recapitulate the prophetic forms of God's address to Israel. The book of Revelation itself is a book intended to be heard, to be read aloud. Its visions fell on the ear – their visual astonishment in fact connected to the enlivening of imagination through sound.

Analogously we may conclude that music is justly called revelatory even if as revelation it is hardly a *precise* new word. Its urgency and its effectiveness as summons to the Kingdom is no less for its indirection:

> My mouth shall speak of wisdom; and the meditation of my heart shall be of understanding.
> I will incline mine ear to a parable: I will open my dark saying upon the harp. (Ps 49: 3-4 KJV)

Chapter Fourteen
Is an evangelical New Zealand contextual theology possible?

Martin Sutherland

Evangelicals have enthusiastically recognised the importance of context. In cross-cultural mission history it has often been low-church evangelicals who have most readily accepted adaptation of practice in order to remove non-essential barriers to the gospel. Just as passionately, evangelical institutions and societies have provided the essential energy for scriptural translation – surely the most symbolic acknowledgement of context. Sophisticated dynamic translation philosophies have emerged from these very efforts. Yet, for all this, evangelicals have been much more cautious about the contextual adaptation of theology. Deep at the heart of this unease lies an anxiety about truth – the fear that contextual theology, if taken too far, will compromise the gospel itself.

In this paper I explore the *possibility* of an "Aotearoa-New Zealand[1] evangelical theology." That is, can there be a Christian theology in *this* place which is at once both truly contextual *and* truly evangelical? This must be followed by the natural next question: what would such a theology look like?

Complexities, of course, immediately emerge when one addresses such an enquiry. There is the obvious one of definition. "Contextual"? "Evangelical"? What do these terms mean? But there are other compounding forces. Not the least is the unstated (at least in the way I put the question), often unacknowledged, but nonetheless undeniable presence of a third critical factor: the influence of theological community – simplistically, denominational distinctives. In a 2003 article, New Zealand Catholic theologian, Neil Darragh pointed out that the challenges for local or contextual

---

[1] It is a common practice to refer to the country using both Maori and European names. In this essay I will use them sometimes together and sometimes singly, as synonyms.

theology may differ according to the theological tradition we come from.² It is, moreover, coming to be seen that the history of "evangelicalism" is better grasped as the stories of many "evangelical*isms*" – that there are subtle but significant differences to be understood between Anglican evangelicalism, Wesleyan evangelicalism, Reformed evangelicalism, Non-conformist evangelicalism, American evangelicalism, and so forth.³

Even the way I have just stated this aspect of the challenge itself exacerbates the difficulties. We too easily concretize our labels, thereby allowing nouns to become fetters. I am a Baptist, evangelical Christian, but does this self-ascription unnecessarily limit my options? What if we were to recast our speaking of ourselves, replacing nouns with adverbs? My disclosure would thus become that I approach the theological task *baptistically* and *evangelically*. Crucially, this very admission places me in a context. In what follows, aspects of what I will appropriate from evangelical debates appeal because they cohere with what I understand to be the dynamics of Baptist theological method. Further, as a Baptist I am naturally concerned with the importance of the concrete and local. So I have an inbuilt desire to find a way of incorporating context as a living factor in theological discourse. The question which heads the paper is thus unmasked as rhetorical. I contend that evangelical contextual theology is indeed possible and that it takes a particular form in Aotearoa.

I will draw first from recent discussions on evangelical theological method and the concept of *truth*, with the intent of identifying approaches which support and enable the ultimate task of constructing a local evangelical theology. In the second and larger part of this paper I will explore some of the possible features and boundaries of that landscape as presented in Aotearoa-New

---

² Neil Darragh, "Contextual Method in Theology: Learnings from the Case of Aotearoa New Zealand," *Pacifica* 16 (2003): 45.
³ See, for example, Timothy Larsen, *Contested Christianity: The Political and Social Contexts of Victorian Theology* (Waco: Baylor University Press, 2004).

Zealand, concluding with some suggestions as to how a contextual theological conversation might sound.

Method, truth, and context

In the first (1992) edition of his influential study of *Models of Contextual Theology*, Catholic missiologist Steve Bevans identified five approaches to contextualization.[4] The first of these was "Translation" which, in Bevans' analysis, regards the gospel as "supracontextual and complete" but accepts that it must be adapted or "accommodated" to local settings. It must be "translated," so that it may be heard in a given context. Bevans suggests that this is the model favoured by (among others, including John Paul II!) evangelicals. His key criticism is that the translation model conceives of revelation as fundamentally propositional. Yet (music to evangelical ears!), he suggests that no other model in his book takes as "seriously the message of Christianity as recorded in the Scriptures and handed down in tradition."[5]

A decade later, in his second, "Revised and Expanded Edition" Bevans added a sixth model: the "Countercultural." This is characterized by its energetic, prophetic voice which seeks to challenge culture at the level of its presuppositions and roots. Given that a key example Bevans cites is the work and legacy of Lesslie Newbigin, it is perhaps not surprising that many evangelicals would willingly associate themselves with this approach. As with his assessment of the first model, Bevans' evaluation of the countercultural model would reassure them. "With the possible exception of the translation model, no other model discussed in this book wants to be as engaging of and relevant to the context while at the same time remaining faithful to the gospel."[6] However (and this is the key point for the purposes of this paper), in the

---

[4] Stephen B. Bevans, *Models of Contextual Theology* (Maryknoll: Orbis, 1992).
[5] Bevans, *Models*, 35.
[6] Stephen B. Bevans, *Models of Contextual Theology: Revised and Expanded Edition* (Maryknoll: Orbis, 2002), 124.

countercultural model revelation is not understood primarily as proposition but as narrative – more particularly "the gospel... is something that has been *done*."[7] That indeed many evangelicals are comfortable with the model, including this aspect of it, reflects recent debate on evangelical theological method, much of it building on Speech-Act Theory.

Typical of those who have embraced and led a shift towards narrative or relational truth, without dismissing proposition, are Stanley Grenz, Peter Hicks,[8] and Kevin Vanhoozer. Vanhoozer reasserts, as he redefines, the principle of *sola scriptura*. "The word written is the critical principle for everything we say and do as theologians. Divine communicative action, embedded in the canonical texts, is the final criterion for the church's communicative action."[9] Nevertheless,

> the canon's primary role is to cultivate good theological judgement so that it functions not so much as a script to be memorized and repeated verbatim but as a guide for learning one's role as a disciple of Jesus Christ. Rethinking doctrine as dramatic direction encourages us to think in terms of *doing* the truth."[10]

Grenz, though from a different argument, presents a similar outcome.

> Through the Bible, the Spirit orients our present on the basis of the past and in accordance with a vision for the future. The Spirit leads the contemporary hearers to view themselves and their situation in the light of God's past and future and to open themselves and their present to the power of that future, which

---

[7] Bevans, *Models of Contextual Theology: Revised and Expanded*, 121.
[8] Peter Hicks, *Evangelicals and Truth: A Creative Proposal for a Postmodern Age* (Leicester: IVP, 1998).
[9] Kevin J. Vanhoozer, "The Voice and the Actor: A Dramatic Proposal about the Ministry and Minstrelsy of Theology," in *Evangelical Futures: A Conversation on Theological Method* (ed. J.G. Stackhouse Jr; Grand Rapids: Baker, 2000), 85.
[10] Vanhoozer, "The Voice and the Actor," 100–101.

is already at work in the world. Thereby they are drawn to participate in God's eschatological world. The task of theology in turn, is to assist the people of God in hearing the Spirit's voice speaking through the text so that we can live as God's people – as inhabitants of God's eschatological world – in the present.[11]

So how is a Kiwi-Baptist-evangelical theologian to translate these ideas for a contextual theology in Aotearoa? A point to reinforce is that issues of context are natural to Baptist theology. Baptists are by nature committed to the significance of the local story. Yet, this local story is not of primary value in and of itself. Rather, the local is valued out of the conviction that Christ is present in the community of those "gathered in his name" (Matt 18:20). There is a particular value placed on gathering in Baptist thought. This aspect of "gathering" is not in itself the focus of this essay and I have sought to explore the wider ramifications elsewhere.[12] However it is worth noting that the gathering is itself an event, an action, a moment in the narrative of reconciliation, in the very mission of God.

What I want to explore here more particularly is the "in his name" element if this conviction of the presence of Christ in response to his promise in Matthew 18:20. Here the Baptist *tikanga* which I am proposing dovetails neatly with the debates over method engendered by Vanhoozer, Grenz, and others. The church experience is the dynamic interplay of *two* stories – the contemporary, local, "gathered" one, and the Christ story as revealed in Scripture. These stories are not equal partners. As the church gathers "in his name," it is seeking to align its story with Christ's story in all its scandalous particularity. Thus, in this dialectic, the Christ story is primary and normative. In Vanhoozer's terms it is "a guide for learning one's role"; in Grenz' model "the Spirit orients our present on the basis of the past" with the additional, crucial

---

[11] Stanley Grenz, "Articulating the Christian Belief-Mosaic: Theological Method after the Demise of Foundationalism," in *Evangelical Futures*, 125.
[12] Martin Sutherland, "Gathering, Sacrament and Baptist Theological Method," *Pacific Journal of Baptist Research* 3 (2007): 41–57.

factor (to which I will return) of a further shaping "vision for the future."

The adaptive, localizing plasticity of this vision of theological method clearly opens up possibilities for a new appreciation of contextual theologies. However it is important to recognise that the emergence (still vigorously contested to be sure, but vitally present in the mainstream of evangelical theology nonetheless) of models like Vanhoozer's and Grenz' demands a refinement of notions of truth. Grenz, following Pannenberg, locates objective truth in God's eschatological world. Truth in the present time is about coherence rather than correspondence. For Vanhoozer, as Roger Olsen notes, "truth is in the [dramatic] performance as much as in the proposition."[13]

I modestly suggest there are other ways still to conceive of "truth," among them one suggested by and highlighted in the baptistic way of doing theology evangelically which connects deeply to the project of a Kiwi evangelical theology.

In the Christian understanding, absolute truth is not some *thing* that you know, share or experience, but a *person* you meet. Christ is truth. Theology can be "true," but in the sense that a builder's set square or spirit level, the sights on a rifle, or a compass can be "true." That is: they indicate a proper alignment, direction, or bearing. None of these instruments is ever *perfectly* true, but good ones indicate measurements or bearings within acceptable tolerances. I suggest theology operates like that, with the implication that it can be better or worse, depending on whether it aligns the church more or less well to the normative Christ story.[14] All theology then is dynamic, provisional, improvising its way in the divine drama. And all theology, if it is "true," will be contextual.

---

[13] Roger Olson, "Reforming Evangelical Theology," in *Evangelical Futures*, 205.
[14] I have explored these questions more fully, proposing an epistemology of "consonance" in Martin Sutherland, "James and the Spirit: Wisdom and Hermeneutics," in *The Spirit of Truth: Reading Scripture and Constructing Theology with the Holy Spirit* (ed. Myk Habets; Eugene: Pickwick, 2010), 73–88.

I will try to illustrate and apply these thoughts in the New Zealand context. I must first stress that I take "context" to be more than physical location. I am nervous about attempts to do theology by Global Positioning System (GPS). Geography is merely one part of the local story, playing its role alongside memory, history, relationships, and media. So if some colonial theologians of the 1880s were couching most of their theological debate in British terms, then that was because for them Britain *was* a crucial part of their context. Their memory, relationships, and most of their history had real anchors in what they still called "Home." What happened there mattered to them. Nevertheless it would be wrong to assume that the physical context did not have an impact. I am most familiar with Baptist examples. Baptists in New Zealand clearly did shape their corporate life in ways very different from their British contemporaries. There was, for instance, a conscious determination not to import historical divisions. In Britain, Baptists had been long divided on Calvinist/Arminian lines. That was very rare in New Zealand. Baptists took up public causes in a very different way here from the pre-occupations of British Baptists. They organised their associations and denomination in ways which reflected the New Zealand geography.[15]

The issue is not whether contextual theology has been or should be done now. It was and is, and always shall be. There is however, considerable room for debate over whether it is being done *well*. Here I return to my remarks about theology being "true." The task of theology is to bear witness to the truth – that is, to Jesus the Christ. It will be "better" – more true – if it aligns us more closely to the Christ story. Here context, geography even, is crucial. If one is in New Zealand and seeking bearings which will direct you to the Statue of Liberty, you need directions which reflect *this* location. If you merely dragged out course coordinates recorded when you were visiting Moscow, you would struggle to find your destination. The bearings would be wrong. They would not be "true" for your

---

[15] See my extended treatment of this in Martin Sutherland, *Conflict and Connection: Baptist Identity in New Zealand* (Auckland: Archer, 2011).

context. Likewise a "true" New Zealand theology would be one which most authentically aligns its participants to the Christ story. It will be different from an Australian or British or Korean theology. It will be "contextual." However this quality will be much more than a matter of geography. It will involve history, art, literature, climate, psyche, and politics.

Thus it is clear that I am suggesting that an authentically evangelical theology can be (and, indeed, at least if approached baptistically can *only be)* contextual. But this is only half of the equation, for no treatment of contextual theology can escape dealing with an actual context. Which pushes us to, perhaps, the harder question: how might a New Zealand contextual theology be shaped? There is not space to define or prescribe such a theology, but I do want to note some limits and possibilities, drawing from parallel debates in New Zealand literature and art.

"Speaking for ourselves"

Theologians are sometimes surprised to discover that others have wrestled with similar problems. In New Zealand, for four decades in the middle of the twentieth century, there ran a debate on what might be termed "contextual art." From the 1930s, an intent emerged among an energetic generation of artists to develop a "National" culture. That is, one which was authentic to the lived New Zealand experience, rather than a mere celebration of the colonial myth of the reproduction of a better Britain in the South Pacific. This Nationalistic urge required the creation of an "anti-myth" to counter the colonial one. Importantly, among the key features of the anti-myth narrative was that New Zealand, far from being a bountiful paradise was, rather, a barren place, even a wasteland. It must be populated, colonised even, by artistic endeavours which would draw deeply on outside forms but which ultimately would find a new voice, authentic to both new place and imported heritage.

As we shall see, the most incisive descriptions of this movement are to be found among literary critics, but the impulse was common to other artistic circles. In a landmark address in 1946, composer Douglas Lilburn (1915–2001) reflected on the New Zealand "Search for a Tradition": "I want to plead with you the necessity of having a music of our own, a living tradition of music created in this country, a music that will satisfy those parts of our being that cannot be satisfied by the music of other nations."[16]

This spiritually satisfying music would not be found easily. Most importantly it could not be contrived. Looking with some envy at the writers who were a step a ahead in their parallel quest for a New Zealand literature, Lilburn noted that "what I found most stimulating about all this activity is that it hasn't happened as a result of people self-consciously setting out to produce a national literature." Rather it was simply the outcome of individuals "getting to grips imaginatively with things about them."[17] This is a gradual, faltering journey, unable to be forced, but essential and inevitable nonetheless. "[T]his context or environment of ours... is slowly but inevitably shaping us into characteristic ways of living, developing in us those qualities that make us different from the English or the Americans."[18] The proper response of the artist is not to abandon the quest as if it were impossible, nor to settle into a creative quietism as if the process were merely external. Rather it is essential to delve deeply enough into the context.

> I feel that the musician in this country must develop his awareness of the place he lives in, not attempting a mere imitation of nature in sound, but seeking its inner values, the manifestations of beauty and purpose it shows us from time to time, and perhaps using it as something against which he can test the validity of his own work... And if we can discover these rhythms of our ways of living and our relations to the environment about us, then we will see the beginning of a music

---

[16] Douglas Lilburn, "A Search for a Tradition," in *A Search for a Tradition & A Search for a Language* (1946, repr.; Wellington: Lilburn Residence Trust, 2011), 21.
[17] Lilburn, "A Search for a Tradition," 28.
[18] Lilburn, "A Search for a Tradition," 43.

of our own, a music that will to some extent satisfy that spiritual need I think we all have, that sense of belonging somewhere.[19]

A further, fascinating parallel is evident in twentieth century painting. New Zealand visual art cannot be accused of ignoring its physical context. Representational landscapes have been its mainstay. Yet, though this may be said to be in one sense contextual, is it significant? Can it be rated "good art"? The issues came to heated debate during the history of the Kelliher art award. The Kelliher award, which ran from 1956–1977, was overtly aimed at encouraging representational landscape art. However it became increasingly criticised by "modernist" artists and critics as lacking imagination or message.

The Kelliher winners and modernist examples from the Fletcher collection were exhibited together in the *Representation and Reaction* exhibition of 2002–2003.[20] Some comparisons highlight the differences of approach. Kelliher winners such as Leonard Mitchell's *Summer in the Mokauiti Valley* (1956), Ernest Buckmaster's *Warrington Station* (1959), or Graham Braddock's *In the Stillness* (1976), whilst not without experiment, nonetheless seem to fit the dictum that "accuracy of depiction provides the standard of judgment." By contrast, pictures exploring modernist techniques and themes, such as Toss Woollaston's *Bayly's Hill* (1967), Robin White's *Hooper's Inlet* (1976), or Owen Lee's *Evening Shadows, North Auckland* (1960) come closer to artist Jean Horsley's declaration that "art is not scenery."[21]

The focus of the modernists' criticism was not that the Kelliher art failed to depict New Zealand subjects – it clearly did – but that it merely looked and represented. Local images might thereby be retailed to the wider world, but there was no *engagement* with that wider world. And, further, no engagement with that world from out of the New Zealand experience. No message.

---

[19] Lilburn, "A Search for a Tradition," 45.
[20] P. Shaw, *Representation and Reaction: Modernism and the New Zealand Landscape Tradition 1956–1977* (Auckland: ABN Amro, 2002).
[21] Shaw, *Representation and Reaction*, 7.

Intriguingly, some of those modernists found the key to that message in a new expression of Christianity. This took a surprising and revealing path. The Nationalist/Modernist artists self-consciously eschewed the European convention of discovering God in nature. As Francis Pound has pointed out:

> God was seen in Nature through the frames of the genres, especially through the frames of the Ideal (His beautiful beneficence), and the Sublime (His awful power). What the nineteenth-century New Zealand painter William Mathew Hodgkins called the "mission of the landscape painter" allowed artists, if not entirely to replace the Reverend, at least to appoint themselves to the priesthood of Nature's Church.[22]

In New Zealand art this was most clearly reflected in the paintings of Petrus van der Velden (1837–1913). For the Nationalist artists this seemed too shallow, too easily won. Unsure how to engage the Maori world, the overriding sense they shared was the cultural barrenness of their context. This was a place waiting to be filled. For the religiously sensitive painters, a spiritual engagement with the landscape would not be through the general revelation of the ideal or the sublime but through the special, in the Christ. Toss Woollaston (1910–1988) declared in 1943 that "the Bible is as good a textbook for art as for religion, and that modern Christian art is due."[23] Nobody took this more seriously than Colin McCahon (1919–1987), who saw that the spiritual significance of the landscape did not spring from the landscape itself, but from the presence of Christ in it. The crucifixion would be enacted here. Ultimately "McCahon emptied out the landscape entirely… so that he could completely fill it with the Word of God."[24]

This is the idea that Lilburn espoused in suggesting that New Zealand music would not spring virginally from the soil, but instead

---

[22] Francis Pound, *The Invention of New Zealand: Art and National Identity 1930-1970* (Auckland: Auckland University Press, 2009), 130–31.

[23] M. Tosswill Woollaston, "Toss Woollaston Explains Himself," *Art New Zealand* 16 (1943): 13, cited in Pound, *The Invention of New Zealand*, 131.

[24] Pound, *The Invention of New Zealand*, 140.

"must be derived in the first place from music written elsewhere." The true shaping of a new tradition would come when enough composers engage in "a deliberate process of selection, or sorting out from the world's music those ways of expression that come closest to meeting [their] own needs."[25] The paradox recognised by these artists was that the authentically local could never be entirely or even seminally local. Rather, "the ancient myths take root in the New Zealand hills, the land's perceived emptiness is filled, the alien is clothed with the familiar, and the land's silence and remoteness is relieved."[26]

> In a country that appeared to Pakeha intellectuals to be without history, in which history was experienced only as a loss, as an elsewhere, the task was to trace over the emptiness, to fill it with the marks of the old legends and myths. In New Zealand the past seemed not an "impediment," as it did to [American Modernists], but an absence, a loss to be made good.[27]

This was also the view which drove the literary Nationalists. The key figure, at least in the theorising on the qualities of an authentically "New Zealand" literature was the poet Allan Curnow (1911–2001). In the "Introduction" to his 1945 *A Book of New Zealand Verse*, Curnow excoriated a 1930 collection entitled *Kowai Gold*. The bulk of the earlier volume, he concluded, reflected "emotional bewilderment" – "verse [which] might be called escapist if it were not so aimless."[28] He dismissed what he saw as an English style and sought something uniquely New Zealand. Importantly, Curnow's concern was not that the poems in that volume failed to use local imagery. Indeed, he acknowledged that there had been "a good deal of honest striving after indigenous effect, words like kowai and rata and tui being new toys."[29] The problem lay in the

---

[25] Lilburn, "A Search for a Tradition," 43.
[26] Pound, *The Invention of New Zealand*, 141.
[27] Pound, *The Invention of New Zealand*, 146.
[28] Allen Curnow, *Look Back Harder: Critical Writings 1935-1984* (Auckland: Auckland University Press, 1987), 50.
[29] Curnow, *Look Back Harder*, 50.

"striving." Speaking of the work of Catholic poet Eileen Duggan he lamented that "the movement is strained, images arbitrary and often unhappy, endless flat comparisons confuse rather than illuminate the statement. She uses the simile as if it were in itself to be admired..."[30]

Curnow was seeking a deeper phenomenon than colloquial phrasing or local flora: "The good poem is something we may in time come to recognise New Zealand by, not something in which we need expect to recognise obvious traces of the New Zealand we know. Local reference ought never to decide our estimate of a poem's worth."[31]

This was the quest expressed neatly by Frank Sargeson (1903–1982) in the title of his 1945 anthology of short stories, *Speaking for Ourselves*.[32] Commenting in 1941 on R.A.K. Mason's poems, Curnow had hinted at the essence of what was sought. "These poems could not have been written... by any other than a New Zealander. The image of isolation, the raw edge, the unformed, the strong man in the wilderness... recurs and recurs."[33] As this passage suggests, Curnow's "Nationalism" took the form of what he later described as an "anti-myth." In common with many contemporaries, he regarded New Zealand in the 1930s as a cultural wasteland, in need of its own literature. But, crucially, this literature must not merely reflect a fascination with New Zealand *things*. It must express the New Zealand cultural experience. For nineteenth-century colonists this might properly be described as a form of exile; in the 1930s Curnow and his friends spoke of isolation.

A deep sense of New Zealand's isolation in part explains the impact on one of those friends, Denis Glover, of service with the British Navy during World War II. Glover (1912–1980), whom few would have guessed would have even been willing to enlist, relished his active service in England. He revelled in the sheer masculine

---

[30] Curnow, *Look Back Harder*, 50.
[31] Curnow, *Look Back Harder*, 49.
[32] Frank Sargeson, ed., *Speaking for Ourselves* (Christchurch: Caxton, 1945).
[33] Curnow, *Look Back Harder*, 29–30.

activity of it, and was profoundly taken with the England he encountered. Like many returning servicemen he felt a deep sense of anticlimax, of flatness, but for Glover this was more than a post-traumatic plunge. New Zealand represented something lacking, something missing, which in its absence was suffocating.

> This sullen and perplexing coast
> Makes no assertion, no boast,
> No positive utterance; and yet
> Somewhere there's concealed a threat
> Somewhere home-coming elation
> Feels an old strangulation.[34]

Ironically, by the late 1950s Curnow and his generation were being accused by younger poets of a too-restrictive nationalism, creating a furore and such ill-feeling that publication of Curnow's next anthology *The Penguin Book of New Zealand Verse* was delayed in press by the reluctance of some contemporaries to cooperate with him. Curnow, by now, was perceived to represent localism, as against poets who wanted to explore universal themes and see themselves as citizens of the world. But this very reaction had at least the potential to be the fulfilment, rather than the repudiation of Curnow's call. The "Nationalist" vision had never been merely local. The context would draw in the ingredients but would itself add (or be) the flavour. As Toss Woollaston had put it, "international influences may give our work manner – environment should give it character."[35] The dismissal of Curnow as localist was thus misplaced, but what was almost certainly happening was that the dream of a Nationalist *body* of literature, recognizable in shared themes, was being discarded. Increasingly artists and writers were finding other lenses, less overtly national, more in keeping with international critical trends. Lilburn saw this happening. Reprising

---

[34] Denis Glover, "Returning from Overseas," cited in Gordon Ogilvie, *Denis Glover: His Life* (Auckland: Godwit, 1999), 213.
[35] Cited by Douglas Lilburn in "A Search for a Language," in *A Search for Tradition & A Search for a Language* (1969 repr.; Wellington: Lilburn Residence Trust, 2011), 64.

in 1969 the themes of his 1946 address he abandoned the quest for a "tradition" and instead spoke of the "Search for a Language." The development of a local language would be the result of a process of the "assimilation" of international languages, "a process which will be lengthy, may be partial only, may prove baffling" but is nonetheless at the heart of the New Zealand creative quest.[36]

> [W]hen any such artist speaks of environment in relation to his work, do not think he is just enthusing about nature, or voicing a narrow parochialism. He is likely to be well aware of the total context of his own living in his understandable here and now, and to be searching for the significant values of all this relevant to his art. Aware of all this, he is likely to be at least as aware of humanity and history, and the complexities of the contemporary international scene, as those of his critics who ignore or negate this immediate context. And in preferring to search the pleasant or unpalatable truths of his own experience, I think he has the best chance of discovering the sources of his creativity, whatever larger thing may give validity to his choice of a language.[37]

The recognition of this tension between the environment and influences from outside in New Zealand cultural life is the great contribution of the Nationalists. As Curnow would put it in 1968, "the theme of *there* in Europe and *here* in New Zealand" is "an inevitable polarity of feeling for us in the South Pacific."[38] More broadly, of course, this is the experience of everyone in Aotearoa–New Zealand. All peoples here are immigrants; all have at their mythical heart a connection with a place beyond, be it Bristol or London, Hawaiki or Dublin, Amsterdam or Hong Kong.

Theology in a Kiwi accent

Theology can draw insight from these debates in literature and art. To be "true" in the sense I have advanced, theology will need to

---

[36] Lilburn in "A Search for a Language," 61.
[37] Lilburn in "A Search for a Language," 81.
[38] Curnow, *Look Back Harder*, 227.

move beyond a somewhat contrived search for local metaphors. A New Zealand contextual theology *is* possible, but only if we incorporate the deep experience of "New Zealandness." We are, to be sure, no longer in the place of the Nationalists. In particular we are all as citizens of Aotearoa more aware and more naturally comfortable with the riches and depth of Maori culture. The engagement with Maori language, Te Reo, whilst still rudimentary for most, has granted opportunity for a more profound engagement with place and places. The change to the population mix and the economic shifts of the last four decades have diminished our sense of being a client state of Britain and opened us to the Pacific world in new ways. Importantly none of these developments still release us from the sense of "*here and there*-ness." Indeed many of our recent cultural trends make it more piquant. A greater comfort with place (in part made possible by the contributions of the Nationalists) makes it possible that, in a globalised world, we can move beyond "exile" and "isolation" to something much more confidently like "dual citizenship." Nevertheless to leave out the *there* and retain only the *here*, will hardly be contextual at all. We are deluded if we believe that we can derive a purely local view, even with the intention of standing in that place to engage the rest of the world. The reality is surely more complex than that, as for us the local already contains the remote. Local theology is not a *pre-requisite* for confident engagement with the wider world; a true contextual theology will be a *result* of such a conversation.

"True" New Zealand theology will be different – as good New Zealand poetry is different – but in the sense that it "could not have been written… by any other than a New Zealander." There is space only to proffer glimpses of what that might mean. In 1946, Curnow suggested a key distinctive in handlings of land and sea.

> To an English poet, in the instances that occur to me… the sea is a feature of the landscape, to be greeted, and left, with a gesture of exultation or surprise. We, if the difference may be

put so crudely, more often take our land for a part of the seascape.[39]

Something similar may emerge in our theology. As islands in an ocean, rather than a land over against the sea, we might celebrate the sense, often unhelpfully translated into cultural diffidence, of being the particular embraced in something bigger and beyond. More narrowly, Curnow's example suggests the importance of the voyages between "here" and "there." New Zealanders are familiar with the practice, only relatively recently decayed, of referring to Britain as "Home." In part expression of that, people used to talk of a "Home Boat." This was not a boat which would merely take you to Britain, but one which plied the trade between the two centres of commercial life – "here and there." This seems to me not a bad metaphor for the theological task in this context: theology as "Home Boat," allowing constant conversation between the centres of theological life.

Which brings us back to the opening discussion on method and truth. Evangelical theology brings a third dimension to the task. If it is to be Christian, if it is to be "true," theology will demand that our cultural "here" and "there" look to a parallel additional "there" of the Christ story and "here" of the Spirit's activity. A dynamic enrichment necessary, especially if we take seriously Grenz' point that "the task of theology… is to assist the people of God in hearing the Spirit's voice speaking through the text so that we can live as God's people – as inhabitants of God's eschatological world – in the present."[40] Is there not an opportunity for Christians, a people who see themselves as strangers, citizens not of this place but of heaven, proleptic exiles from God's eschatological world, to engage creatively with the New Zealand sense of dual-citizenship? Is this not a gift we can bring to a Kiwi society, conscious of its immigrant history, increasingly identifying itself with notions of diaspora? Do we not have something unique to say in this place?

---

[39] Curnow, *Look Back Harder*, 67.
[40] Grenz, "Articulating the Christian Belief-Mosaic," 125.

Evangelicals need not fear this engagement. Indeed, I would suggest it coheres deeply and naturally with evangelical spirituality, theological commitment, and participation in mission. It is only from such dynamic interplay, in its rich fullness, that "true" New Zealand contextual theology will emerge.

www.ingramcontent.com/pod-product-compliance
Lightning Source LLC
Chambersburg PA
CBHW020744160426
43192CB00006B/236